LOTTO

Books by the same author:

Probing Heaven: Key Questions on the Hereafter
   (Baker Books, USA; reprinted UK. Tr. Korean)
*Too Young To Be Old: Secrets from Bible Seniors on How to
   Live Long and Well* (Harold Shaw Publishers, USA)
*Ambushed At Sunset: Coping with Mature Adult
   Temptations* (LangMarc Publishing, USA)
The Trials of Christ: Moral Failings in Four Judges
   (Christian Focus Publications)

LOTTO

FUN OR FOLLY?

John Gilmore

paternoster
press

First published in 2001 by Paternoster Press

07 05 04 03 02 01   7 6 5 4 3 2 1

Paternoster Press is an imprint of Paternoster Publishing,
P.O. Box 300, Carlisle, Cumbria, CA3 0QS, UK
and Paternoster Publishing USA
P.O. Box 1047, Waynesboro, GA 30830-2047, USA
Website: www.paternoster-publishing.com

British Library Cataloguing in Publication Data

A catalogue record for this book is available from
the British Library

ISBN 1-84227-039-7

Cover Design by Campsie
Typeset by WestKey Ltd, Falmouth, Cornwall
Printed in Great Britain by
Omnia Books Limited, Glasgow

FOR

Haydn Lewis Gilmore
Mary Anna Gilmore
Rachel Evans Gilmore Sweterlitsch

Contents

Foreword

I read this manuscript through in one day; it was so interesting and intriguing. It is a thoroughly researched book, historically, theologically, ethically and biblically.

The book is unabashedly Christian. It relates and juxtaposes Providence to gambling again and again. The section on Jesus as the ultimate risk-taker for eternal life is a stirring finale to the book. Throughout, Dr Gilmore states his own spiritual commitment clearly and forthrightly.

The massive amount of well-documented historical data about gambling makes it an excellent history of gambling of which I was unaware.

Wayne E. Oates, Ph.D.
Professor of Psychiatry Emeritus
University of Louisville, Kentucky

Preface

I decided to write a substantial book on gambling. So on a spring day I drove to the city centre's huge Hamilton County Library to begin my research. But before I left the library I ended discovering I had unwittingly gambled. How?

Outside the library I found a convenient street parking place a few feet from the main entrance to the library. The spot was providential. I pulled in and fed the meter an amount for the maximum length of an hour.

Inside the library for one hour I used their computer files to develop a gambling bibliography. The computer monitors were near the main entrance. I faithfully checked my watch to make sure to get out to the street to put more coins in the meter before the time expired.

To my shock and dismay I missed getting to the meter before the arrow went into the red. The meter reader had been there just before I arrived with coin in hand. I had gambled with meter time. And I gambled another way: I suffered loss. I actually lost twice: I lost in getting outside in time, and I had a parking fine. That became a painful irony. I *hadn't been near* a casino, yet it appeared I had gambled!

Both American and English municipalities have slot machines. They are called parking meters. Such 'slots' line business streets. One can avoid slot machines in gambling 'palaces' only to lose money to the street meter 'slot'.

The street meter had no arms to pull, just a little mouth to feed. And I was too late for the feeding. I had an introduction to gambling that I had not anticipated, and one that I will never forget!

Whether one is well off or on benefits, a lottery ticket for a minimal amount is a real temptation to deliverance from being in a financial fix. But what may seem to be a help is more than likely a financial hoax and hindrance to financial security.

Strangely, the Christian church has either been mum about the phenomenon or it cannot wait to unleash a tirade which does nothing but alienate people. Aspects of Christian history seem to contradict or challenge strident critiques of wagering. Some biblical material has been either avoided or superficially examined in Christian books on gambling. There is a place for noting the evils which accompany gambling, but there should also be a place where specific issues related to gambling are discussed. That is the void this book seeks to fill. Fairness and fullness are two aims. No attempt has been made to pound readers into submission by Bible bashing. *Lotto* is not a tract for self-righteous scrupulosity. No repentance form in the back can be found to fill out and mail. Rather the book supplies a balanced historical and theological perspective. Work through what follows. Draw your own conclusions. Responsible attitudes in the use of discretionary money are essential in Christian stewardship. Hopefully, *Lotto: Fun or Folly?* will aid immediate and church-family interaction.

Reading, reflecting and talking about gambling tends to be far more profitable than gambling itself. We don't need to visit gambling venues to get a full-faced picture of the industry. Ample evidence should be followed with ample discussions. Engaging in a discussion of what follows will surely be a profitable experience!

Many of the propositions, principles and practices covered in *Lotto: Fun or Folly?* emerged from discussion within my family. Especially beneficial were the insights, suggestions and reactions of my two sons: John Owen Gilmore, M.S. (Illinois), Ph.D. (Stanford), and on matters mathematical and philosophical, the contributions of my younger son, Martyn Edward Gilmore, B.S. (Ohio State University), were equally important.

My nephew, James H. Gilmore, B.S. Economics (Wharton School, University of Pennsylvania), forward-looking business strategy expert on an emerging economic paradigm called Mass Customization, was especially helpful in interacting with the chapter on stocks and wagering, and in supplying bibliographic information which played an important part in the development of the material.

The inspiration for the book came from the realization of the enormity of the gambling phenomenon from viewing a Spring 1997 CBS-TV 'special' (on Easter Monday) on the gambling industry. Through reading the available Christian books on the subject, immediately afterwards, I was struck by the gaps and gaffs in the arguments on wagering in current information being distributed among Christian readers. I was compelled to enter the controversy to make available information not covered in other books. And I was inspired to develop my own analysis carefully and to engage in drawing my own conclusions on the controversy of lotteries and wagering. None of those who helped me in the project is responsible for the views or possible errors in the work.

xii   *Preface*

I should finally like to acknowledge my indebtedness to the family of Dr Wayne E. Oates for permission to continue to use the Foreword he kindly penned after reading the manuscript shortly before his death.

Dr John Gilmore
PO Box 24064
Cincinnati,
OH 45224

May 16, 2000

Acknowledgments

Special thanks to the many who have contributed to this volume: To the librarians of the Reeves Library, Moravian College, Bethlehem, Pennsylvania, USA, who provided invaluable assistance on the Moravian movement. Appreciation to Dr Curt Daniel for alerting me to Dr Van Dam's doctoral dissertation. Special thanks to the publisher and staff of Paternoster Publishing who accepted, revised, and proofread the manuscript. Also vital to the process has been the interaction with various groups before whom this material was first presented orally in Sheboygan, Wisconsin, USA, in Dayton, OH, USA, and in Cincinnati, OH USA. Other interested persons provided bits and pieces of information and encouragement: Methodist pastor John L. Eshelman, III; UCC pastor Larry Bechtol; American Baptist Deacon Sid Green, MBA; Reformed Baptist pastors Tom Wells and Newton Bush, Th.D. In addition to my two sons and nephew, mentioned in the Preface, I wish to thank my gifted wife, Roberta, for her support behind the scenes, and for her keen editorial eye which helped sharpen and enhance the work's clarity and readability.

The following publishers were gracious in granting permission to quote. HarperCollins Publishers for permission for World Rights to cite from *Something For Nothing*: the Lore and Lure of Gambling by Clyde Brion Davis

Abbreviations

ASV	American Standard Version
GNB	Good News Bible
IGWB	*International Gaming and Wagering Business Journal*
KJV	King James Version
NASB	New American Standard Bible
NIV	New International Version
NJB	New Jerusalem Bible
NKJV	New King James Version
NRSV	New Revised Standard Version

1.

Weighing up the Gambling Pound

Gambling is a hot topic, and – for some – a horrible disease. Leisure-gaming is epidemic. It has impacted modern society with unrelenting vigour. Gambling's scale and side-effects grow each year and should attract serious study and discussion programmes, especially within churches. Justifiably, many are angered by the bad effects of addictive gambling, annoyed by gambling's false claims, and morally repelled by gambling's materialism.

People say they gamble with their 'fun money.'[1] Millions of people like to gamble. Most players lose. Of course, it is fun to win. But how is losing fun? Despite all the loss, gambling money is referred to as 'fun money.' Fun comes from anticipation, from travel, or simply because of time spent with friends. Fun goes with peripheral entertainment, such as variety shows. How is gambling fun?

The evangelical Christian questions the moral value in wagering. Lotteries are a waste of resources and considered to be against biblical norms. It is not just a harmless pastime; it is a misuse of the Lord's money. *The Sword and the Trowel*, published by London Metropolitan Tabernacle, is probably representative of the evangelical questioning of wagering.[2] To many Christians gambling – of all varieties – is patently, plainly, universally evil with no 'ifs, ands, or buts.'

Others wonder, 'Why do Christians bristle with ire on the subject of gambling?' The reasons are quickly heard. In addition to supporting 'get-rich-quick' schemes that prey upon the desperation of the poor, gambling damages society in wrecking careers, in robbing families and in wasting fortunes. All this combines for a conscientious Christian's view that gambling warrants a taboo: it is bad for the nation's health.

'Aren't all Christians against gambling?' Many gambling opponents claim the deplorable ramifications of betting are enough to settle the matter. Because for some, gambling is a major behavioural problem many assume extended discussions must progress to aggressive and progressive action to stop its spread.

Of course, on a practical level, controlling the urge to gamble *is* a major matter. Problem gamblers and pathological gamblers present a unique challenge. How can the cycle of betting be prevented, and if started, broken? Unfortunately, I have not attempted to provide solutions on recovery programmes. One book can only do so much.

The varieties of gambling enterprises are gargantuan. It is impossible to deal adequately with them all in the space of one book. We have decided to focus on the lottery principle rather than pursue all aspects of wagering, such as on sports, dogs, and horses. United Kingdom applications are included. And some American references are used as illustrative of the larger worldwide gambling scene.

Wagering, for the Christian, must primarily be seen through the lens of Scripture. The Bible addresses our attitude to leisure as well as our use of the means of leisure. Surprisingly few current Christian studies of gambling have attempted to trace reactions to gambling in earlier periods when lotteries were in use. We hope what follows introduces you to material not found elsewhere.

Level-headedness is needed as well as wise steward-ship. Full airing of ideas and a review of basic information should precede conclusions. Admittedly, getting exer-cised Christians to cool down on a hot topic is sometimes difficult. The first thing we must do is discuss the matter of how the word 'gamble' is used and what it means.

What does a person mean by 'gambling'? What is gam-bling? And how does a gamble differ from other decisions of risk? Unless meanings are clarified conversation tends to get bogged down by cross-signals and confusion.

In Isaac Watts' [1674–1748] long-forgotten book, *Logic*, he urged his readers to clarify such words as *fate*, *luck*, *chance* and *fortune*. Because Christians accept Scripture's emphasis on God's priority and power none of those pop-ular words, still widely in use, hold an explanation for the origin of events. Watts distinguished between a causative sense of chance and a superficial cataloguing of surprising events as chance:

> ... if by the word *luck* or *chance* [the users] signify the absolute negation of any determinate cause, or only their ignorance of any such cause, we should know how to converse with them, and to assent to, or dissent from their opinions.[3]

How do Christians use the word 'gamble'? More often than not, for them, gambling connotes waste and wrong. The word goes beyond a simple evaluative or descriptive sense: it is used pejoratively. Gilbert K. Chesterton [1874–1936], however, held all betting should *not* be given the bad name of gambling.[4]

Historically, 'gaming' was the first word for 'gam-bling.' The words 'gambling' and 'gaming' were inter-changeable; they meant the same thing. Today casino personnel prefer to refer to their work as part of the 'gaming industry.' Why? Probably because 'gambling' has a social, if not moral, stigma. (In fact the oldest word for 'gambling' was 'gaming.')

I first met the 'gaming' vs. 'gambling' distinctions when I received a church profile from Reno, Nevada, USA, not far from where I lived in the state of Wyoming. The mid-sized church was conservative in theology, congregational in government, and charismatic in spirit. The form specifically said the next pastor was not to preach against gambling as a sin, 'first because the correct name is gaming, not gambling, and, secondly, because many of our officers, leaders, and members are employed – one way or another – in the casinos and hotels.' I never got there. I had a hunch I would not be a winner in Reno.

The traditional definition, the accepted standard of gambling is the legal definition.

The legal definition 'gambling' has three parts:

(a) money put down in the hope of greater gain in return,
(b) the element of chance; no guarantee of gain,
(c) the outcome: some win items of value (often money) and others lose.

Is the legal definition enough?

Gambling, like chance, has two senses: whereas the chance definitions focus on function, the gambling definitions focus on application or how one bets. Gambling has a strict definition and a loose definition. The loose or broad sense is 'taking a risk'. It applies to any number of activities. In varying degrees risk-taking involves all choices and to a greater or lesser degree all decisions have a whiff of gambling. One definition does not exclude or render the other definition invalid. The trick is to clarify how we use the word.

To restrict gambling to the money game would cut out vast areas of life in which people gamble where there is no dropping of cash. To restrict gambling to the legal definition may have greater adverse consequences than any amount of money wagered and lost. Whole sections of life are written off as incapable of being gambled away when gambling is only betting or buying lottery tickets. Gambling has many faces and a variety of appetites. Reformers may limit gambling advertisements and venues, but the loose definition will never be outlawed or eliminated.

We gamble with our diets, thereby shortening our lives. Over-eating or poor nutrition are ways we unwittingly gamble away life. Perhaps the saddest and most destructive sorts of gambling have to do with the risking of our life-direction and destiny. Most anti-gambling rigorists are wrong to limit gambling to the legal sense when the so-called loose sense, the vernacular sense of risk-taking, addresses more serious losses. Is not the gambling away of a life the worst sort of gamble? Do not Christians argue that the wager that God does not exist is the most foolish bet?

Varieties of gambling

Gambling historians distinguish between a variety of money gamblers:[5]

(a) winning at gambling often requires skill, such as at games that involve playing cards,

(b) simple wagering, betting on a horse, dog, or team over which you have no influence, is sports wagering,

(c) lotteries, like raffles, pay to the persons with the win-
     ning numbers, but most of the wagered money goes to
     the state or organization running the game.

Gambling has gone international. Internet outlets provide
on-line gambling. Gambling opportunities already flood
computer messages. We're not just referring to information on the World Wide Web, such as 'Inter-Lotto' that
gives betting updates. According to Eugene Christiansen,
a New York-based gambling analyst, consumers spend
about $300 million worldwide on Internet gambling, and
$2.3 billion is predicted by 2001.[6] Doubtless, computer
gambling may be the greatest challenge to reform move-
ments that want to reduce or limit gambling.

The computer is being used as a slot machine. Internet
gambling is also inter-active. In cyberspace, lottery Web
pages have proliferated.[7] There are even Web 'lottery club'
sites 'that conduct unregulated drawings or act as buying
services for [lotteries]'.[8]

Not just a similarity but a relationship between video
games and slot machines exists.[9] The sheer mechanical
similarities between pieces of equipment (slots and video
games) are less significant than the power felt in their use.
The attraction is the real action. The action is less what one
puts in than what one *gets out*. It is now commonly held
that 'the addictive nature of electronic slot machines is
[like] crack cocaine'.[10] Reports Rex Rogers: 'An estimated
three hundred gambling-related sites can be found on the
World Wide Web, some of which offer real money wagering opportunities'.[11]

World Wide Web gambling is rising rapidly and
spreading exponentially. Gambling via computers is
astonishing: 'Nearly $200 million will be wagered on-line
worldwide [in 1997], most of it on Web sites where people
can enter lotteries, bet on sports events and play normal

casino games . . . promoters see Internet gambling as the next major wave of expansion.'[12] Gaming analysts say off-shore sports gambling is 'taking in 1 to 5 percent of the $100 billion that is bet illegally on sports each year in the United States'.[13]

Law enforcement agents face another problem in stopping gambling, peculiar to US history. After the indigenous Native American Indian tribes were conquered in the western expansion of the United States Federal government, tribes were given independent nation status although put on reservations. Today on their reservations they have the right to build and operate gambling casinos. And Native American reservation gambling is exempt from federal government law.

Website gambling operations currently work out of Australia, Liechtenstein, Antigua, Grenada, Belize, and Austria. For instance, 'of the approximately 60 offshore sports books in operation throughout the Caribbean and Central America, 25 are based in Antigua'.[14]

> On-line betting – primarily through Websites that let you wager on sports events, enter lotteries and play casino games – is still in its infancy. Between $100 million and $200 million will be gambled on-line this year worldwide, says Whittier Law School professor and gaming-industry expert I. Nelson Rose.[15]

Ironically, the casino industry, which is in the business of promoting gambling, is an outspoken opponent of Internet betting. They don't fear computer wagering will overtake casinos, but they express concern that crooked and flawed Websites will undercut their efforts to promote an improved image of casino gambling.[16] (Ironically, casino gambling promoters have active protest from horse racetrack owners.)

The pervasiveness of wagering money has escalated in another direction. Added to gambling through cyberspace is gambling in the skies, for airlines are experimenting with systems that allow passengers to wager at poker, blackjack, and keno video as they fly. 'Swissair now offers the games on its long-haul flights abroad, and other foreign carriers are expected to follow.'[17] But, 'Swissair is not a flying casino. It is trying to have less bored passengers, by offering them a menu of personal entertainment that includes lowstakes, recreational commercial games.'[18]

The trend is spreading. Other airlines that either have or are scheduling this feature for long-haul flights are Alitalia, Quantas, Oasis, Singapore, Virgin Atlantic and British Airways.[19] At the present time 'gambling is prohibited on US Airlines, and foreign carriers are not allowed to operate commercial games on international flights to or from the United States. But this could change.'[20]

Churches are put on the spot. They seem to have been caught sleeping on this social problem. Whereas the social stigma of slavery caught their attention and action, so today they are being called upon to become proactive in regard to lotteries and wagering.

How does it affect churches?

Pity churches near casinos. In the major US cities where casinos proliferate, churches are experiencing hard times.[21] As church attendance goes down, counselling sessions go up, as the number of problem and pathological gamblers put clergy on the front-line, counselling families at all hours. Take the instance in Southern Indiana, US, where the United Methodists, at their 1999 annual conference at Bloomington addressed the increased burden of regional gambling. The Revd Tom Grey, aged 58, the

Executive Director of the National (US) Coalition Against Legalized Gambling, who has spearheaded gambling opposition for the last nine years, and is himself a United Methodist minister, said to the 2,000 delegates: 'The government is escorting a predatory industry into our communities and asking our churches to clean up the mess. It's insulting.'[22] Delegate attender the Revd Bill Helms of Lawrenceburg's Hamline UMC Chapel expressed the opinion that the long-term harm outweighs the short-term economic gains.[23]

British pastors, as well, and United Kingdom church officials wring their hands in despair. But who is supporting 'gaming'? When all is said, among lottery-ticket holders and casino players, there are many from church rolls. Apparently, Christians cave in, join the crowd and play lotteries. Let's be honest – fakery is rampant, realism is scarce; deception is pervasive, moderation is weak.

There is a humorous story told many times, but its point bears mention, because it accurately reflects part of the problem. Allegedly one church near a casino had several birds enter it unnoticed. A stage parrot broke loose, left the casino, and gained entrance to the church. On the first Sunday morning he watched as the choir processed and he watched as the service went on. At the end he commented to the other birds that were with him: 'The Master of Ceremonies is different. The music is different. The floor-show is different. But it's the same old crowd.'

Is charity gambling moral?

Since 1994 in the United States, the growth in charitable (non-reservation) bingo has slowed down. Some see it as 'a long term trend.'[24] 'Charitable bingo continues to be impacted by higher stakes Class II Indian bingo halls, the slower but continuing expansion of casino tables and machine games and, perhaps, nascent in-home Internet bingo games.'[25]

In American Judaism, bingo for fund-raising has been denied as a method for raising money; bingo is 'not to be permitted' among the congregations of the United Synagogues of America, because it does not reflect the spirit of Judaism.[26]

For years, however, US Catholic churches included bingo games as part of their stewardship programmes. Protestants – in the main – have not faced the dilemma of meeting their budgets through bingo operations. For them there is no internal hierarchical disputing on bingo as a way of meeting their budgets. The gambling issue has more to do with individual values.

From the beginning, Protestants have had an anti-gambling and pro-tithing image. Here are four frequent objections Protestants have used against gambling:[27]

(a) Getting something for nothing is not as valued as working for it.
(b) Frivolity should not characterize a Christian's use of time and resources.
(c) The *quid pro quo* ('this for that') useful product argument. To them there is no worthy product gained by gambling.
(d) A 'me win' mentality. Some argue the me-win/you-lose mentality is against the Christian spirit

For Protestants how money *goes out* of church offering plates in funding projects produces less guilt than how the money is raised to *go into* offering plates. For instance, Tony Evans, a prominent Texas black pastor, asked, 'Why does the church have to resort to games to raise the money it needs? There's only one reason I can think of. It's because the church can't get people to *give* money, so it creates a game to get it.'[28]

At the close of the nineteenth century, the once-popular US Presbyterian T. De Witt Talmage [1823–1902] argued that 'we do not read that they had a lottery for building the church at Corinth, or at Antioch, or for getting up an embroidered surplice for St Paul'.[29]

When Christians condone gambling

What separates the occasional gambler from the addicted gambler is not just repeat wagering, but the strength of the urge left after the occasional gamble, and when the urge to wager causes a person to deny the wisdom of restraint.

A keen analysis of the gambling urge should be shared. The compulsive gambler experiences five major moods: risk-taking, the sense of immediate opportunity, and the more compelling moods of fantasy, euphoria, and mysticism.[30] The progression from a series of intense moods from fantasy, to euphoria, to mysticism characterizes the compulsive gambler who idealizes chance to the point that it becomes his character, 'a career organized around an identity'.[31]

The occasional gambler is not compulsive. Many gambling experiences on cruises or on vacations to casino cities are episodic rather than routine. The American middle-class is not about to wager away its assets. 'Despite common worries about problem gamblers, those who monitor the industry say it is rare that a riverboat patron bets away his home or car, or endangers his children's financial well-being.'[32]

Some say the occasional gambler is just an undeveloped compulsive gambler, that the same compulsion is there that is found in the addicted gambler. Physician

Edmund Bergler disagreed. He wrote: 'The person who indulges only occasionally in games of chance is not a pathologic gambler.'[33]

A simple explanation of how one can determine between the occasional vs. the compulsive gambler is found in the following comparison: You know you are an addictive gambler when you drive to a famous US gambling town, Las Vegas, in a $50,000 Cadillac, but ride home in a $150,000 bus.

Is the main lure in gambling fun?

Increasingly, Americans view a casino visit as good use of vacation time, and harmless entertainment. *The Journal of International Gaming & Wagering Business* noted that gambling is a huge entertainment enterprise.[34] At the same time, gambling is probably the most controversial pastime. Most lose at the gambling game. Watched by the non-gambler, the game is boring. Gambling varieties where interest runs high involve those games which go beyond chance and have the challenge of skill. In some instances, a gamble involves the outcome of another game or race: game on game.[35] One way or another, it is a game meant for participation, creating excitement.

Gaming has gained more ground in the UK, as in the US, because of the increased variety of gambling venues. To allow gaming to become the fastest growing industry speaks of the impoverishment of humanity's capacity for intellectual entertainment.

Fans of traditional soccer rivalries expect to lose their neutrality, but not their shirts. But, warn some, when you buy lottery tickets daily or make repeat casino visits, in addition to losing your shirt, you could end up losing your ability to pay for a new shirt, or keeping your house.

Gambling critics view the boom sport of gambling a bottomless rob-the-gullible-public scheme,[36] because where chance rules, the outcome is uncontrollable. In such cases inducement is not challenge, but simple come-on.

Despite the drawbacks from losing lots of money some devotees insist: 'I believe that gambling is entertainment and if it is properly associated with that, then it's OK.'[37] Most gamble for fun. It's part of their entertainment budget.[38] The problem is that eventually a fun-money limit can grow to the point that it covers every last dollar. The pathological gambler doesn't want to limit fun money to a few dollars. Is it more truly fun or folly?

Too much fun can be very expensive. Wagering begins with simple entertainment, and later there is either an economic kick or an emotional kick-back. The lure of the hunt can be followed by the thrill of a win. Satisfaction is what gambling offers. The question is not whether the satisfaction is low or high, but is gambler satisfaction a useful product? This takes us to a new level for discussion. It goes to the heart of what makes gaming attractive.

Is 'satisfaction' ever a 'product'?

Taking a risk has a strange way of bringing enjoyment. The wild hope of winning is not a consumable product, and that is reason enough to shun it. Ann Fabian reflected:

> This is indeed consumption at a very high level of abstraction. Such formulations would have been impossible for those in the nineteenth century who understood that gambling was the antithesis of both production and consumption.[39]

What attracts so many to gambling? Apparently, 'a fun aspect is what draws most participants to gambling.'[40] They have no basis for expecting to become rich by playing. Gaming is neither a good nor a service, but an experience. Do people gravitate to gambling or are they lured, softened, programmed through pre-conditioning? Enter psychological trail-blazing. Whatever answer one comes up with has to include the fact that it is a nurtured inclination. On both sides of the Atlantic it seems today's rush to casinos and lottery outlets is the result of TV game shows, now many of them dealing with quick riches. Like the US networks, the UK ITV has versions of the easy-answer sudden wealth programmes, such as 'Who wants to be a Millionaire?' One specialist of viewer habits is convinced that TV game shows (now replaced by TV talk shows) have primed the pump, i.e., getting the public excited about winning money they don't have to work for. The programmes provide viewers with a 'vicarious gambling experience' with the safe exception that whereas real gamblers lose real money, the game-show viewers lose nothing.[41]

Viewers are increasingly experience-junkies. We are programmed by programmes. And our experiences as game-show spectators have put us parallel with a cutting-edge concept in modern business. Anti-gambling rigourists – usually social-activist Christians – dismiss any value from losses in gambling and even any value from wins. But according to B. Joseph Pine II and James H. Gilmore, forward-looking business strategy experts on an emerging economic paradigm called 'Mass Customization', there exist economic offerings that defy categorization as manufactured goods and delivered services, and transcend traditional worldviews expressed solely in terms of production and consumption.

People are willing to pay money for more than goods or services – whether it is a multiplicity of auras, such as at a theme park, or a single ambience, such as at an 'entertainment' restaurant which advertises the foodstuffs as a thematic event. Customers want more than mere food service; they want a dining experience. Combining a dinner with a play, a movie, or a floor show offers a dining experience which is distinctive, memorable. Customers are willing to pay extra money for added enjoyments.

Similarly, at a casino, customers are willing to participate just for the experience; winning is a bonus.[42] In this light, therefore, the complaint that gambler satisfaction is not a product falls flat. Of course, gambling is not a physical product, nor an intangible service, as Pine and Gilmore point out; but, they contend, experiences are often transformational – that is, they elicit a change in the individual if had repeatedly.

Whether the experiences are impressionistic only and never become transformational is a matter for deliberation and evaluation. One other debatable aspect of the gambling experience and its dubious transformation is that the experience is perceived by Christian moralists to be superficial, transitory, and not aimed at moral transformation.

Moreover, because of the usual losses in gambling there may be no monetary capital left to effect change in society. The thrill of the risk in gambling cannot compensate for the folly of throwing money away. What is left over, anyway, to give to the poor at home when they have paid for their party clothes (goods) and hotel stay (service)? Gambling critics view such a cavalier dismissal as an insensitive rationalization of self-indulgence.

High-rollers or steady gamblers experience heavy losses. How is that pleasurable? The Revd Tom Grey, fiery Methodist minister crusader and Executive Director of the National (US) Coalition Against Legalized Gambling, who sports his striking 'CasiNO ' badge, offered his opinion on the argument that casino gambling is fun: 'There is pain in loss – and since when is it entertainment to lose money?'[43]

I'm no casino gambling endorser by any means, but apart from the hot sociological and statistical arguments against casino gambling, those who seek entertainment *expect* to part with their money (after all, they pay admission to places). But gambling opponents assume that parting with money is not as bad as losing money.

Is *parting with* money as bad as *losing* it?

When a gambler views gambling as an entertainment expense, there is no guilt attached.

Routine reality back home, however, sharpens one's insight into the difference between simple parting and genuine losing, for, as Revd Grey fairly asks, 'How much fun is it to go home two hundred, three hundred bucks lighter?'[44] Even from a non-Christian perspective, the thought should flash across the gambler's mind, 'Now how are the bills back home going to be paid? Could the lost money not have been used to better advantage in getting out of debt rather than adding to the coffers of casino owners?'

Christians view themselves as God's property. God has made us stewards of his money. We trust our needs will be met by God, based on the Pauline re-assurance, 'God shall supply all your needs according to his riches in Christ Jesus' (Phil. 4:13, KJV). Christian faith is of two sorts: God can meet one's needs either with or without wagering, but he has a more difficult challenge to meet our needs after we blow our savings and refuse to invest our incomes wisely.

Good stewards recognize gambled money is tantamount to burned money. Money from reckless gambling in casinos, where the odds are always in favour of the house, goes to an enterprise that is more concerned about personal profits than social services. To make wagering a weekly event, therefore, is considered poor management. And for lottery players to buy daily lotto tickets doesn't make much sense. Stock investment, however, is another story.

Justifiable gambles

If all risky decisions involve something of a gamble, and money need not necessarily be involved, does that make them all inherently evil?

That's a leap in logic we shouldn't take. Why? It would reduce scripturally warranted decisions to evil. But that patently contradicts God's injunction to believe or decide a certain way, to honour and obey him.

Obviously, risk is not necessarily the same as gambling. In the decision to follow God's word our reliance has a solid basis, a firm footing, and such trust will not put us to shame. To trust Christ is not a gamble for he was above gambling himself. He knew what he was about. He knew why he was sent. In addition, on the proven record of Christ's reliability and resurrection, our trust is not misplaced or immoderate.

Before we get heavily into the question of whether risk reduces all decisions to a gamble (which gets fuller coverage in Chapter 6) there is the prior issue of whether gambling itself is evil. What makes gambling a problem? We have already opened the debate and made some preliminary observations. More information needs to be uncovered, more needs to be said and stepping back into history will help. We must begin where ultimate issues are addressed and that is Scripture. Too frequently, we take all our moral clues from cultural analysis and sociological findings, but we must sift Scripture more thoroughly.

Casting lots and lotteries

Some assume casting lots in biblical times encouraged, if it did not give rise to, gambling. Did biblical characters gamble, or at least lend it credibility in the use of ancient lots? What do churches and religious leaders say in regard to the reliance upon random draws as the way to decide and divide spoils?

A two-year nine-member Study Commission, authorized by Congress' Commission on the Study of Gambling, produced in June, 1999, a 300-plus page report with seventy recommendations to Congress.[45] The last such report was published in 1975. Many changes were noted over more than two decades. Principal among the findings was that gambling is legalized in 37 out of 50 states; 28 states have Indian Reservation casinos, and 43 have pari-mutuel betting. But the Report omits any rationale on gambling from a biblical perspective. The Commission was not appointed to decide upon the morality or immorality of wagering. That is why this book fits a need.

What follows is an examination of what the Bible and church history have said on wagering. Be ready for some surprises. Be open to be challenged. Heading up the shocks will be some preliminary observations on Old Testament texts on gambling. Following that will be an in-depth exploration of the relevance of Matthew 25:14–30. Be ready for mind jolts. Through it all you will emerge with a stronger grip of what Christians have said and why. Each reader, and if you are part of a group, each participant should acquire a finer understanding of one of the most significant societal controversies in the New Millennium.

2.

The Bible on Gambling

Does the Bible berate gamblers or condemn gambling? Surprisingly, no. Ever notice? Check for yourself. Run over the verses with an ethical fine-tooth comb. For instance, the Book of Proverbs, usually packed with moralisms, doesn't rip into gamblers. You can't find one verse in which wagerers are roasted or raked over hot embers.

The same cannot be said of those who have commented on Proverbs! In the nineteenth-century *The Expositor's Bible* series, Robert F. Horton wrote on Proverbs. He grouped numerous specific topics appearing in Proverbs (rather than commenting on verses sequentially). He had no chapter on gambling. Why? Because Proverbs has no verses on gambling, *per se*. Moreover, he accused stock investors and counsellors of robbery![1]

Although Horton didn't mention it, there are, nevertheless, at least three significant texts in Proverbs about throwing dice, and these texts are positive, not pejorative. They are,

Proverbs 1:14

throw in your lot with us,
and we will share a common purse.

Proverbs 16:33

> The lot is cast into the lap,
> but its every decision is from the LORD.

Proverbs 18:18

> Casting the lot settles disputes
> and keeps strong opponents apart (MIV).[2]

One would think Proverbs, which hits social sins pretty hard – from prostitution to graft and embezzlement – would have a choice collection of moral zingers for gambling and gamblers. But Proverbs does not mention gambling as an evil to avoid.[3] Scripture does address the motivation to gamble and what makes for a devoted gambler – easy profits, quick riches, covetousness or greed – all of which bolster the gambling business. The closest scolding of gambling may be hidden in rebukes of swindlers and of those who get wealth without work.

Educator Dr Ivan Zabilka considered the picturesque phrase of Isaiah 65:11,12 – those who 'spread a table for fortune' – as being more than an opaque or oblique reference to ancient gambling.[4] His suggestion is interesting, but – unfortunately – a contextual, grammatical interpretation of the passage will not support it. As we shall find when we return to this passage early on in Chapter 9, the so-called gods of fortune are chimeraic, non-existent. We must pass over this passage as being against lottery playing, for the verses deal, not with money made from the fortune gods, but with the honouring of those gods with a special meal. The 'spreading of the table' refers to the spreading of a feast 'for the consumption of the gods'.[5] The spreading reference not only alludes to meals in honour of the gods, but to cushions 'upon which the images of the gods were placed during such meals'.[6] The honouring of the false gods of greater and lesser luck was a 'counterpart of the table of shew-bread' in the tabernacle of Jehovah and, therefore, a supreme insult to the true God.[7]

David L. McKenna's summary of Scripture on gambling is fair: 'A scriptural position on gambling must be derived by inference, not prescription. Arguments based on the stewardship of resources are strong but not conclusive'.[8] Gamblers' huge losses help the average person recognize gambling's evil. A betting urge can grow into an obsessive-compulsive behaviour disorder (OCD). Players beware. Wagering has the potential of escalating from an innocent diversion to an economic disaster. There is no guarantee, however, that an occasional gambler will become a compulsive gambler.

Any consuming pastime, yes, even career obsessions that have no room for God, bring into question Christ's total mastery of us. The Apostle Paul was convinced that a Christian can be a slave to none but Christ. Being a slave to Christ, he could be slave to nothing or no one else (Romans 6:16,17). Money is not our master. We are meant to use it honourably, distribute it regularly, and give it away generously.

Christian books on gambling argue that gambling is wrong because it does not bring any observable product. The sheer possession of wealth has no moral claim. Wealth does not indicate anything about one's relationship with God. A lot of money does not mean we are loved by God a lot, a truth that is often missed. In Scripture money should be used to help others. Paul says we should be willing to part with our money to help others. 'Share with God's people who are in need. Practise hospitality' (Rom. 12:13 NIV).

Back in the 1800s, according to historian Henry Chafetz, 'all [US]statesmen played cards, and gambling was a proper social conduct'. Political moralist and abolitionist, Thaddeus Stevens of Pennsylvania, USA, was one of the hottest, most successful poker players in the nation. One morning, after a big win in a poker game the previous evening, he was ascending the steps of the Capitol in Washington, DC. A black pastor was there seeking contributions for his impoverished church. Stevens graciously 'emptied his pockets of his winnings and reverently cited William Cowper's *Light Shining out of Darkness:* "God moves in a mysterious way/His wonders to perform" '.[9]

In the Old Testament some lack of direction on our part is suggested in the good fortune following the order to 'cast your bread upon the waters' (Eccl. 11:1, NIV) – somewhat related to which side of the boat you throw your net from or what bait you use in casting your line.

A key New Testament passage testifies to a more intentional approach to success in making money, and, from another side, it relates to a side issue in the gambling debate – the claim that no-sweat labour is not real labour. Jesus' Parable of the Stewards in Matthew 25:14–30 is often overlooked as having any application to gambling. But as we shall see, it has both obvious and more subtle reference to gambling issues.

Norman Mailer was interviewed by Maureen Conlan, a *Cincinnati Post* book reviewer, regarding his novel, *The Gospel According to the Son* (Random House, 1997). Mailer said, 'One of the things that appealed to me was how Jesus hated the whole notion of mammon . . . Essentially, Jesus was opposed to money.'[10] The two-time Pulitzer prize-winning author hit on a strand of Jesus' teaching. In Matthew 25:14–30, however, we have another Jesus theme where He values money, especially its wise investment.

Put your money to work by wagering?

The Matthean passage 25:14–30, in particular, sparked interest in an Anglican parish when they planned their annual stewardship drive. In the 1960s the Revd Eric Cook, vicar of St Mary's Church at Chard near London, handed out £50 to his parishioners in a scheme to raise money for the church. Patterned after Jesus' comments of wise talent investment (Mt. 25:14–30), the 62-year-old Anglican vicar urged his parishioners to use the money in such ways as 'buying basic materials and making and selling cakes, toys or coffee.' It was his way of investing to increase the church's income; he took Jesus at his word.

Someone raised the question as to whether it was all right to use the money to bet at a horse race. To the reporter who asked the question the vicar responded, 'I don't mind if they gamble. I am not against gambling in moderation.' He added stipulations, however, for those inclined to triple their 'talent' by gambling: If they bet on a horse and it won, the church should get the money. If it lost, the backer should return the stake to the church. The standard handout was two shillings and sixpence for adults and sixpence for children. Today in Britain betting shops are licensed. In the late 1960s bets as small as three pence were taken.[11]

Lotteries in England

Lotteries emerged in Great Britain in the sixteenth century. Although organized in 1567, the first lottery draw was not held until two years later.[12] The first Irish Sweepstakes were held in 1750. In England, corruptions caused private lotteries to be suspended in 1776. Eventually, only municipal/public lotteries were allowed. Yet by 1826 even public lotteries were curtailed. The ebb and flow of lotteries' popularity had a similar history in the US. (See Chapter 7.)

The road back to lotteries began with the allowing of small charitable lotteries. Closer controls were considered the secret to preventing corruption. By 1956 monitored public lotteries were reintroduced.[13] In 1960, gambling in Great Britain in a variety of forms was legalized with strict compliance to anti-corruption rules. By 1974 there were 15,000 betting offices and 125 casinos.[14]

Within the Anglican church several contrasting attitudes are found. The more tolerant usage of wagering we have already illustrated in Revd Cook's parish. In contrast to Revd Cook, an Anglican theologian, Dr Waddams, considered gambling 'morally wrong'. For Waddams, gambling was wrong mostly on pragmatic grounds. Gambling would be improper 'for raising church funds, since it puts the Church's *imprimatur* on the practice'.[15]

Revd Cook's usage of Matthew 25?

Anti-gambling writers contend that Matthew 25:14–30 'can hardly be used to sanction sharp speculation or gambling risks'.[16] The passage, when reread carefully, does not encourage people to take their money and use it in betting. That is clear. Jesus wasn't saying that you use your money wisely by gambling. That would be putting words in Jesus' mouth that were not there. Nevertheless, we must not conclude that this passage has nothing to say on the wagering issue. It remains one of the key passages dealing with financial risk-taking. We cannot ignore it as a significant section in Scripture on the role of financial investment, financial investment which entails risk or a gambling element.

The passage could be called the parable of investments. There are two sets of investments in the passage. The initial gifts to the servants by the master were the first investments, the second being those of the first two servants. Both master and servants expected returns.

Connected with the investments were the lines of responsibility. Apparently, the master saw himself as part-owner if not sole owner of the initial investments, because he said, 'I shall have received mine' (v. 27), which probably meant the servants were finally answerable to him. Tied to the gifts to the servants was responsibility to the donor. Did the servants who reported gains relinquish the gains? It is not stated. On a higher or another level, however, beyond the gain or growth of the funds was the question of ultimate responsibility and ownership. Jim Gilmore of Strategic Leadership Forum, near Cleveland, Ohio, commented '[God] expects us to make the most of what He provides and is glorified in the increase as well as in the return.'[17]

Matthew 25 and the stock market

The parable is extraordinarily relevant to the stock market issue in the gambling debate. Why is it relevant? Here are five reasons:

1. First, the parable is about the smart use of money. 'Talent' in the passage was not a reference to inner gifts, but to hard cash, real money. Indeed, the Greek word for 'talent' refers to gold, silver, or copper (25:15).[18] A wealthy man entrusted three servants with specific amounts. The first was given five talents, money equivalent to 20 years of wages – a huge amount.[19] Two other servants received

amounts less than the first (the second servant two talents; the third servant one talent). All three were asked to make good use of the money, i.e. to make the money grow, increase, multiply. Servants 1 and 2 doubled the loan. Servant 3, however, did not invest and earned nothing.

2. There is a reference (25:16,17) to winning or gaining.[20]
3. There is a reminder that it is better to gain and not lose (25:18).
4. 'Bankers' are mentioned (25:27).
5. The first two servants were commended for 'doubling' their talents/money (25:28). The initial reading seems to be very relevant to the topic.

The first two servants were wise investors, but the third was self-protective and essentially non-productive. Risk was required for investment, even though it was not presented as a gamble, *per se*. By the same token, not to risk was also a form of gambling, of risk-taking.

The story fits real life. The wealthy man who took a vacation left no detailed instructions on how to invest his money. Apparently, the wealthy man wanted the servants to come up with wise investment ideas. How or what they would trade in, or whether they would start a business was up to the enterprising servants.

One part of the smartness of the two risk-taking servants was a lack of indecision on how best to make the money grow. Jesus emphasized that they actually invested quickly (25:16). What form that took we are not told: some think they set up a business.[21]

Some suggest that it was through trade (NRSV). Still others that the wise servant 'invested his money' (GNB). Where? Jesus did refer to the 'bankers.' In 25:27 Jesus alluded to the money-changers in the Temple.

The money-changers exchanged the foreign currency of the festival pilgrims at a rate of interest. That's how they made money: they charged for their services.[22] It is interesting that Jesus did not refrain from referring to money-changers, especially since on two occasions he personally cleared the Temple of them. Charging interest was apparently in use outside the Temple. As ATM machines today charge the customer for supplying money at any time, day or night, so those who loaned money in Jesus' day charged the customers. That was profitable. Although the Old Testament was hard on 'usury' (Deut. 23:20; interest to Gentiles was permissible), Jesus did not thunder against charging fees for loaning out money.[23]

Investment in the stock market is not referred to specifically. Since, however, earning money by the use of money was implied by Jesus, then there would be nothing inherently wrong or evil about gaining income through stock speculation.

Overlooked factors in Matthew 25

Perhaps the most interesting element of the parable is the most overlooked. It seems to me the parable contains a rebuke to anti-gambling writers of our day in three ways:

1. *The principal character, the wealthy man, had not earned his own money and admitted to it (25:24).*

'The master accepts the description of himself as reaping what he did not sow and gathering where he did not winnow.'[24] Money earned without the sweat of one's brow is frequently berated by opponents of gambling in any form. Consider the following. Methodist seminary professor, Lycurgus M. Starkey, Jr. wrote in the 1960s 'The prevalence of gambling points to a breakdown of the Puritan ethic of work . . . this ethic has been replaced by the something-for-nothing philosophy.'[25]

American theologian Carl F.H. Henry was of the opinion that gambling is 'a vice that encourages the notion that the best things in life can be acquired effortlessly'.[26] The late Wayne E. Oates, Senior Research Professor at Southern Baptist Theological Seminary in Louisville, Kentucky, US, characterized gambling as the expectation of getting rich quickly without working.[27]

Rex Rogers' position went further: 'Gambling encourages people not to work . . . Gambling masquerades as a surrogate for work. It undermines work, rationality, and responsibility.'[28] 'Gambling diverts people from useful labor.'[29] And in his list of eight reasons why gambling is wrong, Rogers put as his fourth reason: 'Gambling undermines a biblical work ethic and human reason and skill.'[30] Similarly, Tony Evans: 'The Bible makes it clear that you and I are not to be involved in any scheme in which we try to get rich quick and bypass the process of productive work.'[31] US educator Ivan L. Zabilka lowered the boom by stating that wagering 'reduces the importance of industriousness, thrift, deferred gratification, diligence, and studiousness.'[32] Are these indictments entirely fair or true in all cases?

Must all rewards be delayed? Must all work be sweaty to justify the designation 'work?' Is not mental work, investigative reading, work? Many avenues of work involve calculated speculation. The critics of stock-market involvement as true work have a narrow concept of labour. Not to call stock investment investigation and speculation 'work' automatically demeans that occupation.

People buy stocks for profit. Sometimes quick profits come, but that does not render the gains evil. If stock investment is a form of gambling (which Rogers admits),[33] then stock investment is a questionable way to earn. David L. McKenna said, 'Jesus actually commended a gambler whose talents paid off ten to one.' In the next paragraph Dr. McKenna lamented that the modern gambler tries to get something for nothing, calling that a 'sin of perverted stewardship.'[34] Didn't the three servants get 'something for nothing?' And didn't two of them double that money by not themselves working but by putting that money to work?

Because no 'sweat' is involved in stock investments, Rogers, among others, is forced into a corner. It would seem that any earning that does not entail physical exertion is unworthy of the word 'work', unworthy of man's dignity and design, and, therefore, unworthy of acceptance. If Rogers is right, earnings from stock can't be noble earning, for it circumvents physical effort. At the end of the nineteenth century, stock buyers were considered evil, but 'by the beginning of the twentieth century, the great market gamblers had moved from the periphery of the financial universe to its moral centre. They had domesticated the vice of gambling.'[35] Two US Christian financial counsellors, Austin Pryor of Louisville, Kentucky and Larry Burkett of Gainesville, Georgia are Christian financial wizards who try to provide sound financial opinions on how Christians can best invest their money.

Are financial windfalls evil 'good fortune'?

Lottery winners, if they are Christian in orientation, speak of God's goodness and providence in helping in the nick of time. But lottery critics say it is wrong to explain it as the result of divine providence, despite the clear text of Proverbs 16:33, looked at earlier in this chapter.

Another disputed element in winning or gathering gain without work is the contention that the only wealth worthily gained and retained is that earned by hard labour. It suggests that riches gained by inheritance or from a combination of winning numbers is inherently tainted. But is non-physical work wicked? I think not. Wouldn't that suggest that the work of being financial counsellors is suspect, even illegitimate? Go back to Jesus' Parable. After all, the rich master didn't work a lick for his money: he didn't plant, harvest, or winnow. In addition, if the principle of not working for what you get lowers the value of the gain, then the valuation of the master's work was deplorable. Indeed, the effort-in, effects-out principle of the Protestant work ethic would demean much of our service for Christ.

The approach to Christian work which puts a heavy stress on our doings is in need of a vast reassessment when what Jesus said elsewhere is taken into consideration. Christ said, 'I send you to reap what you have not worked for. Others have done the hard work, and you have reaped the benefits of their labour' (Jn 4:38, NIV). In Christian or secular work, it is often proud self-importance that would demand individual effort for every penny received. But 'no work, no pay-off' doesn't always fit into God's economy.

2. *A second rebuke is carried in the Matthew 25 parable. It relates to the reluctance of Christians in taking risks with the little wealth they have.*

The third servant was over-protective of the money entrusted to him. He did nothing with it. He hid it out of fear of losing it. He thought the money was secure. To save it without investing, to him, was all that mattered.

But Jesus' parable was a strong statement for wise investment of whatever is entrusted to us. And it makes us think twice about whether seeking gain is evil or good. Tony Evans' most recent book says, unequivocally, that anyone who seeks to make ten millions in the lottery is guilty of greed. In addition, he asks, '... is that the agenda that God has set before you that requires you to win ten million dollars? I suspect the answer would be no. You want the ten millions because it's a lot of money and you would be set for life ... Playing the lottery is not tied to any legitimate goal. Winning the money is an end in itself, and that is evil.'[36]

Most lottery winners would not think, however, that simple winning was an end in itself. To be perfectly honest, they would think of how the surprise windfall would free them to do things they would otherwise be prohibited from doing.

How different Jesus' reaction to making a lot of money! In Matthew 25:14–30, He did not criticize the two servants who doubled their money: far from it. He did not accuse them of seeking improper goals in wanting or making more. Jesus did not accuse them of greed, rather he said to servant 1 and servant 2 the same thing: 'Well done, good and faithful servant!'(25:13).

The third servant was timid and stubborn; he did not use his master's money profitably (25:28). Not to invest is an evil misuse of wealth. The parable is a strong statement on misuse by inaction; on misuse by non-investment. Safe as the third servant's conduct was, he lacked ingenuity, inventiveness and assertiveness. Jesus used the parable to deplore pre-occupation with holding onto one's security.[37]

3.   *The parable raised the respectability of financial institutions and money-making enterprises.*

The non-judgemental attitude Jesus reflected in the banker reference (25:27) should clear the air and clear the way for a more positive approach to today's prime

institutions dealing with money growth: the stock market.
Before the primary application to all of life – that what we
have *from* God should be used *for* God – was the initial
financial spin: that acquiring things and organizing others
to work for us, are forms of work. Paul's injunction that
earning should precede eating does not exclude earning
by investment (2 Thess. 3:10). Our most vital role is not
necessarily that we work, but that we put our money to
work. Somehow in the anti-gaming rhetoric this note is
drowned out.

The simple statement that 'the best gamble is not to
gamble' does not work, does not wash. Stock investment,
of all forms of gambling, has the least risk of losing and the
greatest potential for gain. The seemingly built-in human
need to take risks is best directed to and exercised in
stocks, in land investments, in property ownership and
expansion. The money earned in these ways, the Matthew
24:14–30 passage says, should be earnestly pursued and
highly esteemed. It is money honestly, wisely, truly
earned:

> Learning to take proper risks with our money may be one of
> the hardest, but most-needed lessons that comfort-conscious
> Christians need to learn. It's a lesson that carries with it the
> potential for astonishing growth and spiritual excitement, if
> we dare.[38]

3.

Is Stock Investment Gambling?

Victorian London was blessed with amazing orators, such as the non-conformists Charles Spurgeon and Joseph Parker, and Anglican Henry Parry Liddon. During the same period, Brooklyn in New York had a famous congregational orator, Henry Ward Beecher [1813–1887]. He held that stock investments were a form of gambling: 'Dealing in fancy-stocks are oftentimes sheer gambling, with all its worst evils. Profits so earned are no better than the profits of dice, cards, or hazard.'[1]

Another American preacher, Charles Finney [1792–1875] was equally tough on stock investors. Stock investors needed to repent.[2] Sabbath-breaking by companies made any stock investment in them wicked. To him violation of the fourth Commandment was reason enough not to endorse stocks.

> Reason 3. Owning stocks in steamboat and railroad companies, in stages, canal boats, etc., that break the Sabbath. Can any such owner truly say he does not doubt the lawfulness of such an investment of capital? Can charity stoop lower than to say, that man must strongly doubt whether such labor is a work of necessity or mercy? It is not necessary in the case to demonstrate that it is unlawful – though that can be done fully, but only to show so much light as to create a doubt of its

lawfulness. Then if he persist in doing it, with that doubt unsatisfied, he is condemned – and lost.

Reason 4. The same remarks will apply to all sorts of lottery gambling. He doubts.[3]

A popular Washington DC Reformed/Presbyterian preacher, Thomas De Witt Talmage [1832–1902], found himself face to face with questions about the stock market and its relationship to gambling. In three undated published sermons Talmage commented on stocks. His sermon on Acts 1:19 ('The Field of Blood'), which appears early on (Vol. 6) in his collected sermons, sounded like Beecher. Talmage said, '. . . the man who deals in "fancy" stocks, or conducts a business which hazards capital . . . is a gambler. Whatever you expect to get from your neighbor without offering an equivalent in money, or time, or skill, is either the product of theft or gambling.'[4] But in two later sermons Talmage pulled back his horns. There he softened his position on stocks. It could reflect that some who knew stocks took him aside and enlightened him. In his sermon on 1 Samuel 14:43 ('Forbidden Honey') Talmage said,

> Many men are doing an honest and safe business in the stock-market, and you are an ignoramus if you do not know that it is just as legitimate to deal in stocks as it is to deal in coffee or sugar or flour. But nearly all the outsiders who go there on a financial excursion lose all.[5]

Yet in the same sermon he recognized that stock speculation was still gambling: 'Gambling is gambling, whether in stocks or bread-stuffs or dice or race-horse betting.'[6]

Back in London, Joseph Parker [1830–1902], who was widely admired as pastor of the Congregationalist City Temple, although of a different denomination from

Talmage who was Presbyterian, was of the same persuasion when it came to the stocks-as-gambling controversy. In Parker's published lecture on gambling (1900), he drew a disparaging comparison: 'the Stock Exchange is the bottomless pit of London.'[7]

In Volume 17 of Talmage's collected sermons, however, he showed more accommodation and empathy toward stock investors. He said,

> He who condemns all stock-dealings as though they were iniquities simply shows his own ignorance. Stop all legitimate speculation in this country, and you stop all banks, you stop all factories, you stop all store-houses, you stop all the great financial prosperities of this country. A stock-dealer is only a commission merchant under another name . . . The dollar that he makes is just as bright and fair and honest a dollar as the dollar earned by the day laborer.[8]

Gambling critics say savings accounts are a virtuous alternative to risking hard-earned money at gaming tables. Those with savings accounts have escaped the onus of gambling. But frugal savers' minimal interest earned in deposit and savings accounts is the result of fiscal stock gambles. In surrendering their money to bank officers who consult or retain stock speculators to increase their total assets do not professional money handlers here risk a gamble?

While it is true that gamblers do not speak of 'managing risk' – the way investment counsellors do – does one ever escape the long reach of gambling? If we don't know what we are doing when we place our investments, because we haven't done the research, doesn't that constitute a gamble? Partly, yes, but not entirely. We think wrongly if we imagine that all gambling takes place in dingy betting dives, in the sports palaces of the wealthy or in swank riverboat casinos. 'Gambling arenas' are in bank rooms, in residential homes, in international flights, even at stock exchanges – in England and everywhere.

Rex M. Rogers contends that 'compulsive gamblers only rarely play the stock market'.[9] But that does not fit the findings of a respected money journal. *Financial World* has pointed out that a significant percentage of investors are drawn to high-stakes security trading because they are compulsive gamblers. Experts on gambling addiction say a person who risks more than two per cent of capital on one trade and experiences a rush may be a compulsive gambler.

Even though one may not visit a casino or buy a lottery ticket, one still gambles if buying stocks is a gamble. That's my position. I'll soon tell you why. (Gambling beraters who are heavily into stocks should feel a twinge of hypocrisy if stock investment is a form of gambling.)

The mere assumption that stock investment is gambling is not enough. Arguments for and against this contention need careful examination. Are stock purchases a form of gambling? We will not be losers for looking into the matter.

Henlee H. Barnette has said that 'buying stocks on the stock market . . . is not considered pure chance because the money is risked to provide for the development of industry. Purchasing insurance involves some risks, but these are greatly reduced. Chance is not a predominant and controlling factor in either case.'[10]

How does that contention hold up? Many, like Barnette, maintain it is unfair to lump investments with gambling. Are stock purchases partly gambling, even if not completely identical with typical wagers?

First, take the arguments of those who deny that stock investment is gambling. A central contention of the non-gambling nature of stocks is that a stock share is not a gambling stake. Unlike the gambled casino or lottery dollar, the stock shareholder still owns the dollar, whereas the lottery dollar is down and gone. Secondly, the lottery or slot-machine dollar is total and made on an all-or-nothing basis, whereas the stock dollar has a multi-period life. Lastly, the gambling stake is used in a single, independent event, whereas the stock share is contingent on a variety of factors that can make it grow or shrink. Sounds good so far, right?

Four major arguments emerge against stock shares being a gamble:

1. Whereas in stocks one can 'manage risks', in gambling the claim is that there is no management of risk. (But, as we shall see, that is not entirely true.)
2. Purists argue that risk alone does not make a venture a gamble. Many kinds of risky choices are not gambling. Contests of skill such as chess or golf, even when played for money involve risk, but are not gambles. Such games can be part of the panoply of the phenomenon of gambling but the only gamble is an estimation of the other players' skills. The more skill required or demonstrated the more the element of chance is reduced.
3. Gambling and investing should be separated, many business persons argue, because investors purchase equity. 'For example, common stocks or options to buy some commodity; in contrast, the commodity purchased by gamblers is chance itself.'[11] But both hope and chance unite the stock share and the gamble stake.
4. In the stock market one learns a lot after purchase and performance. Investors, like lottery players, lose. But at least in stocks the investor manages to keep upwards to 90 per cent of the peak price, whereas in

the lottery purchase, unless one wins, everything played is lost.[12]

These arguments constitute the strongest case that investment is not gambling. But there are indications that that conclusion is still too facile and not the whole story. The case is not closed. Consider, now, the arguments which point to investment as reflecting the heart of a gamble if not the heart of a professional gambler. Investment always starts with chance. And chance goes to the very heart of a gamble.

Stock in commodities may be a greater risk than stock in companies. Gold is a commodity, and some companies depend on gold. Historically, commodities were the first stock and were directly affected by uncertain weather and other growth factors. A stable company provides assurance for its future, and its stock can be believed as significantly secure. Company stock is tied in with commodities.

Risk, however, is never far from the most secure company there is. Old companies can fold. Commodities like companies can fail. Since there are no guarantees, even with the companies where we calculate secure shares, the element of chance along with statistical probabilities, is always present. Probability of endurance is strong with 'safe' stocks, but nothing is absolutely certain. Despite the probability of safety, chance is not excluded.

But the complete separation of stocks and gambling is impossible, nevertheless. Why? Because 'some forms of speculative investments are gambling: options on essentially non-deliverable stock-market index futures, in which the underlying equity represented by the index is theoretical and rarely or never changes hands.'[13]

Despite the above arguments the stock market doesn't try to avoid all gambling association. A company with a high performance is considered a good bet. The investor goes through the same psychological elevation and depression as the gambler. There is hope, fear, hesitation, uncertainty, and the satisfaction when the returns are solid. Untenable risks in low percentage speculations create inner reactions comparable to the fear, even panic of the gambler. Like the gambler, the investor has yearning to gain (not necessarily greed) and describes his decision to invest as a leap into gambling.

One can lose on the market floor, just as on the casino floor. 'Gambling on tertiary stocks, like betting on a lucky number . . . takes over in a speculative [pardon his language – JG] "What the hell?" defiance of a part of ourselves that should have known better.'[14]

The riskiest stock investments continue to be not only a problem to the anti-gambling position, but its lynchpin, the Achilles-heel-weakness of the anti-gambling argument. When push comes to shove, anti-gambling Christian writers minimize and marginalize gambling in stocks. One recent Christian anti-gambling writer, William Petersen, admitted: 'Of course, there may be speculative stocks with a high risk attached to them. And if you speculate on them with the sole purpose of making a "killing" for yourself, it would certainly be gambling.'[15]

Norman Geisler has also reluctantly admitted that there is a gambling aspect to investment.[16] Wayne E. Oates is another author who saw an element of gambling in playing the stock market.[17] Barnette's position (the separation of stocks from gambling) was Norman Geisler's. Geisler did not want to grant that stock investment was gambling in the legal sense of the word. He proposed exceptions that made stock speculation different from gambling.

More recently Rex M. Rogers has admitted in his anti-gambling polemic that 'it is possible to gamble in the stock market or insurance . . . Speculators who invest funds hoping for a quick return are in some sense gambling. They have no control of the outcome . . .'[18] Rogers advances two reasons why stock investment is not true gambling: one is that whereas gambling is destructive, the stock market is constructive.[19] But to the occasional gambling winner, his win is constructive. Sure, there are plenty of nasty negatives associated with gambling – from what goes with it and what results from it – but denial of any constructive outcome is an argument that hasn't discouraged charity games of chance from being used. In lotteries, society gains and society is everyone.

Rogers' second argument is that the marketplace still gains even though the speculator loses. The same is not true in games of chance, he contends. Again, his argument doesn't hold water. I'm not a strong advocate of gambling for a variety of reasons, but a gambling advocate could argue in return that because the gambling industry – and in charity games, an organization – succeeds, it makes little difference if the individual gambler loses. Rogers' claim 'that there is no moral difference between gambling and business transactions or investments is specious' has not been proven.[20]

Geisler, like Barnette and like Rogers, wasn't ready to concede that stock-market investment was gambling. Geisler saw two differences. Firstly he says, 'stocks are an investment in a useful product or service'. Rogers and Barnette raise the same issue. Hold up a sec. Does this argument deny that lotteries in the past served good ends, and that present beneficiaries of lotteries yield useful products and services to social agencies as well as benefit to few winners? The benefits to specific moral, religious, cultural, social institutions through charity gambling are consistently either denied or played down by opponents of gambling. Even Larry Burkett found fault with the International Red Cross for launching an Internet-based lottery to raise money to pay for relief efforts.[21]

Another matter that should cause second thoughts to gambling critics: since when has money ceased to be a useful product? The only product a garbage collector wants from his city is his wages. On what basis can money be denied as a useful product?

Many Christian writers use the argument that gambling does not produce new money or goods. Reconsider that point. To all winners, however few, the money *is* new. Why? Because they have never seen it before. Technically, it is not new money, but it is new *to them* and that is important new money; indeed it is the only new money they care about and can use.

In addition, it would seem to me that money, *per se*, is a much better product than some of the so-called valid products stocks support. More importantly, doesn't Jesus' encouragement of investment of money – yes, to make it grow – suggest that Jesus was for money working rather than just the worker working (Mt. 25:14–30)?[22]

Take Geisler's second argument as to why stock-market investing is not gambling: 'the odds of losing on gambling are astronomically higher than on the stock market.'

Having your money in a bank is not without risk. George Gilder, a financial expert, has written: 'Savings accounts, after inflation and taxes, have lost money for decades.'[23]

Geisler's reason against seeing stock investment as gambling is weak, for if one's investments are not diversified but located in a poor stock, or if the entire market falls, then one's losses can be equally astronomical. Geisler's reluctant admission that playing the stock market is similar to gambling goes to show a weakness in the legal definition, that stockbrokers should have some kind of gambler status.

Stock markets are where money grows, shrinks, or disappears. Investments can't escape some gamble. A potential investor who knows nothing about a company whose stock he buys, is necessarily a gambler, but a person who has a handle on the company's growth record, is less so. New-start companies are, therefore, more of a gamble than established companies. Interest dollars, when earned in speculative stocks, are smudged with gambler's ink.

Risk-taking does not prove gambling. True. But while stocks are not of the same species, they are of the same genus. House cats are not lions, but both are cats. Stocks are not as much a gamble as lotteries, but both share risk, the element of financial loss.

A gamble can't be shaken entirely from stock investments. Seasoned financial counsellors have long recognized, for instance, that electing to invest one's entire inheritance in one stock is a high-risk gamble. Commitment to one stock or bond variety has the marks of a gamble. Stock investors who speculate on untested companies enter into a gambling area. The riskiest world of all is speculation on the riskiest stock options.[24]

Speculators may be the highest-flying gamblers in the investment game. But they are crucial to the success of the futures market because they complete a symbiotic relationship between those wishing to avoid risk and those willing to take it. Since hedgers [those interested in commodities; they can be producers or users] are planning ahead, want to avoid risk in what is undeniably a risky business, others have to be willing to accept it. Unless some speculators were willing to bet that orange juice prices will rise while others bet that prices will fall, an orange juice producer could not protect against dramatically increased costs in the event of a freeze, and orange farmers couldn't earn enough money in a good year to pay their production costs. Speculators also keep the market active.[25]

Ann Fabian, in her study of gambling in the nineteenth century, commented:

> . . . young clerks of Wall Street were also singled out as gamblers . . . Although [reformers] attacked gambling, they recognized that profits on the stock markets were often the result of lucky gambles and that it was difficult to assert a vast moral difference between stock markets and gambling casinos.[26]

Gambling has no fixed standard. What we view as a bad bet is coloured by subjective feelings and there are no clues in reality as to which is the safest course. Purchasing a work of art, for instance, may seem to pose little risk and little hope for making money, whereas a lottery ticket may have more appeal because the winning cash amount has been advertised. The risk in buying art is greater than the risk in buying a lottery ticket, for the potential value of the art is unknown, whereas the value of the winning lottery ticket is well known. Whereas shares in an existing company may seem too abstract a risk to induce investment, it may be more to one's benefit to hold shares there.

Horse-track betting is popular in the United Kingdom. Anyone who bets on horses ought to seek information on their track record. The wise bettor tries to manage his risk by studying the horses. A handicapper is one who says his analysis of the field can reduce the risk of losing and increase the odds of picking a winner. Wayne E. Oates, the well-known Christian psychology professor, lived in Louisville, Kentucky, the location of the world-famous Kentucky Derby. Oates pointed out that those who speculate on the likely winner use at least eight criteria before picking the most likely winner.[27] Much of this kind of information is supplied in daily racing forms and guides.

The broker on the stock market plays a role comparable to the handicapper at the racetrack. Soccer bettors had better be students of the strengths and weaknesses of the teams so they don't wager blindly. Again, what one knows about the teams is part of the 'risk management' found in gambling. But such analysis may be flawed, and is no guarantee of a sure bet. No one can infallibly manage outcome.

In sum, it should be noted that what constitutes gambling is risk that involves potential gain or loss of money, and ego-loss or ego-building. (Some are in it subconsciously for ego-stroking rather than simply gaining an economic advantage.) The kinds of gambling where interest runs high are those varieties which go beyond chance and have the challenge of a skill, and there is nothing quite so well adapted to the combination of skill and chance as stock investing. Certainty and chance combine on Fleet Street and Whitehall as much as in New York's Wall Street. What Justin Mamus asked American investors should be asked of British investors: 'Is [the stock market] so pure at heart that investing has no element of gamble to it?'[28]

Contemptuousness in a gambling critic may appear as self-righteousness. To avoid that appearance of evil, the critic must grant some concessions, such as that gambling *per se* is not evil in itself. Some with the mind-set of Protestant Reformer Martin Luther, however, may feel an occasional gamble legitimate, a kind of backhanded show of scorn for the mammon of unrighteousness.

In the Christian scheme of things our life's goal is not to live in financial security, but to live in dependence on God who supplies our needs. We should have no fear that bad luck tags along with us through life, nor entertain a grandiose illusion that good luck is fixed to our persons, because, as God has promised, we are loved by One whose interest in us and whose plans for us exceed any impersonal fate.

Our financial stability, like our health and well-being, is in God's hands. And he who has supplied our needs wants us to manage our resources for profit. Therefore, the wise investment of our resources, entailing unavoidable risk-taking, a kind of gamble, is all the risk we need.

4.

'Casting Lots' Through the Ages

Why bring up lots, argued Geisler, since in the Bible, casting lots is not done for money?

> Divine decision : . . . not monetary gain was sought . . . [I]n the biblical casting of lots there was no money wagered. Biblical lot-casting was entirely different from gambling. Casting a lot for the purpose of submitting to divine determination is the exact antithesis of gambling out of distrust of God's provision for us.[1]

Another Christian author, Rex M. Rogers, demurred. Rogers reasoned that because bones or sheep knuckles were rolled either for games or for gambling, casting lots does have relevance: 'Any study of gambling, and the Bible, therefore, must examine the practice of casting lots.'[2]

Casting lots was used in Scripture for cases of employment and property assignment. The cases where lots were cast dealt with economics, with property, with various monetary values. Casting lots in Scripture was not used to jettison the need for honest employment, hard work, negotiations, but with an equitable resolution to differences and with outcomes that were both humanly uncontrollable and unpredictable.

How will dice role? Human control is temporarily put aside in a dice throw. The outcome involves odds or chance. Chance has to do with randomness. But God is in charge of that too. While there is one view of chance that would rival God's role and urge ridding any reference to a divine providence, there is another view of chance which is compatible with God and with the Bible. Few conservative Christians buy that. But the Puritan divine Thomas Gataker cited non-pejorative uses of 'chance' in the Bible. In those instances chance was taken, not as a rival to God, but as the randomness that the Lord of history has worked into reality through probability and variations.

Casting lots in Bible times had a practical usage. It was done to settle disputes, to come to closure on ownership. But was it a form of gambling? And does Scripture prohibit casting lots today? These issues come up when Christians discuss the degree of divine involvement in our lives. One benefit the present work has is to introduce readers to the various positions and to let them take it from there to form their own conclusion.

An ancient practice

In the Bible there are many references to casting lots. Today people roll dice, pick straws, hold a raffle, sell lottery tickets. In biblical times they sometimes used sticks, marked pebbles, or a select piece of wood.[3] Ezekiel 21:21 mentioned that pagan Babylonians used arrows or arrow points to divine or project the future.

The casting of lots was practised widely in the ancient Near East, including by Jews. Pagan cultures were locked into casting lots as a primal guidance method. Among the non-Hebrews it had evolved into a superstitious use, for example by Phoenicians (Jonah 1:7), Persians (Esth. 9:24–26), and by Babylonians (Ezek. 21:21).

One feature in paganism was the use of 'specialists', i.e. mediums.

> The Graeco-Roman world knew three types of oracles: the oracle obtained through the casting of lots; the dream oracle obtained by sleeping in the sacred precincts, usually connected with healing; and the inspired oracle by which an oracle-prophet responded to inquiries.[4]

Consulting oracles – including casting lots – was used.

A pagan episode on lot-casting with plenty of information about its use occurs in the book of Esther. The character Haman thought he had a lucky day (3:7) for Jewish massacre. He was a thoroughly superstitious person. On his alleged lucky day he cast lots. But a full eleven months elapsed before the result could be effected, time enough to allow the Jews to escape the intended harm (cf. Esth. 3:7).

The word 'pur', which in Esther 3:7 and 9:24, 26, is said to mean 'lot', is not a Hebrew word. Some say it was the Assyrian 'puru', which means a pebble, or small stone, which would be used for casting lots.[5] The Hebrew word *goral*, the standard term for 'lot,' has the added idea of 'destiny' in certain biblical texts (Isa. 17:14; Jer. 13:25; Dan. 12:13). In the Dead Sea Scrolls it meant 'fate.' The noun *pur*, relates to the Akkadian *puru*, in Esther. The festival name Purim is from *puru*. Haman fixed the day for the pogrom. In Esther 3:7, *pur* is specifically identified with *goral*.

In the book of Nehemiah, by casting lots, the community decided to bring one of every ten people in Judea to live in Jerusalem. The late Jimmy Stewart, actor, said the only lottery he ever won was the military draft in the 1940s. A similar lottery system was used during the Vietnam war in calling up recruits. Nehemiah 7:1–5a had also been concerned with the low population of the holy city (Neh. 11:1–3).[6]

When Israel's dependence on God was at a low point, it was not to oracles, that they looked, however, but to the Lord. King Saul represented Judaism at its spiritual worst when he consulted a medium. Unlike pagans, the Hebrews weren't locked into casting lots. Yet, lots were employed under specific conditions. For instance, casting of lots was used in the selection of Israel's first king (1 Sam. 10:16–26). The felon Achen was also discovered by lot as the thief of the spoil from Jericho (Josh. 7:14). By lot, Jonathan was found to be the (unwitting) violator of his father's oath (1 Sam. 14:42).

Old Testament believers saw lots as a sincere turning to God for guidance. Two assumptions were conveyed by lots. First, God's sovereignty was believed to lie behind random selection, and second, casting lots was combined with consultation with God's prime representative, the high priest.

The lot type of oracle occurs in the OT as *urim* and *thummim* (1 Sam. 14:41; 28:6; Exod. 28:29; Deut. 33:8; Lev. 8:7; Num. 27:21) . . . The Urim and Thummim (or ephod) were also oracular media, but answers were restricted to 'yes' or 'no' (1 Sam. 23:9–12; 30:7–8; Num. 27:21). The same results could be gained by casting lots (Lev. 16:8; Num. 26:55–56).[7]

Other selective uses of casting lots in the Old Testament included the following:

1. in the allotment of land or in the parcelling out of property to the tribes (Num. 26:55; 33:54; 34:13; 36:2; Josh. 14:1);
2. in conditions of transferral of the populace in redistribution, including the forced transfer from rural settlements to urban centres (Neh. 11:1);

3. in making decisions on battlefields, such as when and where to attack (Judges 20:9; Ezek. 21:21).
4. in arranging Levite priests' temple schedules (1 Chron. 24:4,5; 25:8; cf. Lk. 1:9) and who got to provide wood for the altar (Neh. 10:34);
5. the division of booty or the property gained through conquest, along with the disposition of a criminal's property (Ps. 22:18; Joel 3:3; Obad. 11; Nah. 3:10).

Bible texts on casting lots

Casting lots is found mainly in the Old Testament and is largely connected with Judaism's moral head of state, the High Priest. The *Thummim* and *Urim*, worn by the High Priest, were probably two precious stones, possibly 'with alternating light and dark sides', and were used in the casting of lots to receive divine answers in difficult matters (cf. Exod. 28:30; Deut. 33:8–11; Lev. 8:8; Num. 27:21; 1 Sam. 28:6; Ezra 2:63; Neh. 7:65).[8] Through these sacred stones of 'yes' or 'no' (1 Sam. 23:9–12; 30:7–8; Num. 27:21) God's will was sought. Casting lots had the same purpose (Lev. 16:8; Num. 26:55–56).

Tomas Martinez suggested that

access to the tools of gambling in earliest times was forbidden, when high priests were the only ones allowed to use the sacred lots to be cast. A non-cleric in antiquity could not participate in the casting of lots (the forerunner of today's dice). To do so was considered an illegal, punishable act.[9]

True, major decision-making was the High Priest's prerogative, but his casting of lots had to do with national affairs. He did not, however, prevent or discourage the average Israeli from casting lots, as three texts in Proverbs testify (1:14; 16:33; 18:18). The latter texts indicate that lot-casting was used to settle disputes between individuals and did not concern the High Priest.

Both personal (Prov. 18:18) and property disputes were settled by casting lots. Consider, for instance, Numbers 26:52–56; 27:12; Deut. 33:8–11; Joshua 7:13–15; 14:1–5.

While Moses spoke to God face to face in a most intimate and direct way (Exod. 12:6–8), Joshua received indirect divine guidance from the priest, using *Urim* and *Thummim* (cf. Exod. 28:30; 1 Sam. 28:6). According to Jewish tradition the name of a tribe was drawn from one urn and simultaneously the boundary lines of a territory from another. This method designated each tribal inheritance. But blind chance did not decide the tribal location, for God was superintending the whole procedure (cf. Prov. 16:33).

With the recording of the allotments by Moses in Transjordan completed, Joshua's account turned to the distribution of the land in Canaan proper to the remaining nine and a half tribes. The resolution of land allotments for the Reubenites, the Gadites, and the half-tribe of Manasseh, and the tribe of Levi was handled in the same way (cf. 13:14, 33; 18:7). Canaan was cut up by casting lots (14:2; 18:8; 19:51).

The casting of lots (cf. Josh. 14:2) would not decide the size of the respective territories then, but only where the tribes would settle in Canaan. If a tribe were large, it would have a large area but only the lot would decide whether it would be in the north, centre, or south. These lots were most likely the *Urim* and *Thummim* of the High Priest (cf. Exod. 28:30).[10] The ephod or vest of the High Priest was where the lots were kept.[11]

Complaints about inequities in the allocation arose from an inability to accept the lots as part of God's purpose. The time for casting lots arrived and the tribe of Judah, receiving the first portion, assembled at Gilgal

(Josh. 14:6–9). Before the lots were cast Caleb, a 'grand old man of Israel', stepped forward to remind Joshua of a promise the Lord had made to him 45 years earlier: 'I will give him and his descendants the land he set his feet on, because he followed the LORD wholeheartedly' (Deut. 1:36).

Although divination texts abound from the ancient Near-Eastern world, little information about divination is derived from the Old Testament. The practice was forbidden to Israel. Some references, however, indicated both the techniques employed to discover the intent of the gods and those used to avert portended evil. Frequently, as in 1 Samuel 6:13, divination took a binary form, that is, a given test would be applied to which a yes or no response would be possible.

Saul, who in other stories is a hidden sinner whose sin has brought divine wrath upon the whole people (e.g., Josh. 7; 1 Sam. 14:24–45)[12] was selected by lot, indicating God's direct hand in Israel's history (1 Sam. 10:17; 1 Sam. 14:1; 1 Chron. 26:1).

Admittedly, 'casting lots' is not a phrase that excites a lot of devotional pondering. Of all forms of decision-making, casting lots does not appeal to many Christians reluctant to abandon rational discussion and negotiation. On the other hand, when it came to a replacement choice for another apostle, the early church resorted to the casting of lots, apparently convinced that it allowed God the right of choice (Acts 2:26).

Sometimes casting lots was not mentioned in the text, although the lots were cast nevertheless.[13] The matter of the choice of who would be the host at the wedding reception is a case in point. In New Testament times the dice roll, like the coin toss at football games, was an easy way to make a decision. We hear a lot about not drinking and driving; but in Jesus' day it was sobre hosts they wanted.

There is an expression in John's Gospel meaning 'master of the banquet' (2:8, NIV) and he was the superintendent of the banqueting-chamber, a position decided by divine selection – or lot – not ownership of whose home it was! Marvin Vincent commented on John 2:8,9:

> This ... view seems to be supported by a passage in Ecclesiasticus 35:1,2: 'If thou be made the master of a feast, lift not thyself up, but be among them as one of the rest; take diligent care for them, and so sit down ...' According to the Greek and Roman custom, the ruler of the feast was chosen by throwing the dice. Thus Horace, in his ode to his friend Sestius, says, moralizing on the brevity of life: 'Soon the home of Pluto will be thine, nor wilt thou cast lots with the dice for the presidency over the wine.' He prescribed the proportions of wine and water, and could also impose fines for failures to guess riddles, etc. As the success of the feast depended largely upon him, his selection was a matter of some delicacy. Plato says, 'Must we not appoint a sober man and a wise to be our master of the revels? For if the ruler of drinkers be himself young and drunken, and not over-wise, only by some special good fortune will he be saved from doing some great evil' ('Laws', 640).[14]

The advantages of lots

What possible advantages did the Hebrews see in casting lots? Why would they resort to a method that permeated pagan cultures? And what advantages did the early Church see in casting lots (Acts 2:26)? What was it about 'casting lots' that would cause Old Testament patriarchs and New Testament saints to both allow and practise it? What value was associated with it? Didn't it short-cut rational process? Wasn't it an unthinking way to resolve

issues? Was there anything attractive about casting lots
that appealed to persons of faith in God? Does casting lots
give justification to modern gambling? There are many
questions here.

'Casting lots' was a form of decision-making. How did
Israel resolve gridlock? They agreed to a voteless decision.
Flip, don't fight, was the solution. At least three positive
values were evidenced in casting lots, which should
appeal to those who admire the democratic process:

Firstly, the major appeal of casting lots was that it took
decision-making out of the arenas of status, hierarchy,
social advantage and personal prejudice. Neither size nor
wealth gave any advantage to the person who threw the
dice. Assuming there was no fixing of the instruments or
their casting, who you were and how much clout you had
had no bearing on the outcome of casting a lot. It represented an agreement that no one person be given the final
decision. The direction to go was left to the random draw.
It had nothing to do, originally, with betting or trying to
make a profit. It was simply a matter of settling property
and ownership disputes.

Positively, casting lots took choice out of the arenas of
rank, politics, petty squabbles and individual dominance.
To the down-trodden and disadvantaged, that was not a
drawback. That was a plus in societies where age, gender
and party dominance dictated who did what when. The
lot was used in Israel as a means of deciding urgent issues
in cases where they were not left simply to the decision of a
prophet, priest, elder, judge or king.

Thus, casting lots levelled the playing-field and meant
that each person had equal chance. In a sense it was an
attempt to democratize a society typically characterized
as monarchical, oligarchic and demagogic.

Secondly, casting lots reduced the importance of primary choice. It put first choice or one's starting position in

a less important role. The first choice was not the final choice. First choice was often less important than subsequent actions. And it may seem to have trivialized the first choice. What mattered most was not whether you were a 'haver' but what you did with what you had. How a primary position was implemented had more to do with its success than the initial gain. What one did with one's choices was more determinative than the initial advantage. It was an indirect commentary on the idea of needing to win everything at once.

Thirdly, casting lots hastened the process of securing goals. Time could be lost over who went first. A lot of time was not meant to be spent quarrelling over who got what. Take the example of 1 Chronicles 25:8. 'Young and old alike, teacher as well as student, cast lots for their duties' (NIV). Instead of rotating and ragging endlessly on portions and positions, a quick dice throw would determine getting on to the next level.

These were three positive traits of casting lots. The same traits appeal to us today, whether we are Christian or non-Christian.

Apparently, today's Christian is not inherently opposed to casting lots, for he too scratches the fast-food game cards, buys a raffle ticket from a Scout troop, or joins the draw at the local supermarket for a free trip to the Mediterranean or to far-off Hawaii. The most devout believer has been known to resort to seeking the 'luck of the draw' and win by random choice.

The unashamed reference to casting lots in Scripture seems odd when dice-throwing was associated with paganism. And that raises the real question: If dice are the Devil's toy, then why does Scripture refer to it without condemnation? Scripture had lists of forbidden foods. Why does it not outlaw the prime tool of chance, dice?

The use of random selection through lottery and raffles, whether in the Bible, or in modern Christian minds, is an endorsement of a world-view that life itself and history is a jumble of random forces, laws, and natural selection. (Chapter 9 offers reflections on chance, providence and randomness.)

A theology of dice-throwing

Instead of insisting that there is a great gulf between dice and divine providence, Proverbs 16:33 (NIV), a pivotal text on lot-casting, combines them.

> The lot is cast into the lap,
> but its every decision is from the LORD.

Chance as a substitute or replacement for God is out of the question. God controls everything. Matthew Henry says three points are being made in the short proverb:

> [1] that divine Providence orders and directs all things, however casual and/or unpremeditated. Nothing comes to pass by chance, nor is an event determined by a blind fortune, but everything by the will and counsel of God. God has his hand in every turning circumstance.
> [2] Even though divine providence was behind casting lots, God must be appealed to by prayer so that it may be disposed aright (*Give a perfect lot*, 1 Sam. 14:41; Acts 1:24).
> [3] In the acceptance of the outcome the person must be satisfied that the hand of God is in it and that God directed it.[15]

The expression 'our lot in life' is derived from the practice of casting lots. It has a definite predestinarian tone. Our lot is due to the Lord's decision. Horatius Bonar [1808–1889] has a hymn that reflects that truth.

Thy way, not mine, O Lord,
However dark it be;
Lead me by Thine own hand,
Choose out the path for me.
    Smooth let it be or rough,
    It will be still the best;
    Winding or straight, it leads
    Right onward to Thy rest.
I dare not choose my lot;
I would not, if I might;
Choose Thou for me, my God;
So shall I walk aright.

Casting lots was not viewed as a trivial method of making choices. Even the heathen looked upon the casting of lots to be a sacred thing, to be done with seriousness and solemnity (Jonah 1:4.), and not to be made a sport of. It is a shame for Christians if they have not a like reverence for an appeal to Providence.[16]

Setting the Temple work schedules of Levite priests by lottery was both practical and fair. Temple coordination of priests in rotation allowed Zechariah's once-in-a-lifetime Temple service (Lk. 1:9). The historical circumstance was explained by Vincent:

Four lots were drawn to determine the order of the ministry of the day: the first, before daybreak, to designate the priests who were to cleanse the altar and prepare its fires; the second for the priest who was to offer the sacrifice and cleanse the candlestick and the altar of incense; the third for the priest who should burn incense; and the fourth appointing those who were to lay the sacrifice and meat offering on the altar, and pour out the drink offering. There are said to have been twenty thousand priests in Christ's time, so that no priest would ever offer incense more than once.[17]

Throughout the New Testament, in the four passages where *lagchano* meaning 'appointed' is used, the emphasis is that what is gained or attained is not by one's own effort.[18] The passage of 2 Peter 1:1 refers to the acquisition of faith as an attainment.

> ... the point of *lagchanein* is that faith has come to them from God with no co-operation on their part. That faith is the work, not of man, but of God or Christ is not stated with equal clarity in all parts of the NT, but it must be constantly borne in mine ... God does not merely give to both Jews and Gentiles the possibility of faith; He effects faith in them.[19]

A modern reference

Indeed, bingo, like lottery, operates as random selection, but whether the word bingo is appropriate in court is questionable. Attorneys can object to potential jurors in the American court system for reasons they need not declare. In the trial of terrorist Timothy McVeigh, accused of bombing the Federal Office Building in Oklahoma City, it was essential to protect the identities of jurors – and a system was used instead, whereby attorneys called out a series of numbers that jurors had already been assigned, for those who wished not to serve on the jury. Prosecutor Joseph Hartzler tried to make light of the situation. 'Like bingo, your honor,' Mr Harzler joked. Judge [Richard] Matsch glared at the prosecutor and said, 'It's a lot more serious than a bingo game.' The newspaper reported: 'Seven men and five women were selected Tuesday to hear the Oklahoma City bombing trial, with the judge using a bingo-style system of numbers to shield the identities of the already anonymous jurors.'[20] The association by lawyers and journalists of numbers with bingo, however, reflects more the saturation of the American mind with gambling terminology than the serious direct implication that juror dismissal is random, or fun.

The Puritans' use of lots

A famous British Puritan, Thomas Gataker [1574–1654], dealt with the popular practice of using the Bible as a lottery. It was done by randomly flipping the Bible open and pointing to specific texts to seek guidance. (The most natural process of seeking guidance from the Bible is to read the text sequentially and deal with the verses in context.) This strange practice was known as 'Bible lottery'. It was used with other books as well, as Gataker painstakingly showed.[21]

Casting lots played a pivotal role in the Moravian Church. Christopher P. Gavaler has summarized the place of lots in the Moravian movement:

> In 1465, the Moravian church justified its division from Rome on the result of a draw of lots. After members asked their Lord whether the sect should separate from the Catholic church, they drew one of three slips of paper. On the first was written 'no', on the second 'yes', and the third lot remained blank. When the affirmative lot appeared, the Moravians agreed to establish a new church (Wallace 1958:8). In 1769, the Moravians expanded the use of this lot system to all significant decisions faced in any of the disparate missionary branches (Olmstead 1991:21). On such a basis, mission marriages were denied, prodigal converts turned away, and individuals chosen for undesirable duties, all under the justification of divine will . . .
>
> Decision derived by lot largely satisfied the Moravians, even in such personal matters as the approval of marriages . . .

Use of the Moravian lots was publicly mandated for all critical missionary decisions 'including convert baptism, proposals of marriage, mission policies, and election of village leadership' (Olmstead 1991:23) . . . The Moravians perceived the blank lot as God's dissatisfaction with an absolute yes-or-no response; perhaps the contemplated matter contained gray areas . . .

Paul Wallace relates that contemporary Moravians 'no longer believe that God uses the so-called laws of chance – whether operating through dice, the roulette wheel, a flipped coin, or bits of paper – to disclose His mind to man' (Heckewelder 1958:8). Accordingly, the church abolished use of the lots during the mid-nineteenth century (Olmstead 1991:23).[22]

For those interested in a fuller version of lots in Moravianism, I have included some basic church histories that cover the practice.[23]

John Wesley on lots

The use of the lot box had an influence on John Wesley. In the citations that follow, not only were the Moravians instrumental in Wesley's conversion, but they had some influence on the way he came to decisions in his Christian life.

John Wesley [1703–1791] picked up the idea of seeking guidance by casting lots from the Moravians. In Volume One of his works, *Journals* 14 Oct. 1735–29 Nov. 1745, he inserted an extract from the constitution of the Moravian Church formulated in Germany (at Hernhuth) in 1733. Wesley's extract was as follows:

16. They have a peculiar esteem for lots; and accordingly use them both in public and private, to decide points of impor-

tance, when the reasons brought on each side appear to be of equal weight. And they believe this to be then the only way of wholly setting aside their own will, of acquitting themselves of all blame, and clearly knowing what is the will of God.[24]

In correspondence with a Revd Church, Wesley outlined Methodist ideas, one of which was his view on casting lots:

For I neither cast lots, nor use that method at all, till I have considered things with all the care I can. So that, be this right or wrong, it is no manner of proof that I do not 'carefully consider every step I take.' . . . 3. I come now to what you expatiate upon at large, as the two grand instances of my enthusiasm. The first is plainly this: At some rare times, when I have been in great distress of soul, or in utter uncertainty how to act in an important case which required a speedy determination, after using all other means that occurred, I have cast lots, or opened the Bible. And by this means I have been relieved from that distress, or directed in that uncertainty . . . This, I firmly believe, is truth and reason, and will be to the end of the world. And I therefore still subscribe to that declaration of the Moravian Church, laid before the whole body of Divines in the University of Wirtemberg, and not by them accounted enthusiasm: 'We have a peculiar esteem for lots, and accordingly use them, both in public and private, to decide points of importance, when the reasons brought on each side appear to be of equal weight. And we believe this to be then the only way of wholly setting aside our own will, of acquitting ourselves of all blame, and clearly knowing what is the will of God.'[25]

The casting of lots was used to select Judas' replacement (Acts 1:23–26) although it was apparently dropped or declined in other cases. In the book of Acts we have later

instances of the process of recruitment concentrating on
rational discussion, protracted prayer, and voting of
church leadership.

But recently, in the US, some have taken a second look
at the practice of casting of lots, not as the abandonment of
a rational process, but as part of it. A Michigan (US state)
Christian Reformed congregation amended the practice
of casting, and saw a way in which it ensured fairness
between equally qualified candidates for church office.

Yes, freedom lovers, a congregation revived and
returned to the casting of lots in church elections!

Why would they want to do that? They found it short-
ened the tedious, sometimes thorny matter of the choice of
church officers, especially when several candidates were
equally qualified.

Dr William D. Buursma, Pastor of Third Church (Christian Reformed), Grand Rapids, Michigan, describes a daring return to casting lots in their yearly election of
deacons/elders.[26] He writes:

> The traditional procedure of electing elders and deacons has,
> over the years, produced in many churches an increasing dis-
> satisfaction with the process . . . Under the old system, two or
> three ballots were often necessary to make our choices. Dur-
> ing the lengthy process of tabulation, bored members began
> to slip away. By the final ballot, numbers were significantly
> down . . . It was also possible (since we live in a flawed world)
> to 'stack' the nomination . . . Now we nominate as many indi-
> viduals as the council feels are truly qualified, and we let the
> lot decide from among them.

Such dissatisfaction was handled differently in the last
few years. After the nominating committee had done their
homework and come up with the best recommendations
for the positions, they decided to revert back to the old

method of casting lots 'in the final step of selecting elders and deacons for the new church year. We are now one of an increasing number of congregations using this procedure. It is done in the context of a morning worship service.'

How did the process work? Dr Buursma summarizes it as four steps:

[1] In February the council informs the congregation that it has started the process of nominating persons for those retiring from office. Input and suggestions are welcomed.

[2] The council makes nominations and announces the names. Opportunity to raise questions is given.

[3] On the first Sunday in June, in the morning service, after the offering and instead of the doxology and benediction, the congregation is asked to be seated for the ceremony of the casting of lots. The officers come forward and the service begins. After the procedure of presenting the cast of nominees . . . the clerk has prepared plastic capsules identical in size, each with the name of a nominee inside. The pastor prays; after the motion to receive the slate, the capsules are placed in an offering plate, then the most recent church member selects the necessary number and hands them one by one to the vice-president, who reads the names aloud and shows them to the pastor and the clerk records.

[4] Upon completion, the pastor congratulates those selected and asks everyone to rise for the doxology.

How has this practice fared? Dr. Buursma writes: 'Looking back on more than five years' experience with the casting of lots, we are convinced this is a more compassionate, sensitive, and Christian method of selecting officebearers.'

In all English-speaking churches and chapels the typical self-governing Protestant way has a rotation of officers known as elders, deacons, and trustees. Filling the vacant positions causes annual anxiety, for part of the problem is getting volunteers to serve in these non-paying jobs. Another problem is ensuring that fair representation among the officers and leaders is attained. How many church officials got into office because they had more relatives voting for them at the annual meeting? One age-old church-life complaint is of unofficial voting blocks. In such cases family ties swing the elections causing one to wonder if the better qualified persons to fill the vacancies were not overlooked. Casting lots among a slate of equally qualified persons would keep the feeling that a democratized process is intact and in use. For churches, however, to break rank and risk a return to the ancient practice of casting lots for its officers may be too risky, too much against the grain of British tradition.

5.

'Gambling' at Golgatha

Soldier scandals; that's news in Britain, in the US, and in any country where military standards are high, where moral fibre is strong. Military professionals both in the United Kingdom and the United States are among the best trained in the world. They are held up as models of decency, respect, and humaneness.

English troops are trained to be disciplined, conscientious, courteous, and respectful. Any breach of that tradition sends shock-waves throughout the nation. Unfortunately, in the last decade several branches of US military have had a number of immorality scandals soiling their reputation.

Those unfamiliar with American news may have missed the navy's Skyhook scandal, the adultery, lying, and disobedience of the first woman B-52 pilot; army drill sergeants who raped women recruits in basic training, and a four-star general whose past admission to adultery forced him to withdraw his name from nomination for chairman of the Joint Chief of Staff.

Soldiers of misfortune?

Soldiers, historically, have abused their power and privilege. In World War II German women feared Russian soldiers would rape them. And German soldiers repeatedly raped and murdered women of the Ukraine. Modern Bosnian women have been subjected to the same inhuman treatment.

Soldiers in Jesus' time were known to have taken advantage of the countries where they were stationed. Roman soldiers didn't serve Israel, they were Israel's captors, in control of Israel. Unlike the Temple police who were charged with the protection of the property and people of the nation's worship centre, a Roman soldier, as Jesus himself admitted, could force a citizen to go a second mile in carrying his pack, or force a civilian to surrender the clothes off his back. Soldiers were armed bullies. They had clout and they used it for selfish purposes.

They devised ways to pass the time when on duty. Archaeologists say that inside the fortress of Antonio was a gambling stone:

> Most moving of all at this spot is to see the markings on the ground where the Roman soldiers used to play the gambling game King, with a skittle, and to realize that here Jesus was given the sceptre, crown of thorns, and the robe, as he replaced the skittle in their cruel game . . . a game called 'Basileus,' or 'King'. A wooden skittle (bowling pin) was moved about markings on the ground according to the throw of dice. When the skittle had moved to the appropriate places for robing, crowning, and being given a sceptre, the person who made the last throw called, 'King!' and collected the stakes laid out by his companions. In view of Matthew 27:27–31, it is clear that soldiers at Castle Antonia played 'King' with Jesus, substituting him for the wooden skittle and using a soldier's cloak, reed, and crown of thorns in their mockery. (Markings for this game can be seen on the paving stones at Gabbatha in Jerusalem to this day.)[1]

But that was not the only place the soldiers were known to have gambled.

Ironically, the soldiers at the time of Jesus' crucifixion in the Gospels were not presented as a band of immoral men, although they had the grizzly task of crucifying Jesus and the other two men. The crucifixion was a Roman act. The soldiers were appointed by Pilate to carry it out. Over the four guards (in Latin, a *quaternion;* in Greek, *a tetradion*), was an officer, a centurion. Josef Blinzler referred to the four soldiers as 'the execution squad'[2] – yet, from the lips of the centurion in charge of the event came the statement which was a near confession of his own sympathy with Jesus, if not an outright acknowledgment of Jesus' Lordship: Jesus was 'a son of God'.

Lloyd Douglas [1877–1951] took Jesus' seamless robe[3] as the central theme for his novel *The Robe* (1942). The soldiers gambled for it. Yet was it gambling when no money was exchanged?

The incident on the roll of dice for Jesus' seamless robe is important for a number of reasons: it is important in terms of attitudes toward Jesus, in terms of attitudes toward justice, in terms of attitudes toward the role of Old Testament prophecy (see Psalm 22 and John's Gospel comments) regarding the Suffering Servant, and no less important in regard to the definition of gambling.

Did the soldiers actually gamble since they did not play for money, but for the robe? Admittedly, the soldiers on Golgatha were not shooting dice for profit. Yet we have a case, in this instance, that relates to the question: Can one gamble without money?

The issue at stake in this episode, some have argued, is not really the question of the rightness or wrongness of gambling. In Rogers' relatively recent book on gambling he commented on this seeming mislabelling of the soldiers' actions. Rex Rogers' polemics against gambling and the gambling industry contain the suggestion that what the soldiers did was not real gambling.

> Even the soldiers casting lots for Christ's robe at the foot of the cross were not gambling. No soldier had paid to play. No soldier was taking any risk. No one was going to win at another's expense. They were simply trying to determine who got to keep the robe.[4]

It appears that what the soldiers did underscores the fact that betting can take place without the exchange of real money. Betting without money at the cross was close enough to call it gambling, but the legal definition was not met. Property ownership was at issue and that was equivalent to money. Joint ownership of the seamless robe existed before the dice were thrown, but they gambled that right for outright ownership.

The gambling or betting over the seamless robe also has some relationship with another question brought up by gambling opponents, who say gambling is wrong because it is trying to get something for nothing. But this is bogus. Why? Because in true on-the-barrel gambling, actual money is put up, or as in the case of the seamless robe, part ownership. People do not wager 'nothing', they wager real money, real property.

Some use the argument that gambling is wrong because though it is something, it is too small a something to be an equitable basis for getting a huge something in return. This amounts to the view that a disproportionate exchange is immoral. But that cannot be valid. Otherwise, life-insurance, accident insurance, or any damage kind of insurance would be improper, immoral. The policy holder only puts up small premium payments in return for the guarantee of a large outlay by the insurance company, if there is a tragic loss by the policy holder. That is not considered immoral. As Anglican Bishop Kenneth Escott Kirk [1886–1954] commented long ago: 'a disproportionate material gain to one party or the other need not be immoral in principle'.[5]

The symbolism of seamlessness

Those who associate the seamless robe with rarity and riches have the non-officer soldiers look upon the seamless robe as a kind of prize, a bonus for their work. For them the gamble over the robe was more than the disposition of the personal property of the deceased. Some see it as a chance to have made some money through resale, so some have speculated that greed drove them to gamble. But that assumes the seamless garment was valuable. Many contend the seamless robe was a normal garment of special quality but not necessarily a costly, luxury item. Isadore of Pelusium, for instance, said that the style of garment gambled for was characteristic of the Galilean poor.[6]

The robe was an undergarment, and it was without seam. Some hold that the article spoke of Jesus' poverty. John Chrysostom [c.347–407], for instance, thought that it established that Jesus preferred simple fashions and that it was a mark of his poverty.[7] Dutch Reformed scholar, Klass Schilder [1890–1952], agreed that seamless clothes were common then.[8] Others have suggested that the seamless garment was of value, that it was intended to last because of its worth. Josephus mentioned that the tunic of the High Priest of Judaism was seamless.[9]

The Johannine passage like the rest of the gospel, replete with double meanings, had a symbolic intent. Some suggested that John's intention was to show Jesus' link with the high priesthood. As far back as Grotius in 1641 this was suggested. Frederick Krummacher [1796–1868], a noted German Reformed pastor, said 'such a dress as the High Priest was obliged to put on . . . That such a priestly garment is found on the body of Jesus was highly significant.'[10] More recently, the late William Barclay commented: 'It is something which tells us that Jesus is the perfect priest, opening the perfect way for all men to the presence of God.'[11]

'Most of the Church Fathers', says Raymond E. Brown, contended that the garment was special and very unusual. Was that imaginative redaction or narrative intention? The conjecture seems fitting, but was it justified? The synoptic accounts had no symbolic purpose. So one cannot appeal to them to establish spiritual symbolism. They would not encourage such conjecture. Their versions are briefer and matter-of-fact. The garment had significance, but did it have sacral character? Some say 'yes', others think 'no'.

John's account contrasts with the other gospels, probably intending to be symbolic. His allusion to the seamless robe, like other physical details in his Gospel, was intended to feed back into the Jewish knowledge that the prominent High Priest was known to wear a seamless robe.

It was ironic that God's final and sole eternal High Priest would have a seamless robe. Irony laces the crucifixion accounts. Also, it was ironic that whereas representatives from the East bore gifts at Jesus' birth, plunderers from the West took his clothes at his death.

Instead of Jesus' priestly role, some see a stronger symbolism: Jesus' unifying ability. Raymond E. Brown, S.S., held that John's chronicle points to the symbolism of unity ('John has shown more interest in unity than in priesthood.')[12] (John 10:16; 11:52; 17:21,22; 21:11). De la Potterie thought it pointed to the unity of the messianic people of God, whereas others see it as a reference to Jesus' unity in the godhead.[13]

Many nineteenth-century commentators focused on the emotions at the scene, rather than on the scene details as post-event emblems of Jesus' role. Charles Haddon Spurgeon [1834–1892], on a Sunday evening at New Park Street Chapel, 1857, said (at the age of 23): 'I have never heard the rattling of dice but I have conjured up the dreadful scene of Christ upon his cross, and gamblers at the foot of it, with their dice bespattered with his blood.'[14] Years later Spurgeon's comments on the event entertained the view that the gambling over Jesus' seamless robe was a sign of profound admiration, rather than of soldier contempt. He wrote for the morning of 7 April in his *Morning and Evening* devotions:

> [Jesus] was provided with *a guard of honour*, who showed their esteem of him by gambling over his garments, which they had seized as their booty. Such was the body-guard of the adored of heaven; a quaternion of brutal gamblers.[15]

When Spurgeon was nearing death he was engaged in preparing his commentary on Matthew's gospel. Regarding the gambling on Golgatha text, he resorted to rephrasing a comment made at the age of 23:

> The dice would be almost stained with the blood of Christ, yet the gamblers played on beneath the shadow of his cross. Gambling is the most hardening of all vices. Beware of it in any form! No games of chance should be played by Christians, for the blood of Christ seems to have bespattered them all.[16]

The robe an excuse to rail against gambling?

Henry Ward Beecher [1813–1887], previously mentioned, gave a long lecture against gambling. He seized upon the gambling reference as an ideal springboard for his lecture. At the start, he launched into the passion narratives about the soldiers gambling for Jesus' seamless robe. Beecher bellowed:

> . . . no earthly creature, but a Gambler, could be so lost to all feeling as to sit down coolly under a dying man to wrangle for his garments, and arbitrate their avaricious differences by casting dice for his tunic, with hands spotted with his spattered blood, warm and yet undried upon them.[17]

Richard Allen Bodey, in an article against gambling, presented the soldiers dicing for Jesus' garment as a wicked greedy wager:

> There is no more ghastly scene in history than that of the Roman soldiers carelessly tossing dice at the foot of the Cross for the possession of Christ's homespun robe. These Romans never heard the seven words of redeeming love which fell from his lips. They were bewitched by a pair of dice.[18]

They were to be viewed as heartless men in the sight of the dead Jesus. Bodey's interpretation is slanted against the Roman soldiers for several reasons. While the evangelists did not moralize about the soldiers in the biblical text, nevertheless, it was patently clear that the soldiers lacked interest in the person of Christ. They thought more of personal gain than in the world's loss. As the angels of heaven bowed their heads in worship, the soldiers gambled for a piece of cloth. At the time Jesus bore our sin, there was the clacking of dice.

The soldiers' insensitivity to Jesus' greatness, agony, and role was apparent and important. How petty for persons to be so occupied with things immanent in the presence of the transcendent. How petty to idle away the time at the most momentous hour in human history. How shortsighted to seek excitement in the roll of dice when the great transaction of the judgment of sin in the sinless sufferer was taking place. One cannot escape the conclusion that harshness, coldness, boredom, and selfishness were at work.

Greed, recreation, or necessity?

Were the soldiers guilty of greed or were they just passing the time? Obviously, they were absorbed in acquiring a valuable garment, Jesus' seamless robe. Was there a greed factor? That criticism seems unjustified when one recognizes their dilemma on the site. There were four soldiers, but actually five articles of clothing: Jesus' clothes were of four parts: 1. headgear, a white hood or *sudar*, which fastened under the chin and hung down the back; 2. the undergarment, usually of one piece, probably grey and red stripes and made of wool or linen. It was also known as a *chifton* or tunic. 3. over this was a vest-like covering, a *talith* with blue and white fringes and, finally, 4. two sandals.

It is common for preachers to suggest that the soldiers gambled for all Christ's clothes.[19] In fact, they gambled over one garment, the seamless robe, not all five articles. Why gamble over the one remaining article of clothing? The famous Anglican F.W. Farrar [1831–1903] noted it would be pointless to tear the seamless robe into four pieces.[20] The garment gambled for by the four-man execution squad was seamless.[21] Some hold that not all four articles of clothing belonging to Jesus were gambled over, for the other pieces, the least valuable ones, had been given to the women (cf. Lk. 7:2,3; Mt. 27:55; see Frederick Godet's *Commentary on the Gospel of John*, Vol. 2:385).

Though recognizing these factors, one should not let them crowd out the decency element evidenced. The most missed significance in the whole event was the intended sharp contrast between the decent thing the soldiers did after the most indecent order they carried through. The overlooked drama was fairness in the presence of injustice.

The soldiers threw dice to decide who got the seamless robe. Casting lots was usually used to settle conflicts of interest. In the case before us, the dice throw was to prevent 'all contention and strife'; and, Thomas Gataker [1574–1654] continued, 'Neither was that act of theirs . . . evil or unlawful, for ought I see or can be said . . . good writers rather commend than condemn these heathen souldiers.'[22]

Except for the pagan and superstitious use of lots, casting lots for mundane gain is never condemned in Scripture. In cases of deadlocks and ties, lots were cast (Prov. 18:18). The soldiers did not fight over the clothes. They did not try to swindle the others out of the prize. They resorted to a democratic neutralized way of handling a dispute, the use of the throw of dice to see who had the best odds, high or low number, in order to acquire the robe. The soldiers were not violating Roman procedure for soldiers, for they had a claim by law to the property of Jesus.[23]

Conclusions

In none of the gospels (all four mentioned the gambling of the soldiers) is there a tirade against gambling. Even though foolish betting was as common as vipers in the desert, the reserve of the biblical accounts on the gambling over the seamless robe is significant. The story was told without moralizing, without condemnation of the act of casting lots.

The passage has long been used as an anti-gambling text, and hundreds upon hundreds of homilies have made the application that gamblers are insensitive to the needs of others, in society, in one's community, in one's own household, just as, below the cross, the soldiers were insensitive to the dead Jesus.

Did God object to the use of casting lots at his Son's execution site? Was he against it as a matter of principle or was he against its use? I think the narratives make clear that the gambling was recorded not as another insult to Jesus, so much as a standard practice. The only extraordinary thing about the incident in terms of gambling was that at the site where Jesus suffered a gross injustice from Rome (and because of the Sanhedrin), God allowed to take place a practice associated with fairness. At the site of unfairness (Jesus' crucifixion), there was an example of decency and fairness (the gambling over the seamless robe).

The so-called incidental details of the disposition of Jesus' last possession was part of God's plan. John 19:24 makes plain that the seemingly insignificant dice throw was part of God's plan for the last hours of the Suffering Servant: 'This happened to make the Scripture come true: "They divided my clothes among themselves; they gambled for my robe." ' Was the conjunction of Psalm 22:18 and John 19:24 contrived?

The soldiers did not cast lots because they wanted to stage a fulfillment of Psalm 22:18 (RSV), 'They divide my garments among them, and for my raiment they cast lots.' While to the educated Jew crucifixion was the sign that

Jesus couldn't be the Messiah, to the scripturally informed Jew it was a sign that Jesus was the Messiah because He fulfilled the description of the Suffering Servant/Messiah down to the last detail.[24] The probability of the concurrence of Jesus' death details fulfilling so many ancient Old Testament predictions being coincidental was reduced by each convergence of fact and prophetic prediction.

During the Victorian age St Paul's Cathedral had an outstanding scholar, Canon Henry Parry Liddon [1829–1890] whose old pulpit, incidentally, is stored in the Cathedral's basement. Liddon counted 333 predictions about Christ from the Old Testament. What chance of 333 items randomly converging on one man at one time in one place? That should point to the uniqueness of Jesus rather than to the contrivance of the New Testament documents.

Thus, we recognize that the seemingly incidental reference to casting lots in the passion narratives had tremendous theological implications, more a reference to the divine character of Christ and the accuracy of the prophetic Psalm 22, than to gambling *per se*. The Gospels were intent on showing that Jesus' character and role as Messiah, fulfilling Old Testament predictions, should receive special notice. Readers were to admire Jesus more than be alarmed at the action of the soldiers.

Though the gambling aspect of casting lots was incidental to the thrust made regarding Christ's personhood, it did serve a small function in rounding out the divine significance connected with a disputed way of deciding ownership.

6.

Is Risk-taking Gambling?

To walk a high wire is very risky. I see a remarkable similarity between the high attributed to gambling and that attributed to high-wire walking. The great high-wire artist Karl Wallenda said, 'To be on the wire is life; the rest is waiting.' One of the sensations important to the gambler, according to Tomas Martinez, is the here-now moment. Martinez wrote: 'While taking a risk of [sic] whether in gambling or on the high wire, the subject has a sense of really living because mind and body are stimulated and become filled with life.'[1]

To attempt a high-wire walk is to gamble with one's life. We all try to reduce our risk of death. We want to see another day. To avoid too great a risk is to refuse to gamble. High-wire walkers probably dread a terrifying goof, a tragic trip. Though seemingly immune to misfortune, famed high-wire walker, Karl Wallenda, got caught in an unexpected circumstance.

On March 27, 1978, the fearless, 'Great Wallenda', Karl, the grand old man of high-wire daredevils, didn't realize that he was taking to the high wire for the last time. When performing in San Juan, Puerto Rico, aged 73, without a safety net, he lost his balance in a gust of wind. He plummeted to the ground below, hitting a parked taxi cab, bouncing onto the ground before hundreds of horrified spectators.[2]

In Greece, young men take similar death-defying risks. Young Greek islanders risk their lives for the humble sponge. In Kalymnos, Greece, native sponge divers use no breathing equipment and carry a large stone to take them to the sea floor. These young men knowingly and repeatedly come under the risk of decompression, and with it possible loss of life.

The Greek government has tried to reduce the casualties by offering low-interest loans for new equipment, but most are too poor to take advantage of that life-saving measure. 'Despite the improvements, fewer and fewer young people on Kalymnos are willing to face the risks and hardships of sponge diving.'[3] Going under without the proper equipment is to gamble with the one life they have.

There are other examples. Even the health measure of surgery can be hazardous. The surgeon George Crile, son of the founder of the world-famous Cleveland Clinic in the State of Ohio (US), would say, 'every operation is a calculated risk. The patient's problem is how to calculate the risk.' It was Crile's opinion we should avoid surgery 'if it means high risk and crippling effects'.[4] To choose a surgeon whose record for patient survival is poor is not only a risk, it is a gamble, a gamble in which the odds are against you.

Financial risks in the business world may not be life-threatening but still fraught with grave consequences. Modern building construction in England and elsewhere uses the steel 'I' beam. It has proven to be the best support design for buildings and bridges. I was privileged to have a tour of Bethlehem Steel plant in Allentown, Pennsylvania, in 1979. Behind the development of the 'I' beam is a story of daring and risk. I never realized how much was at stake to make an innovative switch to produce the now-famous 'I' beams of Bethlehem Steel. The fame of

Bethlehem Steel was due to a high-risk financial gamble. In 1904, Bethlehem Steel's founder, Charles M. Schwab, was fortunate to team up with Eugene G. Grace, a master manager. Schwab saw potential in a new type of mill for making structural steel, a mill that could roll wide-flange shapes of far greater strength and less weight than those rolled on standard mills.

An inventor, Henry Grey, had offered a new process to other steel companies, but was turned down. Schwab wanted to invest in the innovative 'I' beam. But money was lacking and bankers didn't want to risk making Bethlehem Steel a sizeable loan to build a new mill. Schwab wanted to take the risk because of the glimmer of potential growth. He said, 'If we're going bust, we'll go bust big!'

Schwab finally got his mill in 1908, and Grace ran it. Because several men were willing to risk financial ruin, America's major cities are monuments to their vision to what the steel 'I' beam could do to revolutionize building construction.

There are degrees of risk in almost everything we do, even down to the simple choices of which transportation we take. Do we decide to go from point A to point B by automobile or by aeroplane? The odds of being killed in an automobile accident in the US per year are 1 in 5,600. The odds of being killed in an automobile accident in the US per lifetime is 1 in 75.[5] The odds of being killed in a plane crash are significantly lower. Whereas deaths by car accident per 100,000 population in 1993 were 15.9 per cent, deaths by air accident in the same year per 100,000 population were a mere .3 per cent.[6] If you fly to a location and rent a car, be very careful how you drive lest you inadvertently effect your own demise.

In everyday life we are asked to avoid health risks, such as from secondary smoking, car fumes, factory exhaust, sun exposure, pesticides, fungicides and other chemicals, and so on. We readily admit there is a difference between everyday risks in crossing the street and buying a lottery ticket. The relationship of risk and gamble is a fine one and will vary from situation to situation. But we maintain that risk of financial loss is involved in more than the straightforward classic wager found in casino gambling and lotteries.

Of course we can't do anything without risk. Ordinary human reactions entail elements of risk, yes, with lesser or greater gambles. It is hard to imagine circumstances where we do not risk acceptance or rejection. No area is immune from risks of loss or gain. To laugh is to risk being thought a fool. To weep is to risk being thought weak and sentimental. To express your feelings is to risk being thought pushy. To love is to risk not being loved in return. To try is to risk failure. To confess wrongs is to take the risk of having a low self-image. In none of these examples is money wagered but each action is a gamble, however insignificant.

But the gambles most difficult to recover from are the financial ones. One can nurse a bruised ego, but what is there to fill an empty pocket?

Financial risks are among those that leave no visible scars, yet continually chafe. Financial risks that, for many, can be avoided should include gambling. Legal gaming has more financial risk than any business or recreational activity. In gambling you risk profit and you risk loss. Earlier we proposed that playing the stock market is ostensibly, realistically a substantial risk with lesser or greater degrees of gambling.

While probably admitting that some people are risk-adverse, the one-time executive director of the US Gambling Commission, James Ritchie, argued that taking risks is part of being human:

There is in the breast of every person a desire to risk. It may be a desire to run for political office, or a desire by a farmer to plant wheat and see if the elements allow him to reap a crop, or a desire to buy stock or commodity futures. Or maybe it comes from a person who decides he has some disposable income and he's going to risk that money because he has a feeling he'll be coming away with more money, which is called gambling. It makes little difference. It's the desire to risk.[7]

Starting a new business involves great financial risk. Money must be guaranteed before a business opens. The pay-off, if successful, will be profit and a recuperation from investment – or it may be bankruptcy. The courts, however, do not consider starting a business gambling. The less we know about what we are doing, the more the venture will be a gamble than a simple risk.

The person starting a business does everything possible to reduce his or her risk, to take the venture completely out of the field of gambling. He or she tries to sharpen his or her perceptions of the buying public by considering the latest market trends. Risk or loss is reduced, too, by picking the right location, the right staff.

And with each decision comes the risk of failure or of success. There is a risk in putting up or securing capital for collateral. In most cases, large amounts of money must be borrowed. Goods must be ordered, property leased or bought, and advertising secured.

Risk-taking is an integral part of the gambling event. Tony Evans admitted that wholesale condemnation of risk-taking would fault God. 'From God's standpoint, all gambling is not equal . . . God [in fact] encourages risk-taking.'[8] The investor takes a risk when he buys stock.[9] Evans, however, quickly justifies financial risk-taking:

When you make legitimate investments you are investing in something that is productive. It's creating a product or offering a service of producing something of value. The profit comes out of the value. There is nothing wrong with that.[10]

What the average person invests in stocks, of course, can't begin to be compared to what is risked in laying out one's life over a lifetime in marriage. The institution of marriage is usually entered upon with the intention of a life-time investment.

Romantic risk

James Ritchie the US Gambling Commissioner's citations of gambling examples did not include marriage or courtship. Before marriage, when there is repeated dating, love expressed between couples has a risk element. 'A person who chooses to grow chooses also the risk of losing. Love itself, then, becomes a gamble: a person who loves creates not only the potential for his own fulfilment but also the risk that he may be destroyed. And the greater the love, the greater the gamble.'[11]

Is marriage a gamble? Technically, you need only one licence to get married. It is a marriage licence, not a gambler's licence. Marriage a gamble? Not in the sense of huge up-front amounts of money. Yet are there not elements of gambling in marriage?

Firstly, there are more goods upfront than the licence fee. What? Realistically, the goods you risk are all you are and have, person, money, and property. That is what you bring into a married relationship. If you don't think so, dread a divorce court's conclusions. True, the persons marrying are not handing over money, but they are sharing the money and other property.

Secondly, there is an element of risk in the relationship. The marriage may or may not last. Thirdly, there is a pay-off. The pay-off is usually not cash. Ordinarily, a person does not marry 'for money' but for love, companionship, and shared experiences. The pay-off a person seeks is being wanted, loved, respected. These are non-tangible pay-offs, but that does not mean they do not have as much value as money.

So is marriage a gamble or simple risk-taking? The courts say it is risk-taking, not gambling. An individual married partner may see the risk as a gamble, but hopefully, a winning gamble. If you don't really know the person, a marriage is definitely a bad gamble, far more than a risk. There is more room for the element of chance to make it a short-term marriage.

Risk is accepted in marriage. 'As with our Lord, when we give ourselves away in love, the result may be a crucifixion. But there is no other gateway into the joy of a Christian marriage.'[12]

What is a good risk? Not every marriage. Some are bad risks. But the inability to distinguish between good and bad risks is no more apparent than in picking a horse to win. Some have as great a difficulty picking a winning horse as in picking a winsome mate.

Horses are often a greater puzzle to men than to women. Bill Moyers, a former Southern Baptist minister who was US President Lyndon B. Johnson's Press Secretary,[13] once confessed on TV in his early years, 'The only time I ever bet on a horse race, I lost. I saw this Catholic priest standing beside a horse [that was competing] that later came in last. I saw the priest, afterward, and told him, "You're responsible for this Baptist losing $2." And the priest said, "That's the trouble with you Baptists. You can't tell a blessing from the last rites." '

Farming risks

Farming is the forgotten risky business. The farmer invests in analysing the soil, in comparing seeds, in weighing up whether to use the land rented or owned and to what degree to trust soil treatment, and with what variety of fertilizer. He invests in seed, in hiring helpers, in equipment. For a price he must prepare the ground, plant, thin, fertilize, irrigate, harvest the crop. It all takes money. And all the money in farming must be up-front before there is any guarantee of the harvest being successful. More often than not, God is kind and blesses the labour of the farmers with a bountiful harvest whether along the coast of France in Brittany, where cauliflowers are harvested in January, or in harvesting sugar beets in central Wyoming in September/October.

The third element of legal gambling is also in farming. The pay-off can be so many bushels per acre, and the price per bushel will be a certain price. The profit may be gauged another way, by tonnage rather than by containers, but still the farmer expects a profit, a pay-off. If insect infestation ruins the crop, or if hail chops the crop to pieces before it can mature, or if floods or frost stop or stunt the growth, the pay-off is financial loss. Are farmers required to get a gambling licence at the start of the year? No. Because in the eyes of the court, they do not meet the definition of a gambler. Yet the farmer has met the three criteria of what a gambler is. The distinction between gamblers and non-gamblers gets blurry, fuzzy, even crazy.

Farmer Merrill Thornton of Osceola, Iowa, saw himself as a crazy gambler. He said, 'I'd never put $1,000 down on the table over a hand of poker, but here I am gambling thousands or more every year on something that isn't even as sure as that.'[14] Every farmer, even those engaged in irrigation farming, must settle with unpredictable weather and uncertain yield. Too late or too early planting, too superficial thinning, too much sun, too little rain, an infestation of leaf insects or root plant disease can shrivel corn, kill tomato plants. A sudden hailstorm can shred sugar-beet leaves. As one Worland, Wyoming sugar-beet farmer told me, when I lived and pastored there for eight years: 'Farmers are big-time gamblers.'

But for many American farmers, they are less gamblers than they think, because they know their field; in fact, they are outstanding in it. They study the soil and everything connected with farming. Chances are good that they will succeed when they have done their homework and if the weather is ideal.

The difference between the casino attender who gambles and the farmer who gambles is not that farming is not gambling, but that farming is less of a gamble. God's exercise of his creative power in the germination, growth, and maturation of plants is more a constant than the fickle results of dice or cards. Also, we must not confuse the hard-working farmer with the laid-back gambler who is putting all his trust in chance. The successful farmer certainly takes risks and must be a student of his crop, land, and long-range weather predictions, but he is nothing like the fatalistic gambler who doesn't make the same degree of effort as the hard-working farmer.

Many occupations carry high risks, risks that vary in danger. With some you can lose your shirt. With others, such as steeplejacks, you can lose your life. The outcome of life and work on earth is that nothing is certain here. Even those who spend their time trying to play their cards right are surprised and chagrined when they get lost in the shuffle. Businesses fold when the market for the product disappears or because some fluke occurs in transforming raw material into a finished product. Farmers have learned that their occupation contains some heartaches as well as much satisfaction.

The gender issue

Gambling without risk is like a balloon without air. The risk element is what many find attractive in gambling. And risk-taking appeals to both sexes equally. Some contend there are proportionately more women inclined to gamble than men. John Scarne surveyed 25,000 adults, (10,000 women, 10,000 men, and 5,000 professional gamblers). It produced the interesting fact that 80 per cent of women compared to 76 per cent of men answered 'yes' to the question of whether they gambled.[15] The size of the gambling public increases steadily. According to the latest findings, 'Today about 90 million adult Americans – of which 43 million are men and 47 million are women – are gambling the astronomical sum of $500 billion annually.'[16]

The high percentage of women gamblers is surprising. Slot machines are especially attractive to women gamblers, according to Charlotte Olmsted, who wrote that in the Nevada gambling cities, Reno and Las Vegas, 'middle-aged women are the most compulsive players' of the slots.[17] Operators of the two Indiana floating casinos both expressed the opinion/observation that more women than men frequent the boats and many make return trips.[18] Another finding is that 'men generally gamble more than women. But men and women play the lottery at about the same rate.'[19]

[In 1972] 95 per cent of gamblers were men. According to a 1995 survey by Uankelovich Partners and Home Testing

Institute, 55 per cent of gamblers are now women. Casino managers know this and are encouraging the trend with more expensive prizes, colorful gaming lobbies, and free child care.[20]

Women who recognize this statistic are not surprised, for some know their marriages were a gamble.

Judi Hansen, a thirty-two-year old Santa Ana, California woman, won at slots a record $280,000 at the Hilton Hotel in Las Vegas in June, 1972.[21] Slot machines appeal to women gambling. 'If women make the wrong call at the roulette wheel or the wrong play at the blackjack table, they often must endure the ridicule of men. At slots, they can do their own thing without fear of embarrassment.'[22]

Other women seek gambling for what they consider more positive reasons. A retired Arizona beautician, Vera Bradley, told reporter Barry Horstman that she budgets $50 to $100 for a bi-weekly casino visit which results in 'more action than I can get in a month of trips to the mall or the movies.'[23]

The modern family is frustrated by mounting bills and tight budgets. A couple find marriage a nag when bills creep up and threaten to strangle the life of marital bliss. Love is strong but bill collectors are persistent. Couples frustrated at work because the pay is low and prospects for a rise are slim, are forced to try other expedients. The second job is looked into. Some husbands hold down two jobs to try to get ahead. Or the wife seeks employment. That is easier once the children are in school and the mother has plenty of spare time. Few can expect help from playing the slots or throwing dice.

The lure of lotto

Realistically, however much Christian couples may believe the good Lord smiles on their relationship, they can't expect to meet their monthly bills by playing lotto.

> They hope to win big, to suddenly have a large, guaranteed income every year. Unfortunately, few players win. Everybody else still must continue to live on their regular income, which is actually decreased by the choice to spend money for lottery tickets.[24]

Some would prefer not to view lotteries as a loathsome state double-tax on the poor, but as the least likely method of getting out of debt. The Puritan Thomas Gataker referred to buying lottery tickets as 'lusorious', by which he meant that it was a form of playful or recreational spending.[25]

If there is some discretionary money available in a family, a couple may risk a little of it, occasionally, without feeling they are throwing away a future fortune. Others feel indulgence in lotto-buying only keeps one poor, forever in debt. The smarter options are additional jobs, consolidation of debts, better money management, saving toward Conditional Deposits, or going directly into buying smart stocks.

Certainly, lotteries are gambling. But while the lottery is a great risk to the buyer, it is no risk for those who benefit from the bulk of the collection, that the project, city, or cause it sponsors. The first public lottery was conducted by the Dutch in 1434 'in an effort to raise money for the town of Sluis'.[26]

In New England, before 1776, there were 157 separate lotteries, sanctioned by the colonial legislatures, for the benefit of the colonial governments, for individual towns, for paving its streets, building its docks, schools, churches, and to establish industries.[27] Rhode Island, which along with Connecticut and Maryland, were the only colonies that could disobey the abolition by the British Crown, because their charters allowed them to ignore the royal decree, were able to issue 77 lotteries before 1744, most of which were for the improvement of individual towns.[28] 'From 1776 until 1820 over 70 lotteries were authorized by Congress for public works.'[29]

State lotteries, despite their critics, lessen citizenry tax loads, and benefit worthy programmes and projects, with the proceeds distributed to various governmental branches. According to Michael J. Walsh, the vice-chairman of the US Indiana State Gaming Association, '10 cents of each admission tax charged on all Indiana gaming vessel admissions goes to the Indiana Mental Health Division for prevention and treatment of gaming disorders. Indiana gaming vessels contributed nearly $ 2.5 million [in 1997].'[30]

Admittedly, lotteries rarely help the little person struggling to meet expenses. What happens when one doesn't come up with ready cash to meet bills? From a motivational perspective, money rarely gives one the purest desire and drive to meet life's challenges and conquer them. Something internal sought and found in Jesus Christ can deliver a person from inveterate covetousness.

Gambling expenses are usually in increments, and with the money spent, the risk element rises or lowers. Where should the moral fault-line with gambling be drawn? Whether you think gambling is good or evil, risk-taking brings either gain or loss. Even when risks are low there is a small element of gambling. The greater the risk, the greater the gamble. It is rarely that gambling does not leave its sticky imprint on life's trails. James Ritchie would not exclude or eliminate gambling from seemingly risk-free occupations, such as starting a legitimate business, stock investments, land purchases, and farming. Nor should we.

Ritchie's examples do not fit the legal definition of gambling although the risk-element in them is undeniable and unavoidable. It should show the legal definition inadequate to address all of life. Despite that, no one would deny that the legal definition is necessary to deal with inequities and injustices. A hardline approach to gambling delimits the enormity of gambling instances. Gambling critics say the legalization of gambling has desensitized it.

Political pressure by Christians may prevent some gambling initiatives, but to reverse those already in place is less likely. Control by minority voices is unlikely to stop trends. The genie is out of the bottle.

Christians need to take a second look at the basis of their arguments against chance-taking. What Christians can do is continue avoidance of those forms of gambling they believe are unwise for themselves and unhealthy for society. Perhaps the most difficult challenge will be for them to adjust, amend and expand their estimation of what constitutes gambling. A revised view of gambling should include every area where choice presents a poor risk.

Should 'gamble' cease to be a pejorative word? What is evil in gambling is not the word, but the kinds and amounts of the gamble. That automatically expands the moral choice from simple best odds to include other factors, moral parameters derived from biblical directives. What separates a Christian's recognition of what is a bad bet includes more than the best odds. The non-Christian makes a bet primarily on the basis of the odds. The Christian makes a choice not always on the basis of the odds, but on what Scripture says and what has the greater long-term benefits.

The Bible and risk-taking

Scripture honours spiritual risk-takers, especially in Hebrews 11. Patriarchs, prophets and minor characters of faith dared to trust God against seeming defeat. But living for God was not so much risk as a good gamble. But the wisdom of siding with God is never in fact a gamble for there is no risk of final loss. It is more an assured obligation. In Old and New Testament times believers viewed a total secularist mindset the worst gamble possible, leading to or reflecting spiritual bankruptcy.

Early Christians were for the most part not financially secure, yet they had a peace of mind that all financial worries would be taken care of. What prepared them to carry on when resources and comforts were few? They didn't have tranquillisers to take the edge off their anxiety, but they had the Bible, they had access to God through prayer.

One factor was that they felt reconciled to God and in friendly relations with him. That was a wealth sheer cash couldn't deliver. Faced with exile, labelled as insurrectionists and banned as misfits, first- and second-century Christians were both tortured and exiled. But in their furnace of affliction they came out winners. Through God's help they were able to face risks with resolution, patience, and hope.

Perhaps the most famous Old Testament risk-taker was Abraham, who 'went out, not knowing where he went' (Heb. 11:8). But the 'gamble' in Abraham did not leave him even after he arrived in Canaan, for as Genesis 23:1–20 relates, as Paul Pilzer points out, he was 'the first person in the Bible to recognize land as individual property that can be improved, purchased, and sold.'[31]

Later, another famous Old Testament figure decided to stick with an unpopular cause. Moses chose to cast his lot with the adventurous people of Israel (Heb. 11:24, 25).

24 By faith Moses, when he had grown up, refused to be known as the son of Pharaoh's daughter. 25 He chose to be mistreated along with the people of God rather than to enjoy the pleasures of sin for a short time.[32]

Two famous women risk-takers appear in the Old Testament: one was Gentile, the other Jewish, Ruth and Esther. Ruth was one of two Gentile women in Jesus' lineage (Mt. 1:5). Ruth was a resilient woman, a person willing to take risks. 'When Naomi's friends died in the land of Moab, [Ruth] returned to the land of Israel; but when Naomi dies, Ruth will not return to the land of Moab.'[33]

Esther, a Jewess of great beauty, rose from being a humble maiden to become the wife of the great monarch Ahasuerus, the Persian King Xerxes (Ezra 4:6). When Queen, she risked her health and welfare to intervene for her people. If she looked to her own position and self-interest she would not have stuck her neck out. 'Esther was not made Queen Esther that she might make herself glorious, but that she might be in a position to save the Jews.'[34]

Probably the hairiest Old Testament risk-taker was Samson (Judges. 14:12–19).[35] Other Old Testament risk-takers gambled with their lives for the cause of God. Hebrews 11 is a catalogue of those men and women of faith who dared put their lives on the line for the cause of God.

One could argue that these examples establish that risk-taking on the basis of God's Word is not a gamble. From within the circle of God's assured truth-telling, God's total sovereignty, and titanic ability to accomplish all his intentions, commitments, and promises was out of the realm of a gamble. In this connection, the chief gamble was not to believe God, for that would deny God's truthfulness and divine omnipotence. But the risk connected with commitment to God's call would be a gamble where some hesitation or doubt accompanied the commitments. (Even good faith is recognized in Scripture not to be perfect faith.) And new spiritual ventures could be classed as gambles where there was no statistical data or basis for a probability judgment. In that sense the choice was perceived as a gamble.

In the New Testament the supreme risk-taker was none other than Jesus himself. He risked reprisal for speaking his mind and saying things that cut across the grain of traditional Jewish ideas. He risked flak from those who despised Samaritans by giving the parable about the Good Samaritan (Lk. 10:30–37).

Christ's ministry was not a gamble, because he knew the odds that the Gospel would not come across well with with proud persons. He knew, too, that he would conquer death and live to tell more of God's message (Heb. 12:1–3). Despite human aversion to salvation solely by divine grace, Jesus risked ridicule, anger, and alienation by using the Samaritan as an example of unselfish, humanitarian service. Jesus was sustained by the anticipated, guaranteed winning of God's elect (Isa. 52:15; 53:8,10,11). This was one of the joys that sustained him in his ordeals (Heb. 12:1,2). Because of his inner strength Jesus was not ruined by increased opposition when he affirmed his equality with God (Jn. 10:29).

Because of Jesus' insight into human nature (Jn. 2:25), he was not taken by surprise at human unbelief, half-heartedness, hypocrisy, and rejection. From his initial sermon when he offended his own townspeople by using a Gentile woman as a good example (Lk. 4:25–27) to his later daring parable of the good Samaritan, who were then hated half-breeds, Jesus encountered outrage and oppression. And Jesus put his life and ministry in jeopardy by calling the so-called pious to repentance and by preaching

God's grace alone as the grounds of human acceptance before God.

> It was an act of unparalleled risk which Jesus performed when, from the full power of his consciousness of sovereignty, he openly and fearlessly called these men [the Pharisees] to repentance, and this act brought him to the cross.[36]

Jesus himself described his crucifixion as both the epitome and end of his risk-taking on earth. The verb, ordinarily translated 'to lay down', in John 10:11,15,17, could mean 'to risk' as well as 'to give'.[37] But his risk was not a gamble in the sense that what God the Father planned would be effected, completing God's eternal decrees.

Christian risk-taking today

Christians are called upon by Christ to follow him. In the ministry of the Word, in meeting human arrogance and standing up for God, risk is unavoidable. Karl Barth [1886–1968] noted that those who 'put themselves under the judgment of the Word of God, [must accept] the risk that they may be publicly disavowed'.[38]

The Christian's vindication, or his status in the final draw, must wait. 'Just as Jesus did, the Christian takes the risk of entrusting himself and the vindication of his living to God; he is prepared to receive that vindication where Jesus did: beyond death'.[39]

A little-known early convert of the Apostle Paul, Epaphras, was recognized by Paul for his heroism. In one of the last letters Paul wrote, he penned the following encomium of Epaphras: 'because he almost died for the work of Christ, risking his life to make up for the help you could not give me' (Phil. 2:30 NIV). Epaphras' spiritual descendant was Martin Bucer [1491–1551], the forgotten Strasbourg Protestant Reformer, who said in the last paragraph of his *Instruction of Christian Love:* 'We must let no man keep us from the Word of God. For it we must risk honor, life, possessions, and all that which God has given us.'[40]

7.

Puritan Ponderings

Instead of complaining that the undeserving win the lottery, think of how someone, worthy or unworthy, is helped. That is hard to do. But we can learn that lesson from colonial theologian, William Ames [1576–1633].

To the question, 'What is to be thought of publicke Lotteries, wherein many Prizes, or rewards, are proposed to be gotten by Lot?', Ames answered in two parts:

> 1. They might haply bee so ordered, that they might be lawfull. Namely, if there were any need of a contribution to some pious use: and to avoid discommodities [appearance of favoritism], the business should be permitted to Lot who should distribute: and there also which cast the Lots, should onely venture that which they would not unwillingly give and so come to the Lottery, not out of an hope of gayning, but out of an intention of bestowing something. 2. As they are not used, they seem to be unlawful, because they onely aime at gaine, by fraude and flattery, and give an occasion to many evils.[1]

A contemporary of Ames was Englishman Thomas Gataker [1574–1654]. Gataker was highly regarded among the Puritan clergy. To the surprise of many, Gataker also saw some social value in lotteries. As in the seventeenth century, so today, government and state lotteries are a mixed bag. How should we view the modern lotteries?

As an industry and as a major recreation, gambling is hardly a Christian enterprise. Indeed, many Christians contend that gaming is intrinsically evil and only fosters vice. One wonders how seventeenth-century Christians such as the two Puritans, Ames and Gataker, could be so moderate in their assessment of lotteries. Is your curiosity aroused as to how some Puritans could refuse to condemn lotteries?

Significant space, we regret, has not been given to Puritans in recent Christian books on gambling.[2] At best, any mention is so brief it can be missed. With this chapter we remedy previous omissions and minimal reference.

Puritans were models of biblical conformity, intellectual ability, and moral integrity. Puritans were Christians *par excellence, n'est-ce pas?* Most evangelicals grant they were the quintessence of orthodoxy. But before their attitudes, views, and actions are aired and assessed, we should first see Puritans as a by-product of the European Protestant Reformation. Puritanism saw itself as the continuing Reformation of the church. How Puritans viewed life set the tone of subsequent Protestantism. But before that can be looked into, some comment is warranted about Protestantism in Europe.

Two chief Protestant reformers, Martin Luther and John Calvin, made their way into Puritan thinking. Luther's writings were less well known to Puritans than those of John Calvin. Puritans knew Luther more by his reputation than by his writings. Recreational controversies, either in his own nation or in England, did not occupy the Reformer. Luther's time was principally focused on challenging/correcting papal theology rather than on moralizing about German recreation. Nevertheless,

Martin Luther [1483–1546] showed 'an obvious familiarity with [cards] and card-playing.'[3] He drew an analogy that reflects that 'God's chesspieces and cards are great and mighty princes, kings, and emperors; for he always trumps or overcomes one through another ... Lastly, our God comes, deals out the cards, and beats the pope with the Luther, which is his ace.'[4]

Given the popularity of playing cards and Luther's obvious acquaintance with their use, it is not surprising that he and other reformers should address the question of card-playing directly. Little is known about the types of card games played in the sixteenth century, but it seems that most of them involved some element of chance, and therefore, were conducive to gambling. Indeed, gambling and card-playing are generally mentioned together by the reformers. While, in general, they deplore gambling, their attitudes towards card-playing are remarkably mild. Luther calls gamblers 'thieves before God' and says their gains were won out of self-interest and sinfulness but does not censure card-playing specifically.[5]

Gambling occupied the lives of Luther's contemporaries. He admired the ancients who emphasized music and exercise, for they helped prevent men from falling into 'debauchery, drunkenness, and gambling'. At the same mealtime conversation, on 27 October 1536, he saw music and exercise as a prevention against 'habits of drink, lust, and gambling such as we now, alas, see in the courts and in the cities'.[6]

Because of his arduous study and preaching schedules, John Calvin [1509–1564] hardly had time for romance, let alone the recreation of card-playing. He did, however, compose the document *Ordinances for the Supervision of Churches in the Country* of 1547. What he was against was not the use of chance in games, but the use of chance in gambling games. On games he wrote:

> No one is to play at games that are dissolute, or at games
> played for gold or silver or at excessive expense, on pain of
> five sous and the loss of the sum staked.[7]

Regarding the Protestant reformers on gambling, Harvard Professor Smoller concluded: 'Not until the late sixteenth century in England does controversy begin to arise over whether all games of chance, not just gambling, are sinful.'[8]

Puritans asked the same question we ask: 'Should Christians gamble?' Puritan history reflects both the positions of permission and exclusion. Today evangelical Christians, for the most part, oppose all forms of gambling except insurance and stocks, thus keeping alive one form of Puritan opposition.

A significant number of Puritans recorded inner revulsion for a gambler's greed and his all-consuming earthbound attachments. Combined with that, however, some showed flexibility on the role and use of chance.

Not all Puritans urged complete exclusion of lots. Surprisingly, some allowed the role of casting lots for public benefits. Before that position is presented, we need to take a look at how gambling galled the average non-clerical Puritan. How they viewed gambling is best seen in their diaries. These reveal a lot about Puritan attitudes. Puritan diaries fill out how gambling was viewed in the way Puritan lectures on moral issues don't. Both sources are worth exploration.

Puritan diaries

Seventeenth century diaries provide a vast storehouse of information on the times.[9] Although not a Christian,

Samuel Pepys [1633–1703] was perhaps the century's best-known diarist.[10] A friend, who outlived him, was the lesser-known Anglican layman, John Evelyn [1620–1706], second son of a substantial landowner of Wotton, Surrey, who also kept diaries. Rather late in life (he was aged 79), Evelyn came into wealth in 1699. Yet prior to that he had travelled extensively on the European continent in the 1640s, avoiding England's Civil War. He was a founding member of the Royal Society, an author of Christian history,[11] and a witness of many decisive events such as the Restoration of Charles II, the Plague, and the Great Fire of London.

Evelyn hobnobbed with the rich and royals. He attended events where gambling was conducted. His entry for 6 January, 1662 recorded the following:

> This evening (according to custome) his Majestie opened the Revells of that night, by throwing the Dice himselfe, in the Privy Chamber, where was a table set on purpose, and lost his 100 pounds: the yeare before he won 150 pounds: The Ladys also plaied very deepe: I came away when the Duke of Ormond had won about 1000 pounds and left them still at passage, Cards etc: at other Tables, both there and at the Groome-porters, observing the wiccked folly vanity and monstrous excesse of Passion amongst some loosers, and sorry I am that such a wretched Custome as play to that excesse should be countenanced in a Court, which ought to be an example of Virtue to the rest of the kingdome.[12]

On another occasion he described life among the rich. For 16 October 1671, he recorded:

> Came all the greate Men from N: Market and other parts both of Suffolck, and Norfolck to make their Court; the whole house fill'd from one end to the other, with Lords, Ladys and

Gallants, and such a furnished Table had I seldome seene, nor any thing more splendid and free: so as for 15 dayes there were entertain'd at the Least 200 people, and halfe as many horses, besids Servants, Guards, at Infinite expense: In the mornings we went a hunting and hawking. In the afternoone 'til almost morning at Cards and dice etc. yet I must say without noise, swearing, quarell or Confusion of any sort: I who was no Gamster, had often discourse with the French Ambassador Colbert, and went sometimes abroad on horse back with the Ladys to take the aire, and now and then to hunting; thus idly passing the time, but not without more often recesse to my prety apartment, where I was quite out of all this hurry, and had [leasure], when I would to converse with books . . .[13]

Evelyn was present when Charles II died and King James II became his heir. James II decided to keep the same counsellors. At the Coronation ceremony, Evelyn recorded for 6 February, 1685:

. . . Then an Herauld called the Lords Coaches according to ranke, my selfe accompanying the solemnity in my Lord Cornwallis Coach, first to Temple barr, where the Lord Major [Mayor] and his breathren etc met us on horseback in all their formalities, and proclaimed the King . . . being come to White-hall, we all went and kissed the King and Queenes hands, he had ben on the bed, but was now risen, and in his Undresse . . . Thus concluded this sad, and yet Joyfull day: I am never to forget the unexpressable luxury, and prophanesse, gaming, and all dissolution, and as it were total forgetfullnesse of God (it being Sunday evening) . . . I was witnesse of; the King, sitting and toying with his Concubines Portsmouth, Cleaveland, and Mazarine: etc: A french boy singing love songs, in that glorious Gallery, whilst about 20 of the greate Courtiers and other dissolute persons were at

Basset round a large table, a bank of at least 2000 in Gold
before them . . .[14]

Following the Civil War, during the Restoration period,
after a generation of religious disputes the ruling class
indulged in escapist pleasures, such as card-playing.

Opulence led to the opportunity of gaming on a grand
scale. But the grandness, according to the Christian John
Evelyn, was not grand morally. Like many other Christians it grieved him to see the spiritual indifference among
the wealthy and noble. It was a sign of spiritual barrenness
to waste time and wealth on gaming.

The Westminster Assembly

England was deeply divided in many ways, not just socially
and economically, but spiritually. The clash of cultures, the
tension of world-views brought England in 1643 to the brink
of civil war. The Long Parliament was determined to
address its differences and fragile social fabric. One hundred and twenty-one 'divines' or ministers were gathered at
Westminster Abbey to pull together England's Christian
heritage, to formulate its Christian belief. The session began
on 1 July 1643 and concluded 1,163 sessions later in December 1648, (five and a half years later). *The Larger Catechism*
was one of the documents produced.

The Larger Catechism asked, 'What are the sins forbidden in the eighth commandment?' (The commandment
against stealing.) Answer:

The sins forbidden in the eighth commandment, besides the
neglect of the duties required (James 2:15–16, 1 John 3:17), are
theft (Eph. 4:28), robbery (Ps. 62:10), man-stealing (1 Tim.
1:10), and receiving any thing that is stolen (Prov. 29:24,

Ps. 50:18), fraudulent dealing (1 Thess. 4:6), false weights and measures (Prov. 11:1, Prov. 20:10), removing landmarks (Deut. 19:14, Prov. 23:10), injustice and unfaithfulness in contracts between man and man (Amos 8:5, Ps. 37:21), or in matters of trust (Luke 16:10–12); oppression (Ezek. 22:29, Lev. 25:17), extortion (Matt. 23:25, Ezek. 22:12), usury (Ps. 15:5), bribery (Job 15:34), vexatious law-suits (1 Cor. 6:6–8, Prov. 3:29–30), unjust inclosures and depopulations (Isa. 5:8, Micah 2:2); ingrossing commodities to enhance the price (Prov. 11:26); unlawful callings (Acts 19:19,24–25), and all other unjust or sinful ways of taking or withholding from our neighbour what belongs to him, or of enriching ourselves (Job 20:19, James 5:4, Prov. 21:6); covetousness (Luke 12:15); inordinate prizing and affecting worldly goods (1 Tim. 6:5, Col. 3:2, Prov. 23:5, Ps. 62:10); distrustful and distracting cares and studies in getting, keeping, and using them (Matt. 6:25,31,34, Eccl. 5:12); envying at the prosperity of others (Ps. 73:3, Ps. 37:1,7); as likewise idleness (2 Thess. 3:11, Prov. 18:9), prodigality, *wasteful gaming* [emphasis added]; and all other ways whereby we do unduly prejudice our own outward estate (Prov. 21:17, Prov. 23:20–21, Prov. 28:19), and defrauding ourselves of the due use and comfort of that estate which God hath given us (Eccl. 4:8, Eccl. 6:2, 1 Tim. 5:8).[15]

In the above citation it should be noted that a distinction was made between wasteful gaming and gaming. It was argued then, as sometimes now, that there is a distinction between losing much or little in gaming, that big amounts accounted for 'wasteful gaming'.

Surprisingly, there was no universal condemnation of gambling among the Puritans, even among the Puritans who were non-separating Puritans. Among the non-separating Puritans were Thomas Gataker and William Ames, two sterling theologians, and the pastoral leader, Richard Baxter. Yet Gataker and Ames disagreed slightly between themselves on the usefulness of casting lots.

The Puritan Thomas Gataker [1574–1654]

Today Thomas Gataker [1574–1654] is a little-known Westminster Assembly participant, yet in his own age he was highly esteemed.[16] Gataker was one of the great linguists of his time, able, learned, pious. He possessed a photographic memory.[17] And he was a distinguished lecturer at Lincoln's Inn. The famous John Donne followed him in that post.

Gataker was a Puritan whose public discourses on casting lots were misinterpreted and because of that he was maligned. Gataker was 'a considerable scholar and got into trouble with some of his Puritan brethren for writing a treatise approving gambling'.[18] Gataker felt compelled to set the record straight so he published his views. First, the substance of his conclusions came out in 1619, under the title *Of the Nature and Use of Lots*.

After Gataker's first edition on *Lots* appeared, Mr James Balmford attacked Gataker's thesis in his *A Short and Plaine Dialogue Concerning the Unlawfulness of Playing at Cards* (London, 1593). Gataker's initial response was a brief work in 1623 under the title, *A Just Defence of the same Against Mr J. B.* Several years later he issued a fuller defence, a major book which was a revision and expansion of both his 1619 and 1623 works. Another critic Gataker aimed to debunk was fellow Puritan Dudley Fenner.

No present historians seem inclined to examine Gataker's massive *Of the Nature and Use of Lots: A Treatise Historical and Theological*. The second edition (1627) was 416 pages in length. The book is inaccessible to most, so a chapter-by-chapter summary of the work follows in the next Chapter.[19]

William Ames [1576–1633], theologian

Amesius was the Latin name of English theologian William Ames [1576–1633]. He had emigrated to Holland and lived out his life there. Ames authored the most popular theological text in colonial America, *Marrow of Theology.*[20] Ames was a non-separating Puritan, whereas John Robinson [1576–1625], Pastor of the Pilgrim colony that came to America, was a separating Puritan.[21]

The Protestant theology text didn't argue against games of chance, but against the wrong use of them. 'Ames holds that a lot can be rightly employed after all reasonable attempts to solve the issue have been employed, and after both parties agree to treat the result of the lot as a final decision.' Ames' chapter on lots in *The Marrow of Theology* 'is in part an answer to Thomas Gataker [1574–1654]'.[22] Ames wrote in that chapter:

> Those who defend the use of lots in games are sufficiently refuted by one argument, namely, that a lot is held unanimously to have a natural fitness for asking counsel of God's providence in a special manner. It cannot be that one and the same action should by nature be specially adapted to so sacred a use and at the same time to be fit for sports and gambling.[23]

Where did Ames and Thomas Gataker agree? Neither objected to the use of chance in determining a position. Gataker wrote on the nature, use, and abuse of lots or lotteries. 'These discourses were intended by [Gataker to show] the lawfulness of lusorious, or entertaining games of chance, and the unlawfulness of the divinatory lots.'[25]

A favourite Puritan writer among Christians today is Richard Baxter. He is far better known, far more readable, and far more admired than either Gataker or Ames. Many of his works have been reprinted from which all may profit. Baxter was truly dedicated to the principle of the Christian's submission to the Christ of Scripture. Yet Baxter was devoid of the severity usually associated with Puritanism.

Puritan Richard Baxter [1615–1691]

Baxter was somewhat of a synthesizer and mollifier. He sought unanimity where possible. On the controversy of gambling, his position was the same as Thomas Gataker's. Historian John T. McNeill noted on the use of leisure that Baxter was more liberal than the famous Puritan William Perkins [1558–1602].[26]

Interestingly, all three men were contemporaries. Baxter and Thomas Gataker corresponded.[27] Several exchanges show each read the other's published works and both expressed admiration of the other. While Baxter did not say he read Gataker's first work (*On the Nature and Use of Lots*), on the basis of Baxter's omnivorous reading, it is highly likely that he read it, and what he read may have influenced his views.

Baxter's position on lotteries warrants citation. Judge Baxter by his own words:

> Question 1. Is it lawful to lay wagers upon the credit or confidence of one another's opinions or assertions in discourse? As e.g. I will lay you so much that I am in the right?
> *Answer*: Yes, if these three things concur: 1. That the true end of the wager is, to be a penalty to him that shall be guilty of a rash and false assertion, and not to gratify the covetousness of the other. 2. That it be no great a sum than can be demanded and paid, without breach of charity, or too much hurt to the loser (as above the proportion of his error). 3. That it be no other but what both parties are truly willing to stand

to the loss of, if either of them lose, and that beforehand they truly seem so willing to each other.

Question 2. Is it lawful to lay wagers upon horse-races, dogs, hawks, bear-baitings, or such games as depend upon the activity of beast or man?

Answer: Yes, upon the two last expressed conditions; and, 3. That it be not an exercise which is itself unlawful, by cruelty to beasts, or hazard to the lives of men, (as in fencing, running, wrestling, etc. it may fall out if it be not cautelously [cautiously, JG added] done,) or by the expense of an undue proportion of time in them, which is the common malignity of such recreations.

Question 3. May I lawfully give money to see such sports, as bear-baiting, stage-plays, masks, shows, puppet-plays, activities of man or beast? & etc.

Answer: There are many shows that are desirable and laudable, (as of strange creatures, monsters, rare engines, activities, & etc.) the sight of which it is lawful to purchase, at a proportionable price; as a prospect through one of Galileo's tubes or such another, is worth much money to a studious person. But when the exercise is unlawful (as all stage-plays are that ever I saw, or had just information of; yea, odiously evil; however it is very possible that a comedy or tragedy might with abundance of cautions be lawfully acted,) it is then (usually) unlawful to be a spectator either for money or on free cost. I say, (usually,) because it is possible that some one that is necessitated to be there, or that goeth to find out their evil to suppress them, or that is once only induced to know the truth of them, may do it innocently; but so do not they, who are present voluntarily and approvingly. 3. And if the recreation be lawful in itself, yet when vain persons go thither to feed a carnal fancy and vicious delight in piety, and when it wasteth their time and corrupteth their minds, and alienated them from good or hindereth duty, it is to them unlawful.

Question 4. Is it lawful to play at cards or dice for money, or at any lottery?

Answer: The greatest doubt is, whether the games be lawful, many learned divines being for the negative, and many for the affirmative lay down so many necessaries or conditions to prove them lawful, as I scarce ever yet saw meet together; but if they be proved at all lawful, the case of wagers is resolved as the next.

Question 5. May I play at bowls, run, shoot, & etc. or use such personal activities for money?

Answer: Yes, 1. If you make not the game itself bad, by any accident. 2. If your wager be laid for sport, and not for covetousness (striving who shall get another's money, and give them nothing for it). 3. And if no more be laid than is suitable to the sport and the loser doth well and willingly pay.[28]

American Puritan, Cotton Mather alluded to Baxter's last 250-page work (1691), *The Certainty of the Worlds of Spirits*, as one who sided with him on lotteries. Yet Mather alluded to just two pages in Baxter's conclusion. He wrote:

[Young men] do very terribly intimate a peculiar interest of the Devil in ruling the chance of these games; this is an observation which my most Honoured Friend, the Venerable Baxter, has made in the close of his book, about the World of Spirits.[29]

In the light of Baxter's *Christian Directory* comments, what weight can be laid on Cotton Mather's passing reference to Baxter? Did Baxter come out in his last work (1691) with a reversal? Was Mather's name-dropping justified?

Baxter's actual words in his *The Certainty of the Worlds of Spirits* are more important than Mather's summary. Baxter wrote:

Devils have a greater Game to play invisibly, than by Apparitions. O happy World, if they do not do a hundred thousand times more hurt by the Baits of Pleasure, Lust and Honour, and by Pride, and love of Money and Sensuality, than they do by Witches! ... If the Devil can get People (perhaps Lords and Ladies) to spend the Day (their precious Hours) in Cards and Dice, and Feastings, and Stage-plays, and Masks and Musick, and perhaps filthy Lust, he will let you say your prayers at Night, and cry God Mercy ... [30]

Baxter warned of the secular spirit, but there was no outright rejection of the lottery method. It seems Mather used the reputation of Baxter to justify trashing lotteries as well as cards. In his eagerness to find an ally, Cotton Mather stretched Baxter's position.

Baxter's interest in holiness and his ability to raise Christians to a higher plane in following Christ are well known, widely applauded, and deeply loved. But his flexibility on the matter of wagering is less known. And, in fairness to Baxter's track record in commending the inner life, he cannot be faulted for having abdicated his dedication to the spiritual life. On the matter of lotteries, however, Richard Baxter showed astonishing liberality.

It is not known what effect, if any, the writings of Gataker, Ames, and Baxter had upon the significant *The Complete Gamester* (1674) by Charles Cotton, who argued not only that people need recreation, but that gambling was a useful recreation. [31] Yet in gambling at a bowling match, for instance, Charles Cotton warned, ' ... practice must be your best tutor ...; all that I shall say, have a care you are not in the first place rooked out of your money.'[32] Although Gataker, Ames, and Baxter took a liberal approach to play, their views were not representative of most Puritans, who were highly critical of the latitude in recreation promoted by royal edicts.[33]

The flexibility of Gataker, Ames, and Baxter was found in Calvinists who were non-Puritans. These Reformed preachers were godly men, standard-bearers of Scripture as God's Word within the established church. One of the forgotten Calvinists of that time was Robert South, a preacher of brilliant mind and sharp wit.[34]

Loyalist Robert South [1634–1716]

South was chaplain to Charles II and Canon of Christ Church Oxford (1670), and highly critical of Puritan Oliver Cromwell.[35]

In his sermon on Proverbs 16:33, South distinguished between two views of chance: one by non-Christians; another by Christians. The non-Christian held that chance ruled, not God. The Christian saw that while chance did not explain events' first causes, chance did explain 'second causes', i.e. human agency. 'As it related to second causes [chance] is not profaneness, but a great truth.' In addition, he argued that God exercises His royal prerogative 'to have all these loose, uneven, fickle uncertainties under his disposal'.[36]

Puritans, generally, were comfortable with the place of chance (as secondary cause only) in human affairs.

Although Robert South's statements on chance were not in reference to gambling, he clearly held to the existence and role of chance in events, on a secondary level. In the two recent Christian books on gambling, however, neither Geisler nor Rogers gave allowance for a neutral sense of chance having a significant part in God's creation. South argued that Scripture did not deny chance in a service role. In Chapter 9 we shall look more closely at South's justification of this distinction.

Gataker, we previously noted, had been accused of

supporting gambling. Ames held to a similar openness to lotteries, with reservations. Gataker made comments on the use of lots in the election of elders.[37] Translator/editor John Eusden, in his introduction to the *Marrow of Theology*, noted: 'The practice of determining divine will by casting lots continued to be used, especially in America. The First Church of Christ in Middletown, Connecticut, cast a lot in 1715 to settle the location of its meeting house.'[38] Later, the practice of drawing lots grew into selling lottery tickets, and by the selling of tickets, for instance, the First Baptist Church of Providence, RI and the Market Square Presbyterian Church of Harrisburg, Pennsylvania were built.[39]

Cotton Mather [1663–1728], the most published colonial American Puritan, represented those then and now who say gambling is taboo for a Christian. Mather wrote,

> . . . if the [misspending] of the Winter in the excess of eating and of drinking do deserve caution why should not the [misspending] of the Winter in gaming do so too? Especially the games of pure lot whereof thus much at least may be mentioned, that it is best for all Christians to abstain from them. Altho' moderate recreations too much used in the Winter, which in truth is never convenient: such as the games of cards & dice, and those which have nothing but chance to manage them. A lot is a solemn appeal unto the God of heaven; and hence to play with it seems to break the Third Commandment in the Law of our God. Lusory lots are by great and grave divines esteemed unlawful on the same score . . . In every lot, an altar is wholly committed unto a superior cause . . . this thing is to be done rather prayerfully than sportfully . . .[40]

The Mather position on lots was an extension of the views of William Perkins, which probably filtered on down to Mather through William Ames who was his theology tutor.[41] Ames emigrated to Holland in 1610. Arriving in Rotterdam in 1632, Ames got to know John Robinson [1576–1625], pastor of the Pilgrims, who also wrote a small chapter on casting lots.

Mather insisted lots be used 'only in weighty cases'. That was his father's view, too, and that of William Perkins, with whom Gataker disagreed. Increase Mather [1639–1723], in his book, *A Letter to a Gentleman on The Sin and Danger of Playing at Cards and other Games* (Boston, 1755), held that lotteries were appeals to Providence so we 'are not to implicate His providence in frivolity'.[42]

Rational evaluations should be used in matters of dispute. Mather argued that Scripture was against card-playing and gambling because it violated the Third Commandment. Gamblers took the Lord's name in vain when they prayed for a win. In his view, that both trivialized prayer and demeaned God.[43] Mather was not the first ever so to argue. The Venetian rabbi Leon of Modena in his work, *Sur Me-ra* (1584) that argued that 'the gambler trespasses all the Ten Commandments'.[44] Thomas Gataker noted in 1627 some contemporaries in England and France who held that wagering was the 'breach of the whole Decalogue, and of all the Ten Commandments'.[45]

Some leeway, however, already existed in Puritan society on the propriety of gambling. There was some officially sanctioned gambling going on when it came to landing assignments which were determined by drawing lots. 'This precedent weakened the argument that gambling violated the Third Commandment.'[46]

Mather, of course, had been more hardline on gambling than continental William Ames. Ames took a middle-ground position on gambling. While gambling was regarded as wrong, according to Bruce Daniels' thorough study of Puritans and leisure, 'by itself, [it] was not high on their list of sins and crimes'.[47] Daniels continues:

The relative softness of Puritan opposition to gambling was reflected in the New England colonies' ambivalent attitude toward lotteries. English Puritans had made limited use of lotteries under controlled circumstances. William Ames, the Cambridge scholar who shaped much of the reform theology that New England Puritans brought with them, wrote that public (as opposed to private) lotteries 'might haply be so ordered, to some pious use'.[48]

As Puritans did not always dress in drab black, but wore dyed fabric of rich browns, reds, blues, and oranges, so they showed a similar diversity in the use of leisure.

Lots of controversy about lotteries[49]

Puritan ministers, for the most part, reflected the judgment of Cotton Mather, that lotteries were 'scandalous games'. Public policy was influenced by the pulpit, and English colonies, Massachusetts, Connecticut, Rhode Island, and New Hampshire, passed laws prohibiting lotteries. But the public was not behind the conservative magistrates. 'After unsuccessfully trying for a generation to eliminate lotteries, all four colony governments gave up and reverted to the philosophy of William Ames that public lotteries could be harnessed to promote good causes.'[50] (See Chapter 8 for Gataker's views on the social benefits of lotteries.)

Big opponents of lotteries were the Quakers.

. . . virtually no one in the American colonies considered lotteries an evil except the Quakers in Pennsylvania who in 1682 passed a law prohibiting lotteries and 'such like enticing, vain, and evil sports and games'. The Quakers, however, were unable to make their law stick for more than twenty years. When Queen Anne assumed the throne in 1702, she took it upon herself to rescind this colonial anti-gambling law.[51]

Benjamin Franklin, though on the fringes of Quakerism, was an organizer of the 1746 Philadelphia Lottery.[52] Clyde Davis probably guessed right when he expressed doubts that frugal 'Poor Richard' himself patronized lotteries.[53]

At first, lotteries made a swift comeback. 'By 1750 lotteries had been revived in all the colonies.'[54] Many public programmes were financed by lotteries, such as military defence in Massachusetts or new streets in Hartford, Connecticut. In 1769 the British Parliament forbade lotteries in royal colonies. As Daniels pointed out, that was hypocritical, for old England was wallowing in hedonistic excess when they slapped down ascetic rules for New England. 'During the Revolution all the colonies used lotteries frequently to raise money for the troops, defense, provisions, and other civic needs. Buying lottery tickets became a sign of patriotism, much like war bonds would be in the twentieth century.'[55]

Lottery expansion did not diminish but increased after the Revolutionary War. 'By 1790 about two thousand legal lotteries were in operation, and the list of drawings and prizes daily requires a half-column of fine print in the New York newspapers.'[56]

An early winner of lotteries was education. The founding of Columbia University in 1746 was funded by a lottery, and 'many other famous schools . . . Harvard, Yale, Dartmouth, and Williams were likewise helped by lotteries in the early years of their existence.'[57]

But the pendulum swung back against lotteries when lottery tickets were not being sold.[58] 'From the end of the War of 1812 until lotteries were legally abolished in most states the agents and promoters were, in the main, sharpers.'[59]

Conclusions

Should it be overlooked, denied, or minimized that good can come of lotteries? Or should it be acknowledged and appreciated? If all lotteries are evil, then what do you say about house lotteries? House lotteries? You may have heard it said that some stake their homes on a wager. But there is also a lottery in which, for a small wager, the prize is a house, both in the UK and in the US.

Since 1976, the City of Cincinnati has had a yearly 'Dollar House Lottery'. Mike Hunley, director of the city's Homesteading and Urban Redevelopment Corporation, is pleased to turn over the keys to persons who would never have the means of owning a home. The homes were in need of extensive renovation. One winning couple, Brenda and Scott Hardy, who won one in 1993, spent $35,000 in fixing it up to meet city specifications, and are thrilled to be homeowners. Mrs Hardy said, 'It was really a blessing. Our dreams came true. The city really helped us.' After renovations, the couple only pays $285.00 a month for the house they won four years ago.[60]

Today, the modern Christian is faced with state- and city-sponsored lotteries and with numerous charity lotteries, raffles, and bingo. The chance to win in a house lottery and charity lotteries tug more on a Christian heart than state or government lotteries.

Christians like to be perceived as pro-public good, pro-education, pro-church and are usually more inclined to give charity fund-raisers some support and participation. Even so, because the gambling ambiance is associated with excess and evil, Christians show minimal participation even in charity lotteries. Indeed, some Christians actively campaign against the reduction of pro-gambling legislation. We should respect those choices.

House give-aways and charity lotteries have a more noble function than government sponsored or run lotteries. Admittedly, the money percentage actually going to charitable works may be low,[61] but the benefits outweigh the small profits. How one looks at charity lotteries and charity bingo depends on how one looks on a glass partially filled – is it half-full or half-empty? Those who look on the dark side see it as half-empty; those who look on the bright side see it half-full.

The Puritan approach to lotteries was a combination of caution and confidence. They were aware that indulgence could develop into intoxication with money, and that the ruination of spiritual discipline began with small concessions before these grew into unmanageable habits. They were not only cautious about lottery dangers, but they were confident that the use of wagers in secondary matters was no denial of divine providence over all of life: 'Colonists wagered as adventurers, not aristocrats, and American forms of gambling reflected frontier culture more than they mirrored British precedents.'[62]

Puritanism cannot be blamed for either the introduction or the abuse of lotteries in the new nation. At the same time, they can be called upon as witnesses that lotteries have been used of God to bring blessings upon society and to achieve supportable and commendable public goals that compensate for individual small investor loses.

Throughout this book we have noted the many evils associated with gambling. Gambling, one could argue, was not in high gear in Puritan times as it is today. Whatever the age, for the Christian, whether seventeenth-century Puritan, or twenty-first-century evangelical, our use of entertainments should be marked by critical evaluation, caution, and courage. Today's occasional Christian lottery player exercises the same Christian freedom and discretion as the old New England Puritan who had a well-thumbed copy of Ames' *Marrow of Divinity*.

Puritans have been praised for their circumspect lives, for their stewardship, and for the daily scrutiny of their behaviour. Truly, no group of Christians was so aware of secular traps, so dedicated to self-discipline, and to commending models of responsible behaviour. But present-day Christians are shocked that three leading Puritans did not join the easy condemnation of all lotteries. What Gataker, Ames and Baxter wrote, however, cannot be used as a blanket endorsement of all lottery purchases today. The legacy of these men was that lottery-buying must be judged case by case.

Where do we stand? What do we think and why?

8.

Thomas Gataker's *On the Nature &*
Use of Lots

Thomas Gataker's famous work, *On the Nature & Use Of Lots: A Treatise, Historical & Theological*, will shock the modern Christian anti-gambling consensus. Published in 1627 in London by John Haviland, it ran to 416 pages and is so profound – and profoundly unpredictable – that it deserves a complete summary here.

Probably the most thorough treatise ever written on the nature and use of Bible lots was authored by an English Puritan, who lived between 1574 and 1654. Cambridge-educated, Gataker was ordained in 1601 and called to minister at Lincoln's Inn, later served by the famed John Donne. In 1611 he was persuaded to serve the church near the Surrey docks in Rotherhithe, now South London. In 1613 Gataker was chosen to serve on the Westminster Assembly that produced the Westminster Standards.

The expanded 1627 edition of the treatise dealt with critics of his earlier work (1619) on the same subject. Gataker has margin and end notes, in Latin, Hebrew, and Greek, on every page citing from numerous famous classical authors, Christian and pagan. Ambrose, Augustine, and Chrysostom are among his favorite Church fathers. In some instances he put translated portions in the body of his work. He even cited from Geoffrey Chaucer's *Canterbury Tales*, 'The Parson's Tale', about the 'hazarder.'

The book is composed of twelve uneven-length chapters. As might be supposed, the work is a non-circulating rare book, requiring visits to the few libraries that have copies. A leather bound copy, in excellent condition, is in the Rare Book Library of Lehigh University, Allentown, Pensylvania where I read the work. My summary and selections are partly tailored by the present controversy in Christianity about lotteries. Gataker represented a minority viewpoint within Puritan theology on lotteries. Some of the quaint spellings of the period have been altered to conform to modern usage, otherwise the text is as Gataker wrote it.

Chapter 1: 'What a "Lot" is and of Lotteries in General' (pp. 1–9):
Man takes good things and corrupts them; such is also true of lotteries. Lotteries may be wisely or selfishly abused. A 'lot' is defined as a casual event 'purposefully applied to the deciding of some doubt' (2; similarly 5,6). 'A Lot is a child of chance'(3). Chance or probability is viewed as the chief ingredient in lots (4). Gataker notes, however, that everything casual is not a lot (5). He lists numerous equivalents to dice (7).

Chapter 2: 'Of Chance and of Casual Events' (pp. 9–46):
While recognizing that chance may be used as a rival to God, Gataker notes chance is also a part of God's providence, not apart from God's providence, i.e. not opposed to providence.

Not only are lot references non-pejorative in the Bible, there are non-pejorative references to chance both in Old and New Testaments: 1 Kings 22:34; Ruth 2:3,5; Ecclesiastes 9:2,3,11 and Luke 10:31, 32. Gataker cites several church fathers on this question: St. Bernard: 'Chance to us is as a word of God acquainting us with his will' (24). On lotteries: Ambrose: 'a divine trial'; Augustine: 'a divine sentence'; Origen: 'God's hidden will.' (24,25). Gataker sees the biblical usage of chance as 'a secondary cause' only (36,37). He rejects the notion that chance is merely not knowing all the facts (38,39). He admits that ascribing events to chance is often due to a subjective evaluation (41), such as in the cases of 1 Kings 21:20 and Judges 11:34. Gataker holds that foreknowledge was foreordination (42,43), and that full divine sovereignty was not in conflict with secondary causation, viewed as randomness and chance (44,45).

Gataker defines chance as 'a contingency or uncertainty severed from forecast and foresight'(12). 'Where necessity is or certainty, there can be no casualty' [i.e. accident cf. *Oxford English Dictionary*, (Compact Edition, 1971)] (16).

Cites Old Testament usage (1 Sam. 10:1; Josh. 7:16, 18; 1 Sam. 14:38,45; Prov. 1:14; 16:33; 18:18; Jonah 1:7; Lam. 3:37 [lots assumed].

Chapter 3: 'Of the General Sorts of Lots' (pp. 46–50):
Deals with the matter of chance being used to come to a conclusion (49); cites William Perkins on four ways to settle a dispute/strife: dice toss; the diabolical use of divination; lot-casting for political decisions; business use of lots to settle bankruptcies (49).

Chapter 4: 'Of Ordinary Lots' (pp. 50–115):
Cites Ambrose and Origen, to deny his critics who argued that the use of lots was an unfair dragging of God into controversies (58,59). 'Angels in heaven have their charges by Lot assigned them, who shall rule this or that Province, who tend this or that person, who govern this or that church' (Dan. 10:13,21; Mt. 18:10; Acts 12:15; Rev. 1:20)

(61). Cites use of lots in civil service and in military matters in the Old Testament (Neh. 10:34; Num. 3:45,50; Judges 20:11). The section on Old Testament use of lots (92–99), including the cases found in Judges 17:14; 19:9; Numbers 26:55, 56; 32:33; 34:7,8,13–15; Joshua 11:13; 14:1–3; 21:4,5, 21,43; 1 Chronicles 6:54. On the pagan use of lots he cites its use in Athens (70–75) and in Rome (76–91).

Old Testament minor (Levite) priestly rotation used lots (1 Chron. 16:13–20), a fact reflected in the New Testament case of Zechariah (Lk. 1:9) (61–65, esp. 64,65); he points out that Reformed pastors in Geneva used lots for the selection of those who would visit the physically infected during an epidemic, a fact noted in Theodore Beza's 'Life of John Calvin'.*

Lots play a secondary role to decision-making (99,100). Hiding fingers behind the back and bringing them forward (such as used in playing cards) was 'a kind of lottery' (101). Other Old Testament usages included Ezekiel 24:6; Leviticus 16:1,9,10; Micah 2:5; Isaiah, 17:14; 34:17; Jeremiah 13:25 (102 *et passim*). Lot-casting was used in the Old Testament tithe/gifts (100, 108,109; see also 112,113). Romans used lots in meting out punishment to criminals (112,113).

Chapter 5: 'Of the Lawfulness of such Lots with Cautions' (pp. 115–150):
Gataker advances six arguments against those who saw no sanctions necessary in the use of lotteries (116–118) and follows that up with nine cautions (120–124).

Throughout the book, but beginning in this chapter, was Gataker's treatment of texts in Proverbs 1:14 (101); Proverbs 16:33 (116,162,163,181,188,195,196) and Proverbs

---

* Beza's 'Life of John Calvin' is included in *Selected Works of John Calvin: Tracts and Letters* edited by Henry Beveridge and Jules Bonnet, Vol. 1, (Grand Rapids: Baker Book House, 1844, 1983).

18:18 (118,162,172,192,207,209,211,212,213); gives endorsement of lusorious[1] lots (119,133,134).

Lots used to pick elders (130,131) were also used in the simple procedures in ancient time as to who was to see the doctor next (similar to our grocery store take-a-number queing system) (134); more on use of lots in Roman history (137–139); on the social benefits of lotteries (142). He concludes with a fine statement on lots being secondary to Scripture (144).

Chapter 6: 'Of Ordinary Lots Lusorious and of the Lawfulness of them' (pp. 150–177):
The role of lotteries in games of skill and of chance; dealing cards was seen as an extension of the lottery principle (154). On lottery in games: 'The use of a Lot in games . . . is but the putting of a matter of mere indifference to the hazard of an uncertain event' (165). Similarly, 'the use of Lots in games is not in itself or of itself a sin either against Piety or against Charity' (166). Gataker has an open mind toward civil lotteries which 'are not [a violation of holiness] and therefore the lisorious [another spelling of "lusorious"] use of them is not the profaning of any holy thing. And if neither the unhallowing of anything hallowed, nor the hallowing of anything unhallowed, then can it not be brought within the compass of impiety or sin' (169).

Chapter 7: 'Answer to the Principle Objections made against Lusorious Lots' (pp. 177–223):
Takes exception to William Perkin's view on lots (which was later perpetuated in the publications of Increase and Cotton Mather). Duplicates the arguments of two Puritan contemporaries on lots, then rejects them: Dudley Fenner and James Balmford. Balmford's treatise was called *A Short and Plain Dialogue Concerning the Unlawfulness of*

Playing at Cards (London, 1593); refers to this as a 'long discourse.' (289). Makes frequent citations from both authors and indulges in dismantling their arguments point by point (see 178–190, and 214–220).

Shows that oaths and lots are different (192–195,213), and that lots are not to be considered part of God's oracle (198–206). Deals with the question of how decisions are considered sanctified (210–212); much comment on hunting (219–220,272; see also 262,293), leading to a discussion of other types of recreation (221–223). What constitutes recreation is not fully addressed; recognizes that what is regarded as recreation is subjective.

Chapter 8: 'Answer to the Argument less Principle against Lusorious Lots' (pp. 224–281):
Addresses ancillary arguments used against gaming. e.g. that lots are evil because they come with evil: cursing, loss of time, decay of heart, unlawful gain, or desire of gain and the wasting of wealth; deals with the argument at length that because some who used lots had an 'evil disposition' lots were therefore off-limits for the believer (225f). The use of lots was not spoiled by human wickedness, nor spoiled absolutely or universally, for the acts of the Creator and the acts of a creature must be kept separate (226).

Therefore, in casting lots there is 'no tang or taint at all of impiety, or blasphemy' (226). Deals with pagan use of dice (276,277).

Chapter 9: 'Of Cautions to be Observed with the use of Lusorious Lots' (pp. 282–315):
Knocks the hypocrisy of those who object to lots yet 'give themselves wholly to game and play and all kinds of excess' (284). Gataker was for the moderate use of lots; comments (28) on the danger of excessive wagering; targets partying (290–292) and especially intoxication which

included more than alcoholic beverages (291) e.g. sleep intoxication (292); observes the over-valuing and danger of the use of sport (293–294), and of the misuse of the Sabbath (295). Returns (300–305) to the argument of not using lots lest a weaker brother be offended. Earlier (278) he made the point that if the scruples of others become the absolute criterion of what is allowable, then we are potentially restricted from engaging in anything. When desire to win is modest, lots are not evil (307); gives five replies to those critics who say there were abuses in gaming to warrant their non-use. (309–311).

Chapter 10: 'Of Extraordinary and Divinatory Lots' (pp. 315–347):
Extraordinary lots are lots that seek to divine hidden matters and/or the future (316, 317). These 'require an extraordinary power and providing for the disposing and directing of them' (315). Hidden information related to such questions as whom to marry and who should serve in office; cites Chrysostom, in discussion of the case of Isaac and his future wife who used a special prayer, not a special lot (319). In the choice of Matthias through lot (Acts 1:23–26) the practice was not repeated in the Book of Acts. (321). In the Old Testament lots were sometimes used in judgment (323,324). Other Old Testament incidents noted are 1 Samuel 5:6,9,12; 6:7,10; 13;l; 14:24,27,36,37,38; Jonah 1:4–10; Joshua 7:11,12,13 (323–329); cites some instances in extra-biblical history.

Treats 'Bible' lottery (340–346); discusses the pagan use of lots, giving more attention to Ezekiel 21:21 (334,335); Gataker cites references to the use of lots in Chinese and German history (337).

Chapter 11: 'Of the Unlawfulness of such Lots' (pp. 347–381):
Gataker continues his discussion from the preceding

chapter. At this point he has little to add, save numerous instances of lots for divination in Old Testament times, and that they were not approved of in Scripture (352–380).

Chapter 12: 'An Admonition to avoid divining Lots with answer to some arguments alleged in the defense of them; and the conclusion of the whole' (382–416):
Gataker ends his exhaustive study. Reviews earlier material to reinforce it. One final matter treated was the oddity of identical results from repeated lots (398–401). His bottom line on the controversy reads as follows: 'So take the ordinary abuse from the ordinary Lot, and it will prove an ordinance of no evil life . . . As for the extraordinary Lot, the very ordinary use of Lot is a mere abuse of a Lot.' In the use of lots 'God be not dishonored who has given us the freedom to use them' (416).

In the above summary not enough space was given to lengthy quotes of Gataker. The advantage of the longer quote is to see how his argument develops. The longer citations have the advantage of giving more of Gataker's perceptions and conclusions.

Citations from Gataker's work *On The Nature & Use of Lots* (1627)

Ch. 1 On Proverbs 1:14:

> . . . he brings in these companions, not so much inviting him whom they would persuade to adventure his part with them . . . as promising him that he shall cast Lot with them, that is, shall have an equal share with them in whatsoever they get: as those are wont to do and to have that deal by way of lawful traffic together in joint stock [101].

Ch. 2 On Proverbs 16:33:

In these words the holy Ghost manifestly not allowed only and approves the use of Lots in such cases, but commends it unto us as a wise and discrete [discreet] course of the taking away of controversies and questions in this kind, and the preventing of law-suites or other quarrels that thence otherwise might arise [118].

Ch. 3 On Proverbs 18:18:

But a Lot may be ordinarily used . . . by the express authority of God's Spirit speaking by Solomon, for the ending of contentions and matters in suite of strife be they weightier or of less weight [162].

[The text is] rather a permission than a precept, or not so much a commandment as an advice and counsel, commending that to us as a wise and prudent course [172].

Ch. 4 On games and lotteries:

If Lots in general, even civil as well as sacred, be holy things, they may in no case without no Caution be made matter of sport and pastime, or of gamesome recreation; nor can the light use of them be so corrected and qualified, but that it will have deadly poison even in the heart and pith of it not adhering or cleansing unto the bark or outside of it only. But civil Lots are not such; and therefore the lisorious [sic] use of them is not the profaning of any holy thing. And if neither the unhallowing of any thing hallowed, nor the hallowing of any thing unhallowed, then can it not be brought within compass or impiety or sin against the first table [168,169].

Which therefore so long as the use of it is kept otherwise free from superstition and impiety, or from injustice and dishonesty, ought no more to be exiled from a Christian man's recreations, than any other creature or ordinance whatsoever, that has any natural power to delight and give contentment in that kind [170].

If question be whether bowls or chess be lawful or no: what can there be said in justification of them more than this, that recreation in general is by God's word allowed; the matter in particular not determined: these games not prohibited; therefore lawful and allowable. Now the very same may be said of Lots and Lottery. Game in general is allowed: no particular matter or manner of it prescribed: any therefore lawful that is not against the general rules of God's word: this of Lottery such; and therefore allowable [176].

Ch. 5 On chance:

Chance or Fortune is not any distinct kind of cause, but an assertion or adjunct only . . . cleaving unto, and accompanying some cause and so differencing [differentiating] them from others by the manner of their working in the producing of some effect [36]. The disposing of the chance is secret, that it may be chance indeed, and wholly of God, who directs all things (182).

Ch. 6 On sports betting:

If we consider the nature of those things that are wont to be, and may lawfully be put into a Lot, according to the rules and cautions before delivered, we shall find a Lot no more unfit for sport, nor more unlawful in it, than it is fit for, or lawful in any other ordinary employment . . . the using of a Lot in game (or the using of it in any business, be serious or lusorious, qualified and cautioned as before) is but putting of a matter of mere indifferences to the hazard uncertain event, to wit, who shall join or stand out . . . The use therefore of a Lot in such cases, and the putting of such matter to the hazard of a Lot, is not evil simply of itself [165].

Ch. 7 On using the word 'luck' in everyday conversation:

Suppose a man riding on the way through the forest, where a deer rushing suddenly out of the brush makes his horse start and throw him: in this case for a man to say, 'What luck was this?' or 'What a cross accident was this?' is no blasphemy, nor any accusing of God's providence, but a complaining of the creatures' act and the event of it [227].

Chapter 8 On the social benefits of lotteries:

... in a matter of common or public benefit, as bridge repair, hospital renovation, school building, or the like, for divers men of good ability to agree among themselves to put it to hazard what sum each of them shall distribute or dispense toward the discharge or support thereof, the sums being no greater than the estate of them may well bear [142].

Ch. 9 On the evils associated with gaming:

[Some] raise the evils and abuses that usually accompany these games to a whole Alphabet, even as many as there be aces or points on the dice ... These, I say, I might well pass by ... partly because in effect they bring no new matter; and partly because these evils are equally common to all games, and do not so much concern the nature of this kind of play, as contain general abuses of all kinds, though applied more especially to these: they are the faults of the gamesters, not of the games: as one said well of Lots ... so say I of game, and of Lots used in game. The lawful use of them must be distinguished from the unlawful abuse. For it is one thing to consider game as it is game, another thing to speak of it as it is abused [237,238].

Ch. 10 On wagering being a bad influence and example to others:

[1 Thessalonians 5:22 advises avoiding all appearance of evil] . . . the commandments that forbid any sin, forbid those things also that may be occasions of that sin. But they inhibit not generally the use of all things to all, that any does or may take occasion of evil by. They forbid them to those to whom they are that way dangerous [i.e. compulsive personalities], not to those that may and do use them without danger in that kind [i.e. the casual gambler] [238,239].

Ch. 11 On question of playing for gain:

[Some] forbid all playing for gain at them; which yet at some other games with some kind of caution, and at these also upon somewhat stricter terms, as for somewhat to be spent privately in common, they allow. So that is not the games themselves that are simply condemned, but the evil and hurtful usage of them, to wit, either the immoderate and customary, or the excessive and expensive use of them; as both by the letter of the law itself plainly appears [245, 246].
. . . neither ought any man to seek or desire by play to increase or advance his estate, or to make a prey and spoil of him that he plays with [298].

Ch. 12 On moderate use of Lots:

the immoderate use or abuse of them is of evil report, the moderate and sober use of them is not [277].
. . . that in our lawful recreation we go not beyond our ability; and therefore that either we play without staking or wagering, or at least without staking and wagering more . . . [286].
[Civil law prohibited participants] not to cast their wealth

away at them, playing night and day for gold and silver, and jewels and plate . . . [even the law allowing some games] forbids any man to hazard at them above a shilling a game. [286,287; on page 288 Gataker had cited the folly of excessive wagering arguing that it robs the family and is a form of self-robbery, indeed of self-murder: 'so he that robs himself by wasting his own state on such courses, is little better than a murderer or destroyer' (287)].

As we may not spend our life in sport: so much less may we spend our life on sport [290].

The following passage probably refers to what persons invest in wagering, not the large gain from it:

Where comes to be condemned again that eagerness in game, that we spake of before, that playing for great sums, not in regard of itself alone, and the loss that it brings with it, but further also in regard of those grievous abuses and enormities that is usually occasion men to break forth into. For let men say what they will, that is all one to them whether they win or lose, (as a reverent Prelate of ours, whose words I willingly use oft in this argument, well said,) 'in such profusion of substance as the loss cannot but pinch, so men's passions cannot but bemoved, and a troop of wretched sins commonly ensue, swearing, forswearing, cursing, banning, defying, heart-burning, quarrelling, fighting, spilling of blood, insupportable sorrows of heart, cursed despair, self-executions, weeds able to blemish and disgrace the lawful recreation that is, wheresoever they be found, as the [herpes] defiles the cleanest meat [304].

Gataker warned against excessive wagering.

Where comes to be condemned against that eagerness in game, that we spoke of before, that playing for great sums, not in regard of itself alone, and the loss that it brings with it; but further also in regard of those grievous abuses [304].

As we exclude not God's presence in play; so we call not in his providence to further our play [308].

Ch. 13 On the question of jobs around gaming:[2]

... it is one thing to play at dice or cards, and another thing to be dicer or a carder [275].

Is Gataker making reference to gambling hall workers i.e. dealers, or, as seems more likely according to the context, those who are compulsive gamblers or lottery players?

Ordinarily those may be said to live lawfully by game, whose trades and professions are employed in whole or in part in making, providing, selling, and making such instruments, or other furniture as are used commonly in game, as bowlers, fletchers, and turners, and dice carvers, and card-makers, and haberdashers of small wares. For if the games themselves be lawful, the callings are not unlawful, whereby men are set on work to provide necessaries for the same, which could not otherwise so commonly, or so conveniently, be had [297].

Ch. 14 Gataker on dice (references highlighted in italics are of especial significance):

58,107 [dice sometimes used in deciding which name to use for a new-born]; 134 [in hiring], 135, 153 [in the choice of magistrates]; 155,158,171 ['all of a piece are shuffling of arrows, the drawing of tickets, the dealing of cards, the fall of a die']; 233,237,*240,241,* ['some play away more than they should, so some note the laws of the Land we live in; wherein all dicing is said to be generally forbidden'; dicers taken, punished with six days' imprisonment, and with sitting in the stocks; keepers of dicing houses punished with three years; players in dicing houses with two years' imprisonment. Notes the state of Geneva condemns the very making of dice: a certain 'clerke' or clergyman in the Decretal is found deposed for being a 'dicer' and a 'usurer'; and the Canons of two General Councils forbidding clergymen from dice and knuckle bones, either to play with them or to be present at such play]; 246–249 [more English laws on dicing], 252,253 [examination of the game of craps, which uses dice]; *253–258* [cites church fathers Cyprian, Tertullian, and Augustine; corrects a criticism of Augustine: he did not write against dice, but is *said* to have written against dice]; 260, 261 [Chrysostom cited]; *262* [notes Bernard of Clairvaux, enjoyed chess and dice]; 263,267 [cites pagan writers on dice]; 269 [the use of dice in Parthia); 271 [pagan poets warned against dice use]; 277 [in response to the critics who said that cards and dice were 'things of evil report,' replied that 'the immoderate use or abuse of them is of evil report, the moderate and sober use of them is not.']; 307,340,353,366 [some use of dice even as some 'Bible lottery' (random opening of a Bible for decision- making) is of the Devil when it makes moral decisions that way].

There is much covered in the preceding, material which needs a second reading, and sustained scrutiny. Not everyone will agree with Gataker's arguments, but it is possible to justify his positions by looking at them from various angles.

9.

Luck: Chance or Providence?

Here is the next big question – Does chance automatically rule out God's sovereign control? The bottom line is not the question, 'to gamble or not to gamble', but what is the Christian response to chance? This side of the gambling question pops up faster than prairie dogs in West Texas.

Non-Christian gamblers look to luck for a win. They assume that a pair of dice is paradise. Superstition is rampant among lottery players and hoodwinks casino players. Is so-called luck real? Should one think that luck is behind good fortune?

Lottery players and casino visitors are subtly programmed to think that a thing called luck is working for them or against them. Players think favours fall their way or against them before they buy a lottery ticket, before they enter the casino, before they buy chips, before they roll dice. Casino owners induce people to roll dice by throwing gratuities at them like bait, which, they hope, will be picked up. Free transportation, complimentary drinks, and cheap food are offered as inducements to play and incentives to stay. Already luck, chance and fortune seem to edge out God in bringing them to that moment.

The die-hard gambler believes luck alone is the secret to winning. To look fondly on game cards, lottery tickets, and casino wheels as omens of winning, means our world-view has been deeply etched by superstition. We've been cheated out of a belief in God's all-wise involvement in life. In the process what we lose is the best philosophy of life, not just our savings.

Ask yourself: What's all this talk about luck? Is the world really run and ruled by whimsy? Kenneth S. Kantzer, in an editorial in *Christianity Today*, spoke representatively, if not officially, for evangelicals: 'The fundamental Christian objection to gambling is that it represents a denial of the God of providence. It replaces him with the universe of pure chance and a dependence on blind luck.'[1]

But before we deal with a Christian view of chance and providence, consider the slick gimmicks habitual gamblers use to psyche themselves up to gamble. Mindgames are invented to weigh chances of winning in their favour. Superstition in gambling is common. Some wear 'good luck charms'. Or some feel bad luck happens on Friday and they will not bet then. Luck is credited with being a supernatural force. An impersonal good fortune is dragged into gambling in an attempt to guarantee winnings.

Around the world people gamble and they resort to unusual tricks to try to sway odds in their favour. When British currency was in use in Korea, a missionary there reported that a gambler bought a New Testament because he believed that if he sat upon it while he was gambling, he was bound to win. An ironic but beneficial result was that he lost one pound the first night, and twelve shillings the second night, so he decided that Scripture was against gambling.

Lady Luck is a misleading mistress

Superstitions are thought to increase good luck. Some gamblers imagine that their routines must be changed or that something about the day or casino visit affects the outcome of the game. In his book, *Break the One-Armed Bandits:* Frank Scoblete quoted some typical superstitious gamblers. What they said could just as well be any gambler in Great Britain:

> Leonora of Staten Island, NY: 'I walk around the casino at least three times before I decide on what machine to play. I always pick a machine that has the coin light on the top of it flashing but no one is playing the machine. I think this signal is my lucky signal.'

> Joe of Pittsburgh, PA: 'I only play dented machines. I've had my best luck on dented machines.'

> Kid Nostrels of Atlantic City, NJ: 'Man, I can smell when a machine is ready to hit the big one. I think the wiring gets hot because they'll be pumping a signal through the line that says to the machine: "Get hot, buster". '[2]

Smart gamblers work on the basis of the best odds. Not-so-smart gamblers base their hopes of winning on luck alone. Chance, of course, is something over which they concede they have no control. To stimulate good luck, some place their wagers on a specific day. Bad luck is thought to accompany a losing streak which continues.

Instead of conceding that the laws of probability play a key role in his chances in winning, the superstitious gambler relies on personal hunches or kooky charms to increase his or her advantage. According to John Scarne, described as the world's foremost gambling authority, 'As a class, gamblers are superstitious for the usual reason – ignorance. They don't understand how chance operates or know what luck really is.'[3]

The higher the stakes the greater the desperation in the gambler. But whether the losses or gains are great or small does not matter when luck is credited as the cause.

Scripture does not allow for belief in luck as the cause of either good or bad.

Isaiah deplored Lady Luck

The chief Christian alternative to secular 'luck' is divine providence. In the eighth-century BCE Israel had been bamboozled into believing that luck could be gained by appealing to foreign gods – the gods of luck. Isaiah 65:11 (ASV) refers to their dependence on the hollow gods of supposed good fortune: 'But ye that forsake Jehovah, that forget my holy mountain, that prepare a table for Fortune, and that fill up mingled wine unto Destiny…'

Here we have the first Hebrew word for the pagan god, 'Gad'. I once knew a lady who had the habit of using 'gad' as a pause word in her conversation, a cover for 'God'; although 'minced oath' would be the proper description. The Hebrew word in Isaiah 65:11 was 'Gad', but not the 'gad' of the woman's conversation. *'Gad'* was a Syrian divinity[4] and meant 'the god of good luck'.[5] The NIV translates *'Gad'* here as 'Fortune.'

'Meni', the second foreign god mentioned in Isaiah 65:11, was an Arabian goddess Manat,[6] and stood for 'Destiny'(NIV). These false deities were representative of those who believed in good and bad luck. 'The LXX [Septuagint] suggests that they bore opposite functions, favorable and evil destinies, as in Arabic astrology.'[7]

Also, Gad and Meni had astral connections. Following Hebrew philologist Gesenius, Franz Delitzsch held that they referred to 'Jupiter and Venus common among the Arabs, as the two heavenly bodies that preside over the fortunes of men; and understands by Meni Venus, and by Gad Jupiter.'[8]

Israel saw no harm in mixing Gad and Meni with Jehovah. Isaiah, however, said God saw it differently. For them to trust in luck was a denial of the Lord. 'The prophet's protest was against those Israelites who trusted to chance rather than God. It also involved those who sought a syncretized religion that included both the God of Israel and the gods of luck.'⁹

In Isaiah's time people were superficial in their beliefs. They did not think deeply into causation or origins. It was sufficient to chalk up their good or ill fortune to a supposed entity, an impersonal fate or fortune. Similarly, today, many explain their gambling winnings, health, and successes as flukes of good fortune, or good luck. Unwilling to look behind and beyond wins, wagerers brush it off as chance. God is nowhere to be found in the ordering of the universe and especially absent from their lives.

To non-Christians caprice dominates the odds for or against winning. God is nowhere to be found in whatever happens. The alleged capitulation of history to chance is an outgrowth of spiritual ignorance. But gaming or reliance on chance outlaws God. Writing as a Christian, the late American Professor, Wayne E. Oates, confessed: '[F]aith in luck is not the substance of our being. The substance of our faith is in the steadfast love and constant providence of the living God.'¹⁰

At best, non-believers see God as part of the game, but unable to influence the outcome. In man-centered philosophies, God has no control of the outcome of history. For them God has no influence over the turn of events. Steven J. Brams is representative. He writes:

> Since God does not always get His way, He can properly be viewed as a participant, or *player*, in a game. This is so because a *game* – as the term is used in game theory – is an

interdependent decision situation whose outcome depends on the choices of *all* players [author's italics].[11]

When chance rivals God

People are accustomed to credit 'chance' alone as the cause of the good or evil they experience. Chance becomes an alternative to God. Anytime causation is attributed to chance, chance becomes God's rival. The argument Christians have with chance is primarily when causal powers are attributed to it.

The word 'chance' has two senses. Most think of chance as causation. But that rubs Christians. We need to confront that form of chance first. Chance is used in reference to origin and in reference to order of outcome. There is a second usage of chance: chance as a comparative factor, chance as mathematical probability.

The acknowledgment of the existence of chance even on a secondary level runs against the grain of Christians who, in postulating God, deny that God would stoop to use chance as a secondary part of the process. The argument is made that chance does not exist because it has no being. But to argue that chance as probability must have being to belong to reality and be an operative element is like arguing that motors must be alive to run.

The theologian R.C. Sproul came out with a thorough study of chance and its philosophic and scientific ramifications. He covers numerous issues in physics, philosophy, and theology. Only the first three chapters deal specifically with chance. The rest of the book addresses Christian and anti-Christian theories. The following passages bring out the deep-seated clash between chance and divine control of life:

The mere existence of chance is enough to rip God from his cosmic throne. Chance does not need to rule; it does not need to be sovereign. If it exists as a mere impotent, humble servant, it leaves God not only out of date, but out of a job . . . If chance exists in any size, shape, or form, God cannot exist. The two are mutually exclusive.

Attributing instrumental causal power to chance vitiates deduction and the rational . . . Perhaps the attributing of instrumental power to chance is the most serious error made in modern science and cosmology. [Non-Christians espouse 'spontaneous generation'. Sproul rightly argues that to so believe attributes a self-creation to chance.] . . . The fatal flaw of chance scientists is that they impute real being to the name chance. To say things happen by chance is to make a statement about reality. It is a false statement about reality . . . Chance as a substitute for real causes not only obscures real causes; it threatens the very heart of scientific inquiry, because ignorance expands to such a degree that it ends up in attempts to justify irrationality . . . to grant causal power to chance is not a matter of faith, but of credulity . . . As a causal force, chance remains, ever and always, a fiction.[12]

Sproul has less to say about chance as mathematical probability. It is mentioned so slightly that some readers miss it. He admits that chance in the realm of mathematics serves a real and vital function. 'Here *chance* is merely a formal word with no material content. It is a pure abstraction.'[13]

One of the earliest representatives of Calvinism wrote differently about chance in the secondary agency sense. Thomas Gataker [1574–1654], whose work on lots has repeated reference in these pages, pointed out how 'chance' was included in biblical descriptions of events. In the Old Testament, he pointed to 1 Kings 22:34; Ruth 2:3,5; Ecclesiastes 9:2,3,11, and in the New Testament, where even Jesus alluded to it, in Luke 10:31,32.[14] These texts are not the result of philosophic diversification, but the owning up to the reality of God's providence which allowed for randomness. It would be patently unfair to attribute or dismiss these allusions to baseless abstractions.

Previously, Sproul forcefully and properly argues that things do not happen by chance, since chance is powerless.[15] Gataker could heartily agree if chance were confined to a rival to God, but he would disagree if chance as a secondary phenomenon, i.e. randomness, was said to be in conflict with God's control. Chance as a secondary factor was powerless, but present, for in coin-tosses and card-shuffling there is randomness. Sproul admitted to a secondary meaning to chance. For comparison purposes it means 'uncertain outcomes . . . measured by probability quotients translated into odds'.[16]

Sproul reluctantly acknowledges some presence of chance in lifeworks.

> Bringing chance back into the affairs of the world may work in terms of providing useful models of predictability of atomic behavior and the like. Chance as a calculation of probability factors certainly 'works' in a bridge game or dice bet ... As an aid to mathematical models, chance surely works. As an aid to grasping real states of affairs, it fails – and fails miserably.[17]

Sproul more positively admits chance as a mathematical function is important and serves useful purposes. Christians and non-Christians benefit or suffer from it in their various calculations. But, Sproul – in my view – grudgingly and weakly mentions chance as mathematical formula. The secondary presence of chance is not a fiction, a non-Christian construct, nor a word to cover up human ignorance on causation.

Chance is not always to be explained by our ignorance, but is a functional law.[18] For instance, chance is very much involved in weather patterns. Tides may be easy to predict, but not weather – there are too many variables. Weather ingredients are extremely complex and constantly changing. Chance explains why your local meteorologist is sometimes wrong. Chance is in play for Christian travellers even though they rightly and rigorously argue against chance as cause. To admit chance in storms and other acts of nature doesn't mean, however, that God is helpless to control nature. Whatever variables occur, God is always and completely behind them and works through them.

In the second chapter of Thomas Gataker's work on lots, as we noted, he pointed out that chance as secondary agency is given space in Scripture.[19] In addition to that, the principle of chance stands behind the lots references. Some Calvinists find it hard to admit there is uncertainty in God's world, but God has built the world so that uncertainty continues.

The balance of Proverbs 16:33

The two usages of chance are reflected and advanced in Scripture. Watch for it. Perhaps the text that bears most immediately on the two aspects of chance is Proverbs 16:33: 'Lots are cast into the lap; The decision depends on the LORD' (NIV).

In the Old Testament the casting of the dice was not the determiner of the decision, but the Lord over the lots was (cf. Num 26:55; Job 18:6–10; Neh. 10:34).

Calvin's summary of the significance of Proverbs 16:33 is 'that God directs by His counsel the things that seem most fortuitous.'[20] A few pages earlier, in the same treatise, Calvin said,

... of this providence ... there is a beautiful description in Psalm 107. For there the prophet shows that what in common estimation are thought whims of fortune, are in fact so far from being imposed by blind chance, that they clearly mirror the goodness or wrath or the justice of God.[21]

The eighteenth-century commentator, Matthew Henry's comments minimize chance:

Note, 1. The divine Providence orders and directs those things which to us are perfectly casual and fortuitous. Nothing comes to pass by chance, nor is an event determined by a blind fortune, but every thing by the will and counsel of God. What man has neither eye nor hand in, God is intimately concerned in. 2. When solemn appeals are made to Providence by the casting of lots, for the deciding of that matter of moment which could not otherwise be at all, or not so well, decided, God must be eyed in it, by prayer, that it may be disposed aright (*Give a perfect lot*, 1 Sam. 14:41; Acts 1:24), and by acquiescing in it when it is disposed, being satisfied that the hand of God is in it and that hand directed by infinite wisdom. All the disposals of Providence concerning our affairs we must look upon to be the directing of our lot, the determining of what we referred to God, and must be reconciled to them accordingly.[22]

The traditional view of this text is that it says chance has nothing to do with causation. Also typical was Ralph Wardlaw's explanation [1779–1853].

In no case is there a more thorough disavowal of chance than in the use of the lot. It is the strongest and most direct recognition that can be made of a particular providence, – of the constant and minute superintendence of an omniscient overruling Mind. While it assumes our own ignorance, it equally assumes divine knowledge.[23]

But the reality of chance as a secondary agent finds defence in the writings of the Anglican Robert South [1634–1716]. Like Gataker, he argued Solomon had no problem balancing chance and providence. Chance is not denied in the text. South correctly saw that chance was used on a secondary level.

South was far as the East is from the West from Sproul. Sproul and South represent two Calvinists in disagreement about the significance of two kinds of chance. There is a causal element in the lot. The causal role was as a secondary means. Sproul refuses to think of chance in any other capacity than primary.

South, however, saw chance as secondary. Primary versus a secondary cause is worth consideration. South said:

> Some there are, who utterly proscribe the name *chance* as a word of impious and profane signification: and, indeed, if it be taken by us in that sense in which it was used by the heathen, so as to make anything casual in respect of God himself, their exception ought justly to be admitted. But to say a thing is a chance, or causality, as it relates to second causes, is not profaneness, but a great truth; as signifying no more, than that there are some events, besides the knowledge, purpose, expectation, and power of second agents: and for this very reason, because they are so, it is the royal prerogative of God himself, to have all these loose, uneven, fickle uncertainties under his disposal.[24]

A century after South, the English Baptist Charles Haddon Spurgeon [1834–1892] kept the two roles, God's and that of lot casting, in balance.

> And if the disposal of the lot is the Lord's whose is the arrangement of the whole life? . . . You know when Achan

had committed a great sin, the tribes were assembled and the lot fell upon Achan. When Jonah was in the ship they cast lots and the lot fell upon Jonah. And when Jonathan had tasted the honey, they cast lots and Jonathan was taken. When they cast lots for an apostle who should succeed the fallen Judas, the lot fell upon Matthias, and he was separated to the work. The lot is directed of God. And if the simple casting of a lot is guided by him, how much more the events of our entire life – especially when we are told by our blessed Savior: 'The very hairs of your head are all numbered; not a sparrow falleth to the ground without your Father.'[25]

When chance and providence are not in conflict

In the mid-twentieth century, the scientist and theologian, William G. Pollard, superbly rephrased the point in Proverbs 16:33 and the distinctions ably represented by Gataker and South: 'Providence . . . is to be found in the appearance of chance and accident in history.'[26]

Chance cannot be denied without denying the reality of which it is a part, without denying the Creator of it for the functioning of the world. Although chance has functioned in all history and in the universe from its formation, it does not have an independent existence or the power to bring matter into being. The role of chance in keeping randomness alive and probabilities intact does not precede or supersede God. *Chance is God's instrument, not to destroy determinism, but to weaken, prevent, or destroy man's ability to predict with certainty.*

Chance does not undermine determinism. That is a huge statement though a short sentence. But it is what separates my view on the subject from R.C. Sproul's. Sproul begins with the notion that chance undermines determinism. I think he steps out without his conceptual shoes tightly laced. Chance does not exclude God, but has been with the world ever since God made it and will continue to operate in what happens.

Chance is important for the Christian and was important for God because it factored in unpredictability in the world. Certain aspects of the world are predictable, but over a long period the element of chance ensures that total predictability is impossible.

Perhaps the best recent explanation of the significance of chance in God's creation is found in the new mathematical principle of chaos. This is important for it underlines the thesis that predestination and predictability are not equivalent. Rather than the principle of chaos being a denial of divine sovereignty, it shows how control reaches into areas previously thought untouched by causation. R.K. McGregor Wright, Ph.D. – of Jonesborough, Tennessee, pointed out:

> [In chaos theory] there may in fact be no strictly chance events in the world at all. Even things like the upward curl of smoke from a cigarette, the branching of capillary tubes in our blood vessels or the fall of leaves from a tree, which we previously assumed to have a large element of chance in their structures, turn out now to develop according to mathematical formulas. The same seems to be true for social events like the movements of large crowds and other events made up of large numbers of human choices. Perhaps the ignorance gap can be closed, if only in the abstract world of statistics. This should give freewillers pause.[27]

Divine determinism is a reality, but from our perspective that does not allow us the luxury of anticipating an event as absolutely settled. That does not diminish or deny that what God wills God accomplishes. From God's perspective there is no separation or lack of equivalency between knowing and causing, pre-determining and predicting. For God, what he knows, he achieves.

> An apparent paradox is that chaos is deterministic, generated by fixed rules which do not themselves involve any elements of change. We even speak of deterministic chaos. In principle, the future is completely determined by the past; but in practice small uncertainties, much like minute errors of measurement which enter into calculations, are amplified, with the effect that even though the behavior is predictable in the short term, it is unpredictable over the long run. The discovery of such behavior is one of the important achievements of chaos theory.[28]

It is now known in science that determinism and predictability are not equivalent and that within the same system of order there can be chaos. A causality factor can be involved where there appears none. And chaos and chance can co-exist where there is evidential causality. For the same reason one can have chance and providence. Proverbs 16:33 allows, indeed, even requires that viewpoint.

William S. Pollard, as a Christian physicist, grappled with the problem of the place of chance in God's world. Chance exists within nature, not as a controlling system, i.e. as something independent from outside influence, but as part of our reality, in Pollard's words, 'an indeterminate one involved in alternatives and latitudes.'[29]

One fault a Christian should find with Sproul's presentation is that he has not allowed enough room for chance in the world. It is there, and there in abundance, but it is there because God wants it there. It is there to keep man humble. It is there to make sure that man cannot think he has everything figured out and that outcomes are totally predictable.

Neither certainties nor probabilities are excluded by providence. Pollard continues: '[We live in a world] in which indeterminacy, alternatives, and chance are real aspects of the fundamental nature of things, and not merely the consequences of our inadequate and provisional understanding.'[30]

And divine providence is not an outside fluke, nor a new or additional force, as in vitalism, but it is the prime cause of history's movement and conforms to God's purposes. Pollard, who was a physicist, kept chance in perspective.

> When we speak of chance as a factor in history, we have in mind the existence, as a typical feature of natural processes, of alternative responses to a given set of causative influences for which the laws of nature specify only the relative probabilities. Insofar as alternatives are typical of all natural processes, chance becomes a universal ingredient of history.[31]

Sproul underplays the role of chance in nature and in the development of God's purposes. He essentially confines chance to atomic physics and games, which I believe is a weakness in his book. My point is that chance blankets all reality and is involved in much more than the outcome of a coin toss, a game of bridge, or mathematical calculations. The beauty of Proverbs 16:33 is, in my interpretation, that with chance's continuous functioning in God's cosmology his role as supreme is both preserved and honoured.

Unpredictability is the main mission of chance in nature. In keeping reality that way, God is not a spectator, and is more than a participant. He is Lord over the operation. He guides and hides the outcome. He caused the dice to come up a certain way, now, and in any future roll.

Pollard's articulation of the resolution between chance in nature and divine sovereignty is worth careful and repeated reflection. He wrote:

> The Christian sees the chances and accidents of history as the very warp and woof of the fabric of providence which God is ever weaving. Seen in this way, they can be gladly and joyously acknowledged and accepted. But apart from this revelation, chance and accident mean anarchy, sheer meaningless random incoherence, and utter chaos from which the soul recoils in horror. The truth then may be concealed and some substitute for Christian providence, or as the Bible would put it, some idolatry, must be found which will give a source of hope in spite of chance and accident. But every such hope is false, a temporary whistling in the dark, a concealment of truth.[32]

In your next 'pot-luck church supper' no one knows how many, or if any, will bring baked beans, and whether pies, not cakes will be part of the dessert menu. Some Christians are hesitant to use the word 'luck' in conversation. And for good reason: after all, the secular mind grants no validity or reality to God's intimate involvement in history.

I heard a publisher/pastor in western Pennsylvania share his hesitations about Christians using 'luck' in the 'pot-luck supper' designation. For theological reasons, he said, he has scrubbed the use of 'luck' from church notices. Instead of referring to an up-coming church supper as 'pot-luck' he calls it a 'pot-providence' dinner. Other churches have used the expression 'pot-faith suppers.'

I wonder, however, why some in the Reformed tradition don't flinch when, in their discussions on gambling, they admit to a role of 'pure chance'. 'Pure' with 'chance' seems contradictory. But if it means total probability, it has no theological conflict or contradiction. For the same reason anyone, Christian or non-Christian, should wonder about the validity and value of saying, 'the best of luck to you'. If luck is only probability, it may be a well-intended well-wishing, although somewhat hollow. Well-wishing is fine but whenever an opportunity arises a Christian should say, 'the Lord bless you'.

Seventeenth-century Gataker worked with fellow Puritans who had similar scruples against the use of 'luck' and 'chance'. Because a pagan association seeps through 'luck' and 'chance' they studiously avoided repeating them. Gataker was charitable in commenting on those who use 'luck' but were solid Christian believers. He tried to allay fears that to use these words does not necessarily send the wrong message.[33] He was for verbalizing Christian faith, but recognized that sometimes Christians fall into repeating cultural clichés.

Whereas the words 'luck' and 'chance' drip with God's exclusion from life, for the most part Christians don't hesitate to refer to something 'happening'. How far should a Christian pursue his critical attitude? Should one knock the book of Ruth 2:3 (KJV), where it says, 'As it happened, she came to the part of the field belonging to Boaz.' The word for 'happening' here is the Hebrew word *miqreh*, which means 'chance' or 'event'. The same word 'chance' or 'happen' is found in Esther 6:13 and 2 Samuel 1:16.

Gataker, early on, noted the Old Testament references acknowledged a form of chance.[34] Christians also face the same problem in the use of the words 'fortunately', 'accident', and 'charming'.[35] The original sense of these words was that something other than God had a hand in history. Should we refrain from describing a person as 'charming' once we realize the connection of that word with superstition? Should Christians refuse to use 'accident' in conversation and in writing when they are called to report damage to their car?

Proverbs 16:33 suggests no such apologies were necessary to use the word 'pot-luck supper'. We do not refer to chance in action, in primary agency, i.e. as a causative force, for that would make chance a rival to God. Chance in that sense has no reality. The non-Christian is committed to a world-view that excludes control and is run entirely and exclusively without God. But as a mix of unpredictable outcomes, as a built-in, and operational procedure under God, chance as probability has a place both in reality and in our vocabulary.

I submit that Christians must distinguish between the different usages of chance. And Christians should have a clear view of how others use the word. We should always sort out how a person uses 'chance', for one may not be aware that the bare expression can carry a double message. It would be a golden witness opportunity gently to suggest that 'chance' has several meanings and that any ascription of origination to 'chance' runs counter to Scripture's assertion that God is the source of every blessing.

I believe behind everything is God's rule, even when a person unwisely gambles away his wealth or gets himself in a financial quagmire because he has bet his money when he should have invested it. There is a randomness in events and occurrences, under God's sovereign good hand, which are unpredictable. It is that very unpredictability or uncertainty where it is proper to refer to chance.

To say that is to deny neither divine sovereignty nor determinism, but something within the ordering of the universe by God. We should not look to luck as a life-force to make our lives easier or brighter. As Christians we do not look to a mystical manipulation of reality by a fictional Lady Luck. Luck is neither a lady nor a lord, but a fabrication invented to supplant the only true God. The God of Scripture is the only sovereign of the universe. We are held in his hand. We are the sheep of his pasture.

10.

Probability: The Only Sure Thing in Lotto

Anti-gambling researchers charge state and government lotteries with cynical exploitation of the poor, and of double taxation. Gambling generally has been denounced as a perilous thrill and a dreadful waste. And gain from gambling has been called a dangerous obsession.

There is even bigger money, contends financial expert George Gilder, to be found in the lawsuit gamble. 'One of the best remaining ways to strike it rich, the best remaining scene for gambling, with the odds against the productive* stacked ever higher by government, is the civil suit: malpractice, product liability, discrimination, antitrust, libel, pollution, whatever.'[1]

But the Christian is not out to make money 'any which way'. Whereas the secularist thinks of nothing but money and more of it, the Christian is not trying to use the system to line his pockets and feather his nest in a selfishly aggressive way. To better one's economic base is neither proof of greed nor the result of graft, but a God-honouring way to free one from the encroachment of debt which eats away at our freedom to enjoy God's creation and to advance the spread of the Gospel.

---

* This word's usage is unclear, but probably a reference to profits made.

Two kinds of probability

Probability has two senses and the first relates to gambling. It is statistical probability or likelihood and odds. Statistical probability is based on the long-run stability of frequent ratios. In everyday gambling ventures, how many times will the dice come up in favour of the player? The second concept of probability has to do with the likelihood of a proposition or position being right, based on given evidence. This latter sense has to do with intellectual, moral, and spiritual values. Whereas a gambler can't escape percentages and probabilities, a world-view evaluator faces the inductive probability of whether a moral judgment is more likely to be right or wrong.[2]

But the two are not always isolated and separate. Sometimes moral questions arise in wagering. For instance, what is the probability that stocks are squeaky clean compared to the ethical issues in civil lawsuits? Don't moral values weigh as much as statistical probability? But the two areas – numerical probability and moral valuation – are not inherently incompatible.

Historically, stock-market buying found itself moving up the moral scale. At the turn of the century, according to historian Ann Fabian, stockbrokers stood midway between 'the most diabolical of gamblers and the most vicious of investors'.[3] But the progress along the spectrum of respectability continued. The stock market was able to impress the average citizen that market speculation was 'an inherent part of nature'.[4]

Now stock investments are looked upon with respect, sometimes with awe, rarely with disdain. But it has been a long road and an uphill climb towards such acceptance. According to gambling historian Ann Fabian, 'By purging a world of vice and corruption on the edges of their market, they purified the speculation practiced within it and thus transformed their agrarian critics into deluded victims in need of their professional protection and sage advice.'[5]

We have next to see if there is anything such as luck behind financial bonanzas in stocks, or whether the force is only a fluke.

Is acceptance of a phenomenon called 'luck' warranted? What does it bring to the table?

Luck: illusion or reality?
Does luck rather than probability favour the player? Does luck level the playing-field? What one thinks about this presupposes the existence of luck. The gambler is only setting himself up for bitter disappointments if he or she believes luck is going to kick in. Those closest to the gambling game, who have no theological agenda to push, know that luck is a chimera, a phantom, a false justification of what happens in wagering.

> Superstitions about the miraculous powers of luck defeat thousands of gamblers by blinding them to the realities of the games they play. A casino is a recreation center, not a temple of the occult. Nothing could be less supernatural than the percentages that rule the games. Most of these numbers have been known for centuries . . . Persons who do not appreciate the probabilities, and regard them as somehow secondary to luck, take foolish risks that multiply their chances of grave losses.[6]

Anyone who gambles and thinks good or bad luck explains his or her win or loss has been hoodwinked by superstition. A gambler may have been the recipient of a win due to the law of probability, but 'it is sheer superstition to say that a person will be lucky or unlucky'.[7] Luck can't get a win, but knowing the odds increases the odds for winning. In addition to the general odds, are the added, built-in odds of the gambling operator.

Probability, i.e. the secondary agency some call chance, works for or against the gambler. False hopes drive the gambler to try again and again. But the probability of winning is usually so slim gambling hardly seems worth the expense. Especially sad are those whose expectations are unrealistic and who spend more than they should.

Of course, where the skill of the player is a factor, the odds of the player winning increase. Games that operate on pure chance are craps (the rolling of two dice), baccarat, and roulette. Lotteries operate on the same principle of pure chance. The volume of players reduces the chances of winning. The national lotteries of the British Isles allow a chance of winning of 1 to 450,000. In the United States a 'Powerball' lottery – a six-figure combination win – offers little hope of winning: the odds that one ticket will hold the precise numbers is a fixed 80 million to one. ('The odds are determined by the number of possible combinations.')[8] One statistician consulted by the *National Review* agreed, and added a comparison that makes sense to golfers: 'It would be likelier to shoot twenty consecutive holes-in-one.'[9]

What are the odds in casinos games? Back in the 1970s, the odds were as follows:

> In casino games, the house gets its share of the odds. On Las Vegas roulette wheels, which have two zero spaces, the house benefits by 5.26%. (In Monte Carlo, where the wheels have only one zero, the house margin is 2.7%) In blackjack in Vegas, the house has a basic advantage of 5.9%, though this can vary depending on the skill of a player. The best casino odds are in craps, where the house is only 1.4% better off than the player. Slot machines vary, keeping 3 % to 22% of the coins they swallow.[10]

Now casinos distribute cards listing the house's statistical edge, which 'ranges from about 0.5 per cent on blackjack –

the only game in which some player skill is involved – to 5.3 per cent on roulette'.[11] To induce customers to bet more and more, casinos lessen the odds of their winning. For instance, 'whales' – or those who gamble more than $1 million a visit and who may have credit lines up to $20 million (there are only 250 gambling 'whales' in the world) – pick baccarat as their game of choice for that 'has only a 1 per cent advantage for the house'.[12]

People foolishly ignore the odds and pay for it dearly. The strength of the gambling urge goes against sound judgment. A truck driver from San Antonio, Texas, reflected on the plight of fellow drivers who blew their profit at a pit-stop gambling place. Gary Stevens, aged 36, said, 'I'm totally against these things. I've seen drivers drop $200 in these machines and walk away with nothing. It takes 1,000 miles on the road to make that.'[13]

Probability not heeded
Do not bet on probability to bale you out of bad decisions. Les Wilson of Lockland, Ohio, former editor of the Ohio-based suburban newspaper, *Reading-Lockland Valley Courier*, testifies to this. An otherwise model citizen, the former editor-columnist, over the years, had previously written columns containing touching stories of needy children and families. Concerned readers began to donate money. The Purely Personal Christmas Fund was started. Thousands of dollars were donated. Mr Wilson took the donations and squandered them on rub-off lotto tickets. Over a long period of time he dishonestly used gifts for the needy and gambled them away. At the last count 'authorities estimate that Mr Wilson stole as much as $10,000 from the Purely Personal Christmas Fund'.[14]

Unfortunately, Mr Wilson, aged 71, pleaded guilty to a single count of theft for taking more than $6,000 from the Purely Personal Christmas Fund. The actual amount

stolen was $4,000. more. In his final column entitled
'Purely Personal', he announced his resignation from the
paper and apologized to readers for stealing from the
charity fund he had administered for years. Instead of
buying food, clothing and Christmas gifts, Mr Wilson
spent the money on scratch-off lottery tickets.

Court papers show that Mr Wilson misspent the money
between 1 November 1996 and 19 January 1997. Police say
'he played the tickets so often while sitting at the bar at
Sandaddy's in Reading that he left a dent on the counter'.[15]
Before there was a dent left on the bar, some critics could
justifiably mutter that there was a dent in his head for
doing it. Not only were the needy deprived of help and the
donors betrayed, but Mr Wilson stole money from generous citizens and tried to defy the law of probability against
winning at lottery scratch-offs.

The case is strong against winning at gambling on the
basis of probability. But what kind of probability are we
talking about?

> Probability theory supplies mathematical methods for dis-
> covering what can be expected to happen when the results
> depend upon chance. It states, for instance, that each player
> in a game of chance has an equal chance to win in the long
> run. If during a long evening of play at poker or bridge, you
> never get a decent hand, or when you get a halfway decent
> hand someone else always gets a better one, you may doubt
> this. But your experience does not contradict the theory of
> probability, because the theory does not pretend to state that
> you and the other players will get an equal number of good
> hands in one evening of play. It states that the longer you play
> the more likely you are to get approximately the same
> number of good hands. [Don't think that results must 'even
> up' in the long run.][16]

During US frontier days of Dodge City, Kansas, according to records, 'virtually everyone, in and out of the church, gambled and regarded it as *the* frontier pastime'.[17] It was the habit of a minister, a regular visitor, who wouldn't begin his card game until he had hung his black coat on the back of his chair. And he always opened the game with prayer. He said he regarded chance as God's means of favouring the elect and punishing sinners.[18] Only a skilled card player could make that claim. But the claim was clerical hype.

In gambling, probability doesn't play favourites. Depending on the vehicle, gambling usually has a sliding scale pitched against players. Unless the results are fixed, unprejudiced mathematical probability is the inescapable ingredient in all gambling. More often than not the odds are against winning. Winners are rare. Christian and non-Christian alike are subject to the same laws of probability. 'The theory of probability has revolutionized the theory of games.'[19] Someone may try to defeat the odds and risk a small amount, hopefully, much smaller than the amount to which driver Gary Stevens referred.

True figures over false weights
King Solomon inveighed against the sin of false weights. Gambling decks have been known to be fixed or stacked against the players, roulette wheels have been purposefully adjusted off-balance, dice tooled unsymmetrically, skilfully but deceitfully balanced with a bias for the gambling house. Sometimes probability is never in one's favour. Whenever odds are rigged against the player, losing is assured. Whether mixed for fun or gain, fraud is still fraud and leads to our loss.

Other kinds of fraud are being used to cheat the public. In February 1978 the CBS news programme, *60 Minutes*, warned carnival and circus attenders that the midway game of razzle-dazzle is 100 per cent slanted against the participant.[20] Such a game is now illegal in California, but not everywhere.

Fraud helped make the lottery an illegal activity. Early lotteries were often conducted by outside companies. Some of those who ran the lotteries disappeared with the money and the winners never got their wins. At other times, unscrupulous persons printed bogus lottery tickets and pocketed the money. Because of graft and other inequities lotteries fell into ill repute and were banned in the latter part of the nineteenth century.

But when first introduced, lotteries were noble enterprises. In 1665, the city of New York (then New Amsterdam) raised money to benefit the poor by running a lottery. The prize to the winners was a Bible, not money.[21]

Times have changed. State lotteries, once occasional, are now, seemingly weekly! One can buy scratch-off lotto tickets night or day, seven days a week. The ease with which one can be in contact with gambling has increased. One recent book on gambling provides gambling newcomers with a tour guide to the gambling spots of the nation, state by state. Entitled *Where To Play In The USA: The Gaming Guide*, this 338-page guide supplies the details about where to gamble and how to get there. All-in-one locations include play and accommodation whether hotel or campground.[22]

By 1910, most states had enacted legislation *against* gambling. State legislators had voted in anti-gaming laws. But gambling supporters worked to reverse or to remove the onus against gambling practices. Gambling went underground to survive. The tide gradually turned sympathetic toward gambling interests. By 1976, 44 US states had some form of legalized gambling.[23] By 1985, state treasuries had cleared a total of $3 billion.[24] Today, with the exception of Hawaii and Utah, all states provide some form of gambling. Today '27 states now offer some kind of casino gambling; 37 states and the District of Columbia operate lotteries' and other forms of gambling.[25]

Indian reservation gambling is another story.[26] Scattered across the nation are more than 150 Indian casinos, even in states that don't sanction casino gambling, 'which produced $1.3 billion in revenue and $400 million in net profit [as long ago as 1991], according to the National Indian Gaming Commission'.[27] In the state of Connecticut, the Mashantucket Pequots' Foxwoods Casino, a massive 4.1 million-square-foot complex, is both the largest and the most profitable casino in America, with estimated '*daily* profits of about $1 million'.[28] No state can prohibit casino gambling on Indian land reservations. Some Native Americans are against casinos, and a few tribes have voted casinos down.

Another temptation faces the Christian Native American that would not face a citizen of the United Kingdom. Should one turn down winnings that come to members of the tribe? Christian Native Americans face the option: should they accept or endorse cheques from guaranteed shares in tribal profits? Should any balk at benefiting from those profits?

Without needing to gamble, non-gambling tribe members automatically benefit from Indian reservation gambling. A big question is whether or not they should decline, for conscience's sake, accepting a percentage of casino profits from the tribe treasury. For the Pequot Indians, at least, the benefits are enormous:

Tribal members who once sold maple syrup and lettuce, raised pigs and cut firewood to eke out sub-poverty level incomes now receive annual stipends that reportedly range from $50,000 to $100,00 plus, based on incentives that reward them for their level of education, jobs and for residing on the reservation. Cradle-to-grave social services funded by the gaming revenue include free medical, child and senior care, free post-secondary tuition through graduate school, housing stipends and $30,000 annual payments with medical benefits for Pequot mothers who choose to stay home to raise their children.[29]

Now tribal members can pursue a college education through to a doctorate. Advanced education is no longer an impossible dream.[30] Although overall Native American gambling represents only 11 per cent of the $50 billion US gaming industry, casino profits provide the impoverished tribal members with new economic stability and educational opportunities.[31]

The pendulum of gambling's acceptance has now swung – almost everywhere – to the side of favouring it. Consequently, gambling has swept the nation. Not far from Cincinnati, in Lawrenceburg, Indiana, off-shore gambling is licensed on Ohio riverboats. Billboard ads line the Interstates in and around Cincinnati luring drivers to venture trips to nearby Indiana, the latest hot-spot of midwestern gambling.

Gambling in the tri-state

Local Radio stations promote regional gambling. Station WSAI (1530), 'Cincinnati's Original Hits Station', was the chief sponsor of a 16-page circular containing various business promotions to every household in Cincinnati. The prominent back page was all about 'The Grand Victoria' casino resort in nearby Rising Sun, Indiana. Its particular pitch was to retirers (55 or over) who are promised 500 free points to belong to their '55 Senior Players' Club'. 'As a Grand 55 member, you enjoy all the benefits of Club Victoria Players' Club, plus $1 off any gaming session any time and 10 per cent off food and gift shop purchases!' Along with that is the lure of being in the running to win free merchandise at draws on Tuesdays and Thursdays.[32]

The publicity blitz is relentless and effective. A weekend insert of *The Cincinnati Enquirer* for Friday, 11 April, 1997 had two full-page ads aimed to inducing new customers to Indiana's Argosy Casino in Lawrenceburg. Whereas the by-pass (Ronald Reagan Expressway) billboard had the statement: 'It's Close. It's Easy. It's Fun', the newspaper ad had 'It's Fun! It's Easy! It can be Very Rewarding!' (No promises or guarantees, however, are given!) In the Friday insert, then, were pictures of eight local people who made it to the big winnings: $25,000, $10,000, and $9,000.

What is true of Cincinnati is probably true of other metropolitan areas. Accessible gambling opportunities are within a short drive, a quick phone call, or the click of a computer mouse. The casino hotels are new and inviting. Their gambling booths are open, the blackjack tables are set, the roulette wheels spin, the slot machines hum.

Farther west, the state of Iowa has a significantly large casino gambling business. It used to be that only Nevada, Delaware, and Montana provided legal betting on sports events like professional football, where illegal bookies get most of their action. Now the trend is for state-sponsored lotteries.

At the risk of losing betting dollars and the revenue that generates phenomenal profits, legislators can't resist dipping into the financial pie. A domino effect explains the willingness of states to open the gate to legal, state-sponsored gambling. State legislators see gambling profits going to nearby states and they want part of the action to meet their budget. After New York state got into off-track betting, Connecticut and Massachusetts soon followed.

State lotteries have proliferated and citizen acceptance of them has expanded. Food chains such as McDonald's, Burger King, and Wendy's, which are worldwide, and make their way into nations such as the UK and others, set up and subliminally soften customers to risk winning on another level. The promotional gimmicks of scratch-off game cards fit into a culture which softens opposition to lottery playing. Customers unwittingly weaken to the free participation in the company lottery of winning free food and drinks, or cash prizes.

The leap of lotto
Today, buying lotto tickets is super convenient. Motorized drivers can buy lotto tickets at the same time as they pay to fill their fuel tanks – all in one motion.

Floyd Pearson of McPherson, Kansas, combined lotto playing with his gas purchase. One winter day in 1997, he bought eight lottery tickets when he filled his tank at the local gas station. Everyone said 'wow' when he won $100,000. He confessed, 'I'm not what you'd call a serious gambler. I usually pick up a couple of tickets when I am buying gas.'[33]

For a year or so the closest grocery store to our home, a Kroger grocery, had an upright lotto machine tempting customers to finish their shopping run with a stab at recouping their food bill. A few weeks later, at the same exit, I saw an interesting competition.

Next to the lotto rub-off ticket machine was a uniformed volunteer Salvation Army person with an extended tambourine inviting direct giving to their social programmes. A case can be made that more social good is done by donating small change into a circular tambourine than dollars into the upright lotto machine.

A little-known feature of store lotto machines is that the machines make money for the stores. I heard of one case in which social good resulted for the store owner from supermarket lotto tickets. A former resident of Lake Bronson, Minnesota, told me how the town's Sele's grocery store was spared from going out of business because of the percentage received from the state for selling lottery tickets.[34]

Lotteries are definitely the fastest growing form of gambling available. Lotteries are near the top of all forms of legalized gambling. But despite their popularity lotteries are not the smartest use of money to make money. From a statistical viewpoint the prospects of winning are poor. Sure, they offer massive prizes, but that's only because there are lots and lots of losers.

Nevertheless, lotto has swept the nation. But in one poll it came second to cards.[35] That poll, however, was before state lotteries escalated. After the general lottery ticket, 'Super Lotto' was introduced. Then, after that, came a 'Powerball' lotto ticket. A number of states now have them, promising substantial potential earnings, and thereby increasing its appeal to more buyers.[36]

Powerball was the brainchild of physicist Ed Stanek and was set up in 1992 as a way for 'relatively less populous states to gain access to large money-generating player bases'.[37] On 30 July, 1998, thirteen machine-shop workers from Westerville, Ohio, pooled ten dollars each for Powerball tickets, as they had done for six years. Whoosh, they won the largest Powerball ticket in history! One of the group motored one hundred miles to the closest Powerball outlet (in Richmond, Indiana). The ticket and trip netted the thirteen $250 million, a record amount. Each of them got $12.4 million pre-tax dollars.[38]

The big appeal of a Super Lotto or Powerball lotto ticket is the prospect of becoming an instant millionaire or an instant billionaire. Psychologists now refer to it as 'lottery fantasy syndrome'.[39] George Blackburn of Pensacola,

Florida, is representative of the typical attitude of the lotto players. He thought lotto players 'got a chance to be a millionaire'. According to Terri La Fleur, senior editor of *Gaming and Wagering*, lotto players 'continue to spend billions of dollars annually on their favourite pastime – dreaming about the day when they fax their boss their resignation because they hit the big one'.[40]

Desperate, the financially strapped continue to go beyond moderation. According to Curt Suplee of *The Washington Post*, 'Statistically you are seven times more likely to get hit by lightning than to become a millionaire in state lotteries.'[41] Millionaire wannabes beware.

Fair game?

The appeal of lotteries is strong among minorities, the poor and the under-educated. The top five per cent of state lottery players spend an average of nearly $3,400 annually on tickets, which amounts to 51 per cent of all lottery tickets. The top ten per cent – who spend $2,250 annually – account for two-thirds of total lottery ticket sales.[42] Frequent or core players are the persons who can least afford it. The final report of the National Gambling Impact Study Commission – over 300 pages – came out on 18 June 1999.[43]

Understandably, some see increasing addiction in lottery use. The anticipated summer report to Congress in 1999 contains specific criticism of state governments (37 states have lotteries, plus the District of Columbia) by some members of the National Gambling Impact Study Commission such as James Dobson who said, 'governmental lotteries remain shameless in their exploitation of the poor . . . and the vulnerable'.[44]

Early New England Puritans ironically endorsed lotteries that funded towns, cities, states, and churches! Puritan

Theologian William Ames has already been cited to the effect that lotteries can serve the public good (see Chapter 7).

On the other hand, warnings against lottery playing are pervasive in Christian publications. And much of lottery use is abuse. Although the total number of lottery addicts is small in relation to the number of players (2.5 pathological gamblers and 3 million problem gamblers have recently been tabulated),[45] many consider the social cost too high to warrant participation and promotion. Seventeenth- and eighteenth-century Puritans saw the principle of probability behind the gaming as a key issue. Although recognizing addiction as one of the evils, they were also able to see God's hand in lotteries for public benefits.

In colonial times lotteries supplied the struggling colonies with an educational edge. Columbia University was founded with £2,250 raised by lottery in 1746. Harvard College, later University, held a number of lotteries to pay for new buildings.[46]

In 1931, New South Wales in Australia, conducted a state lottery that turned the proceeds over to struggling hospitals. The Swedish state lottery, after meeting budgeted needs, turns over its proceeds to support Red Cross hospitals, museums, music, art, and drama.[47]

Lotto gains go into state budgets. Educational, senior-citizen services, recreational, urban improvements, law enforcement are among the benefits of state lotteries. Take one small example in Colorado. On the East side of Durango, Colorado, Bayfield's Little Pine River Park was one of the recreational facilities to be funded from state lotteries. It received the Colorado Lottery Starburst Award 'for excellence in the use of Lottery Proceeds'. Two-thirds of Colorado state gaming revenues for 1996 were earmarked by the Historic

Preservation Commission for refurbishing home exteriors in Cripple Creek.[48]

The probability of any personal winning at a state-run lottery, however, is poor, next to nil.

> Each person who purchases one ticket has three chances in 1,000,000 to win one of the prizes . . . as a bet, the ticket holder has odds against him of 6 to 4. If he purchases two tickets, his chance to win first prize becomes 1 in 500,000; that to win one of the prized 3 in 500,000, the odds against him remain the same. In spite of the unfavorable odds, buying lottery tickets is attractive to many people, because the price of the ticket is so small, the prizes so large.[49]

Rogers described the likelihood of winning the lottery as 'astronomical odds'.[50] Researchers at the University of Nevada at Reno's Institution for the Study of Gambling have put that in realistic comparison. If a person bought 200 one-dollar lotto tickets every week for his entire adult life from the age 18 to 75, his $296,400 investment would still leave him with less than a 1 in 100 chance of hitting the jackpot.[51]

The Eighteenth-century Frenchman, Georges Louis Leclerc Buffon, put the odds even stronger. He wrote:

> Only a fool would invest in a lottery ticket when more than 10,000 other tickets are being sold . . . the possibility of any event for which the odds are less than 10,000 to 1 should neither affect nor occupy our feelings or our minds for a single moment.[52]

Current comparisons make the prospect of winning far harder, and multi-dollar participation far more stupid. Several years ago an Ohio jackpot of $27 million made headlines. Then, the maths department of Miami

University figured the odds against winning a single lottery were 7.5 billion to 1.[53]

The odds of winning are measurably increased when fewer enter the lottery. For 21 years the City of Cincinnati has conducted a lottery for qualified low-income people to win a new home, sometimes costing $50,000 to renovate. People who qualify must not own a home already, have an annual income between $21 and $22 thousand and agree to live in the home for three years after it is renovated.

In 1997, 1,000 people applied, but only 150 were qualified to take part. In the June draw, 15 families and individuals became instant homeowners for a dollar. It was a lotto dollar and it won them a bona fide home that needed repair to make it livable. More than 500 homes have been given away since the lottery started in 1976.[54] The odds in the 'Dollar House Lottery' are usually excellent, because of the small number that apply and because of the smaller number that qualify for the draw. Surely, lotto opponents would not be opposed to such a lottery!

The only sure thing in lotteries is probability. But probability can be low or high. Probability is no guarantee of winning. Where the odds are good, such as in the 'Dollar House Lottery' in Cincinnati, then the chances of winning are increased. Anyone who plays lotteries should do so to benefit society, not for the prospect of real personal gain. Most buyers of the tickets consistently and regularly lose each time they bet.

Therefore, waiting for probability to turn in our favour for gain is ultimately unrealistic. The non-Christian as well as the Christian should find that fact a strong deterrent against excessive lottery playing, and for some a brake against even occasional lottery playing. Probability against winning should discourage both over-indulgence and excessive participation entirely.

Yet for the occasional lotto player there is the consolation that some needy cause or persons are being benefited. Whether that cause is the state budget or the few citizens who win should console the participant. As we should pay our state and federal taxes without complaining, so we should not feel our money is wasted in lottery losses, for it helps state government to function better on behalf of the total citizenry.

'Lottery advocates emphasize their games return an average of 32 percent of their sales revenue to state governments, while only about 9 percent of casinos' profits go to the states.'[55] For illustrations of lottery winning, take the income from several US States. In Ohio, for instance, more than $748 million of 1996's lottery income was earmarked for education. In 1998, Ohio lottery money to education was $724 million.[56] Kentucky turned over $151 million to its general fund and Indiana generated $181 million for its general fund.[57] A favourite rag is to say lotteries are a tax on the poor, the ones least able to afford tickets. Nevertheless, in lottery revenues some social benefits are documented and demonstrable.

Those who are critical of lotteries had more ammunition available in the expenditures needed to secure Connecticut Powerball tickets by residents of New York state. Wm. F. Buckley, Jr., for one, raised the question of the wisdom of New York state's Westchester County residents driving three hours in slow traffic to cross the border into nearby Connecticut's Fairfield County to make Powerball purchases. If one were to calculate the driver's time – 'say three times the minimum wage, or $15 per hour' – for 100,000 drivers (assuming one ticket per driver) that would amount to $4.5 million dollars.[58] The vendors get .05 cents per ticket. They profit.

But what did the Powerball buyers lose in trying to gain? Ironically, what is put out should put the kibosh to investing heavily in Powerball lotteries. There is a better way to make money: stocks. The argument of Chapter 2 was that it is not necessarily greedy to want to make money – or to make it grow – but that wise investments have divine approval and recommendation. Stocks, though sometimes proving to be disappointing risks, are far better than wagering risks in lotteries.

11.

False Hopes in an Uncertain World

Sometimes knowing what is best for us is not too hard to figure out. For instance, if you had a ladder with some loose rungs and a crack half way up one side of the wooden frame, would you venture to climb it to paint your rain gutters? Not a chance. How about if you don't need to climb a ladder, but must get to work every day? If you got into your car to drive to work and you put your foot on the brakes and the brake pedal hit the floor, would you start the motor and head down the street? Not a chance.

The risks in both cases would not warrant the try. You'd want both a safe ladder and a safe car before you would venture up or venture out. No one wants to hazard a needless fall or crash. You would not want to become a predictable accident statistic.

In the circumstances cited, predictability and safety certainly encourage or discourage your use of the ladder and car. But in the case of gambling, the odds are predictable against winning. So why risk money on gambling?

Why do people gamble?

Non-gamblers ask this question of gamblers. Gamblers do not usually ask it of themselves. Since unpredictability and uncertainty are upsetting to people, and because gambling has a large dose of uncertainty and unpredictability, why is gambling found fascinating? When the odds are against participants, is it a particular lunacy that drives one to gamble?

Why do people gamble? No other question has the same ability to cause the gambling impulse to lose its power over people. When there is skill required to do well, some persons won't venture to wager. They know enough about themselves not to gamble at games which require a razor-keen memory, maths skills, and aptitude for numbers. Forget about playing bridge if you hate numbers and can't remember what cards have been played. The more complicated the gamble smarter people will be discouraged from trying.

The need to study, such as in horse-track betting, puts a brake on those who tolerate only the easy modern gamble. And that puts track betting off-limits.

> Compared to casino slot machines and table games, betting on the ponies is a complicated and time-consuming task. In the time it takes a horse player to handicap a race, place a bet and then wait perhaps 15 minutes for the race to begin, a casino gambler could have wagered a small fortune.[1]

Other forms of gambling attract a person because they require no talent. Is it because some gambling allows the mind to be idle that makes it so attractive? Also, one wonders how that kind of gambling can be referred to as a 'recreation' (re-creation)?

Gambling is precisely attractive to some because it only requires money, not brains. The stupidest person on the planet can gamble simply because he or she has the money.

Survey of why people gamble

Why do people gamble? The answers, of course, are complex and comprehensive. Gambling specialist Scarne's survey asked the question 'Why do you gamble?' Respondents gave the following answers: 75% replied that they gambled primarily to win money; another 25% said that they gambled for pleasure, and, of this group, one-fifth put it in stronger terms by saying that they found nothing more exciting or thrilling.[2]

Gamblers generally don't admit to greed as their prime motivator. Those who view casinos as places to relax tend not to want to characterize the attitudes reflected in the business. The accusation of greed turns casinos into places of 'institutionalized covetousness' not simply entertainment.[3] Covetousness is a biblical word. Rex Rogers says, 'Gambling maximizes covetousness.'[4]

What is covetousness? The sin of covetousness, mentioned frequently in Scripture, has lost its meaning in a society often illiterate both in word derivation and in the Christian content of words. In biblical context 'covet' means extreme desire; a selfish craving beyond self-preservation. In the nineteenth century a Revd John Harris, an independent Protestant, wrote a whole book (311 pages) on the subject.[5]

For the moment forget trying to condense our moral climate, or forget about giving descriptions of what is our consuming social passion. (It's easier to forget than to avoid!) Off or on screen, everybody's slogan is truly, 'Show me the money'.

The illusion is that money comes freely and fast at casinos. The lure of casino gambling first begins with the suggestion that a casino visit saves money. Inducements include low hotel rent, cheap buffets, and free alcoholic drinks. Then the casino visitor is encouraged to think of making money quickly, and large amounts of it, while lotteries hook customers by their convenience. Millionaire wannabes play and lose both at lotteries and casinos. In the nineteenth century the saying went that the only way to win at lotteries is to run one. Today the only sure way to win in casinos is to own one.

Sports betting is a year-round gambler's recreation. And the mega-million contracts for good players in the particular game may fire young athletes for similar huge-paying contracts. Indirectly, that's a little-recognized morale boost to gambling. Everyone would like a piece of the profit pie, but most are prohibited from partaking because of age and other limitations.

Desire drives; desire is a psychological drive. The oldest New Testament book (gauged by the date of writing) is the letter of James. He understood behavioral motivation. The apostle James referred to buried, even in-born, desire as what sucks people into the cycle of sinning (James 1:14): 'but each one is tempted when, by his own evil desire, he is dragged away and enticed' (NIV).

The insights of Scripture

Wealthy citizens must beware lest their accumulation of money replace their desire to know God. Jesus said it was difficult for the rich to enter the kingdom of heaven (Mt. 19:23; Mk. 10:23; Lk. 18:24).

C.S. Lewis [1898–1963] saw Jesus' warning as a reference to money, but more than money. 'I think it really covers riches in every sense – good fortune, health, popularity, and all the things one wants to have, all these things tend – just as money tends – to make you feel independent of God, because if you have them you are happy already and contented in this life.'[6]

A pastor friend, Revd Larry Bechtol, who has served the same church for over twenty-four years, tells of visiting a family in College Hill (on Aspen Drive) in Cincinnati. The wife was a believer and active in her church, but the husband had no ties with the church or with Christ other than his wife being a Christian.

Pastor Bechtol made a visit to the home. The wife was not there, but the husband was. The husband began the conversation by saying that he was a 'stock market gambler' and that that day he had lost $120 thousand dollars. His sizable loss was proof he was a gambler. Most people would not have that much to lose, but he apparently had much more and didn't feel threatened by his loss. (He owned a meat-packing business and had done very well.)

He was a man who had great financial resources, but he had no interest in God, the Bible, or the church. And when his wife became gravely ill, she was taken to the hospital, and later died. The husband was inconsolable, shaken, and without comfort. He had oodles of money, but no sense of God's goodness, grace, and forgiveness.

Some years later the same man had serious health problems that required hospitalization. He came near to dying himself and in Revd Bechtol's visits showed even greater agitation and alarm. All the money he had, all the stock he possessed, did not provide any source of assurance about his life here or his life beyond the point of death. He illustrated the state of those who live for things, sense, material gain, and wealth, but are not right towards God.

Matthew 16:26 applies to those who have great wealth on earth, but are spiritual paupers.

> 26 What good will it be for a man if he gains the whole world, yet forfeits his soul? Or what can a man give in exchange for his soul (NIV)?

The late German theologian Karl Barth [1886–1968] described the man to whom Revd Bechtol tried to minister. Barth wrote, 'In his objective misery he plays the rich man always and everywhere. But engaged in this game he is necessarily closed against God.'[7]

The world gambles away life, not just money. Compulsive gambling is symptomatic of a disruption of God's image in man. The gambler tries to drown his or her anxiety and apprehension about universal flux.

A non-Christian approach to life's vicissitudes is to be gripped by despair and hopelessness because God's role in life is usurped by Lady Luck. Scripture gives an entirely different picture: numerous Bible verses credit God for our material blessings.

These texts are a wealth all their own. They can do more for us than watching Wall Street ticker tapes. Before they can be re-examined, they must be reprinted. They include:

Proverbs 10:9 [8]

> The blessing of the LORD brings wealth,
> and he adds no trouble to it.

Proverbs 11:4

> Wealth is worthless in the day of wrath,
> but righteousness delivers from death.

Matthew 6: 24

No one can serve two masters. Either he will hate the one and love the other, or he will be devoted to the one and despise the other. You cannot serve both God and Money.

Luke 12:15

Then he said to them, 'Watch out! Be on your guard against all kinds of greed; a man's life does not consist in the abundance of his possessions.'

Colossians 3:5

> Put to death, therefore, whatever belongs to your earthly
> nature: sexual immorality, impurity, lust, evil desires and
> *greed* [emphasis added], which is idolatry.

1 Timothy 6:10,17

> For the love of money is a root of all kinds of evil. Some
> people, eager for money, have wandered from the faith and
> pierced themselves with many griefs.

> Command those who are rich in this present world not to
> be arrogant nor to put their hope in wealth, which is so
> uncertain, but to put their hope in God, who richly pro-
> vides us with everything for our enjoyment.

Christians should realize how wealthy they are in Christ,
for they have a heavenly friend in the highest place, and
access to him anytime. God's eternal presence has a form
accessible to us on earth. By consulting God's self-revelation (the Bible) we are in touch with God's presence, at
least His mind. And through contact with Scripture we are
supplied with resources that can't be found in stocks and
bonds. For anyone weary with the cycle of wins and
losses, there is life and new hope in the book where we
look for help last, the Bible. Christ gives an assurance that
troubles cannot destroy, a peace that remains.

In 1825, at the height of his fame, and when he was living at Abbotsford, Sir Walter Scott [1771–1832] had a
printing house that failed. In his diary for that period, he
wrote, 'Naked we entered the world and naked we leave
it; blessed be the name of the Lord . . . I have walked my
last in the domains I have planted – at the last time in the
halls I have built. But death would have taken them from
me if misfortune had spared them.'[9]

Daily manna that kept Israel going in the desert lasted but a day. Mammon, another word for money, like manna doesn't last and can't be taken with you when you die. Mammon stood for luxury and greed. The noted Pascal, scholar of a former generation, Emile Caillet [1874–1981], wrote in his highly acclaimed *The Dawn of Personality*:

> God is ultimately dethroned the moment Mammon is enthroned. Mammon is the perfect incarnation of unlimited power because wealth is the surest path of access to power. The insidious danger of that path, moreover, lies in the fact that it often appears to be a safe, legitimate way.[10]

Craving for more money is the standard Christian explanation of gambling. While large wins entice gamblers, large profits entice corporations to get into the gambling business. The same is true of the illegal gambler.

> A bookmaker is a very different breed who never gambles and generally wins. Unlike the gambler, the bookie carefully calculates odds and then spreads the play around so that, for example, in a seven-horse race with one winner there are six losers. The six losers provide the pay-off for the one winner, plus a small built-in percentage of profit . . . for the bookmaker.[11]

Not just a fanned deck of cards, but greed is on the lap of the card-playing gambler. But is greed confined to the gambler? We are self-deceived if we think that covetousness is the peculiar fault of the financial risk-taking gambler.

London's Charles Haddon Spurgeon [1834–1892], a minister endowed with remarkable intellectual abilities and enormous oratorical talent, would not let the non-gambler get away with thinking that he had escaped the clutches of greed. On Sunday evening, 21 September, 1884, at the age of 50, Spurgeon said,

> Look at a miser; he will not fall into licentiousness, because it is expensive, and he cannot afford it. He is greedy for money, so he sins by covetousness, which is idolatry. He does not go and get drunk, for that is an expensive sin, and he thinks he cannot afford it. The love of money is his besetting sin; his covetousness is like Aaron's rod, it opens its mouth, and swallows up all the other sins.[12]

Smug non-gamblers cannot take pride in their anathemas against gambling and their abstinence from various gambling activities. They are not guiltless, though gambling is not their particular vice.

The profit motive

How badly gain has gripped our society is illustrated by the case of the man who stole an estimated $405,000 for playing lottery rub-off tickets and then left the country. *The Cincinnati Post* reported that a former Anderson Township resident pleaded guilty to laundering only $405,000 from an investment scheme and spending it on the Ohio lottery.[13]

After cheating unsuspecting people in phoney investment schemes (importing military-style night-spy binoculars, clothing and cosmetics), from November 1993 to August 1995, Samuel Dagan, 51, defrauded people of more than $800,000. He then took that money and wasted it on the lottery. When his theft was discovered, he quickly fled the US and went to Australia, where he was found and extradited. The actual sentence in the US District Court of Ohio by Judge Weber on 5 September 1997 was remarkably light, yet it had some heavy penalties. After the defendant pleaded guilty to Count 165 S, he was ordered to serve two years in prison – it could have been twenty – after which his release would require three years of supervision and the restitution of $405,000. The remaining 164 counts were dismissed.

I live in an area where the gambling business has experienced phenomenal growth. Now in nearby Indiana there are several towns with riverboat casinos. Those who funded the operations and those who own and manage them, from a business viewpoint, must be enormously pleased.

A report of their profits for May 1997 indicated a substantial increase. To the east coast there is Atlantic City and to the far west is Las Vegas, two cities with large gambling operations. I've not attempted to report on the gambling activity there. But consider, briefly, just a small section of one corner of Indiana, near Cincinnati, Ohio. I'll spare you a visit and fill you in on one segment of the gambling world.

Gamblers on south-eastern Indiana's two riverboat casinos set a record for betting in May 1997 as more than a quarter of a billion dollars was wagered in Lawrenceburg and Rising Sun.

Nearly 240,000 people flocked to the two floating gambling halls and wagered a whopping $259 million in May – the highest month total since the boats opened in autumn 1996, a report by the Indiana Gaming Commission showed.

The two riverboats' 'win' in May – the amount of money that gamblers lost – totaled nearly $22.2 million. Of that, Hyatt's Grand Victoria Casino in Rising Sun won nearly $11.6 million – out of $ 145.5 million wagered – while gamblers left behind about $10.6 million of the $113.4 million bet at the Argosy Casino in Lawrenceburg . . .

With the summer months ahead – which traditionally are among the strongest in the casino industry – the Rising Sun and Lawrenceburg riverboats are on pace to easily eclipse officials' pre-opening predictions of a combined annual wagering total of $2 billion.[14]

Summer profits exceeded expectations.

South-eastern Indiana's two riverboat casinos saw a record month in August [1997], with gamblers leaving behind more than $27 million at table games and slot machines.

Grand Victoria Casino and Resort in Rising Sun made more than $15.5 million from its casino games, according to an Indiana Gaming Commission report released Monday. That's 23 percent more than July's $12.6 million.

Argosy Casino in Lawrenceburg made more than $11.8 million from its games, up nearly 8 percent from the $10.96 million the casino made in July [1997] . . .

Attendance at Grand Victoria jumped 36 percent in August to 379,624, up from 279,013 in July [1997]. Argosy Casino also saw more people board its riverboat – -278,842 in August compared with 274,505 in July.[15]

The business of gambling is making the owners rich, but leaving the players poor. What has happened close to where I live (Lawrenceburg is 25 miles from my home) is being repeated, even exceeded in the Midwest. Impressive as the monthly gambling figures are in Lawrenceburg and Rising Sun, they are dwarfed by those at the state's highest-producing riverboats, located in north-western Indiana just outside Chicago.

The wagering in May 1997 at the Empress Casino in Hammond, for example, nearly equalled the combined total of the Rising Sun and Lawrenceburg boats. Last month, gamblers bet more than $229 million at Empress. At the Showboat Casino in East Chicago, the monthly wagering total was more than $183 million.[16]

Further west the story is the same. Take Colorado. In addition to money spent in Native American casinos, in the state of Colorado three towns were granted gambling permits in October 1991: Black Hawk, Central City, and Cripple Creek – all relatively close to Denver. All three mountain towns do a brisk gambling business – buses and cars stream in and out, seven days a week.

Colorado's recent casino revenue statistics show a similar growth pattern to other parts of the nation. Their figures for June 1997 vs. June 1996, at Cripple Creek, for instance, were up 7.5 per cent. The town's twenty-four casinos posted $9.9 million in adjusted gross proceeds. Statewide, for the same month, from all gambling enterprises there was $37.2 millions in receipts or 3.3 per cent higher than those of June 1996.[17]

States that don't allow casino gambling have bingo. Bingo profits are small compared to casino gambling. Nevertheless, some go bonkers over bingo.[18] It's a huge favourite with senior adults. They go to bingo halls to socialize, to support a cause, possibly to win. Many bingo events are now advertised as 'smokeless', but what is good for your lungs is not necessarily good for your wallet.

Lotteries have surpassed bingo in revenues. In the glacial spread of lotto a crevasse for evil occurs not in the collection of lottery money but in its distribution. In the UK the otherwise useful reputation of lottery revenues for promoting public good has shown some flaws. Now the distribution of lottery gains has caused Christians to flag its promotion. The National Lottery Charities Board voted in 2000 to fund project Citizen 21 which is a training-workshop on gay and lesbian issues for employers and state agencies[19] While the National Lotteries Charities Board probably argues that such is not a tacit endorsement of homosexuality, the move nonetheless indirectly fosters a form of tolerance which drains opportunity to register outrage against a patently anti-Christian stance. Education support in the traditional sense does not include sexual indoctrination, especially homosexual preferences. Such projects appear to cross the line from education to endorsement and doubtless would never have gained broad support in the seventeenth-century lotteries whose projects such as road improvements, dock renovations and public buildings benefited all citizens. Lottery profits should contribute to the public good.

Opponents of lotteries point out scandals associated with state lotteries. For the most part, however, both state and national lotteries in the US as well as the United Kingdom are safeguarded against and scrutinized for scandals. In a few rare cases corruption occurs. This is the exception. Government-run lottery seems an innocent activity with significant civic and social benefits, not only for the few winners, but for the citizens and the government agencies.

Some, however, like journalist Richard John Neuhaus, think state lotteries play tricks with the public. On lotteries he wrote:

> It's a cheap and dishonest way of raising money. States typically claim that gambling revenues go to 'education' and other motherhood programs, but it is simply a device for exploiting human weaknesses to go generate funds that the government can slush where it will. It is a taxation by another name, but taxation of the vulnerable, and taxation without accountability, which is another form of taxation without representation – which was once in American history a matter of lively concern.[20]

The latter comparison, however, doesn't float historically, although it flies rhetorically, for the simple reason that whereas King George would not allow the colonists a vote through representation, state senators do represent state taxpayers.

The merry-go-round of questions continues: Is lottery's lure extravagance a sly way of avoiding raising of taxes, or a sincere drive to deliver the poor from the pain of their plight? Is the appeal of sweepstakes the temptation to avoid work or the prospect of freeing oneself for more productive avocations? We may always come down on the same side of these issues or we may weaken and grant credibility to opposing views.

Many Christians and non-Christians alike hold that, in moderation, playing lotto is innocent wagering. Few scorn playing small amounts of money because, combined with other money, it finances the nation's and state's operations and fosters admirable social and educational programmes. On a smaller scale, a church may raffle a new car to improve its funds.

Should the wide acceptance of wagering be such a shock? No, according to a former sociologist at New York's Cornell University, who foresaw the legitimization of gambling. He predicted, 'Our society [has moved toward] secularization, to rationalization, to the collapse of real commitment to public morality. Gambling fits into our whole Machiavellian rationale that anything goes if it works.'[21]

Noble reasons or crafty rationalizations?

Again we ask – 'Why do people gamble?' Some creative explanations – or rationalizations – have been offered. A California novelist, William Saroyan, with a number of successful novels and plays several decades ago, reflected on his gambling addiction in his autobiography, *Here Comes/There Goes/You Know Who*.

Getting something back is part of the fantasy of the gambler
. . . not getting back anything, not getting back the money, the
time, the abandoned sequence, or anything else I may have
lost. I have gotten other things, some of them better than the
things lost . . . I may say that every time I have lost enough
money to be deeply annoyed by the enormity of it, which has
always been picayune, even when it has been fifty thousand
dollars, I have gotten something I could not otherwise have
gotten. My money losses are picayune . . . Money itself is picayune. Even so, every time I have lost, and have been
annoyed about the difference between right and wrong, with
the edge of the wrong moving to me, I have made up my
mind to somehow right the wrong, to balance the imbalance,
to earn more than the sum lost. What's more, I have done so,
and it has always been by means of writing. But the point I
am trying to make is that I believe all such writing is writing I
would not have done had I not lost at gambling. Hence, while
I have not always won back the money lost, I have gotten a
number of things from having lost . . . But most important of
all, my annoyance has conditioned what I have written. Consequently, I have a new book, a new novel, or a new play,
with a style I could not have otherwise put into it. The annoyance about the loss of money, of time and sequence, gave the
work its style, and now and then that style has been rare
enough to please me.[22]

Greed explains our thirst for wealth. But it does not go far
enough in uncovering the dynamics of the gambling act.
What is behind the willingness to risk, what drives the
greed? While we may be satisfied with the explanation
that the small-stakes, occasional lotto player isn't consumed with covetousness, how can taking some extra
money, 'fun money', be a grave evil? And where do the
urges that overwhelm those who wager huge amounts of
money come from?

Gamblers are blindly gullible, entering a hope that is based more on fantasy than fact. It is an unbounded, indestructible, even irrational expectation. These wagerers willingly stake their lives, their savings, their families, their reputation, their integrity for the illusive prospect of recouping their losses and of winning huge amounts of money. Maddened by their losses, they are consumed by a desire to recover and become instantly rich.

The stories of recovered gamblers tell how they progressed from normalcy to dependency, from success to bankruptcy, from family wholeness to personal disintegration. How were their hopes aroused? How were they fed? How were they dashed? How were their normal desires replaced? Testimonies of going from riches to rags, phases few would want to repeat, are often heart-wrenching, sad tales.

Clyde Davis introduced a dimension that may go deepest in explaining what propels or draws people into the gambler's web or cycle of risk and lose. In his penetrating *Something for Nothing* he offered the following theory:

> [Are] the minority of Americans who are not at all tempted by any gambling game – are they simply more sane than the average man or woman? Are they well-adjusted individuals who know the value of money and do not care to take a chance where mathematical odds are obviously against them? Indubitably this is sometimes the case. But other individuals, I think are saved by sheer timidity. Then there is the inconsiderable group which refrains from betting because of moral scruples, the group which opposes all sin – with gambling close to the top of the list ... [gamblers have] a sublime, actually mystical, faith in their eventual triumph. It is the indomitable ego. It is the unconquered I AM speaking from the shadowed depths of being, giving pleasant reassurance

to the poor weight that he is, after all, a very, very special person and blessed with subtle powers that given proper opportunity will blossom forth into honest-to-God pre-science or second sight, especially when assisted by his own particular guardian angel, saint or pagan control. . .

'Gambling', said Dr. Theodore Reik, 'is a kind of question addressed to destiny'. In other words, to gamble is to send up a trial balloon to determine how the winds of fortune are blowing. No matter how he may express it (if he expresses it all), everyone longs to be in a state of grace, in tune with the infinite, on the ball, in the groove, riding the crest of the wave, in favor with the goddess Tyche [the Greek Goddess of Fortune] or Lady Luck, in step with the rhythm of the spheres or just plain 'hot'. . . . I do not mean to say that many gamblers go to a casino or race track with the definite idea in mind of finding out whether they are in tune with the infinite or in a state of grace. But I do believe the impulse to gamble is generated more often than not by a subconscious longing for assurance that they are this day in with the strange force or anthropomorphic agency that sees, records, judges and passes out rewards and punishments.[23]

We should go one step further. In the lunge to get rich there may be a subliminal drive to atone for one's inability to achieve great wealth, i.e. the spectacular win at gambling is subconsciously an attempt for man to atone for his failure to be rich. And that goes back to a low self-image. These dynamics are rarely mentioned. It may be part of the picture of what makes a person risk his material possessions.

The gambler is seeking acceptance.

On the surface he is seeking thrills, but they don't come cheap.

What gambling winnings can't do

We know that money can't buy us a clear conscience. It can't buy happiness and inward peace, but a lot of people still love money. We all like as much around as possible. But what inner or eternal good does heaping up money bring?

Money does not satisfy the human spirit, for even after one reaches the pinnacle of earning and acquires enormous financial holdings, one is unsatisfied inside. Our natures are not satisfied until we make contact with God.

> All my life long I had panted
> For a draught from some cool spring
> That I hoped would quench the burning
> Of the thirst I felt within.
>
> Feeding on the husks around me,
> Till my strength was almost gone,
> Longed my soul for something better,
> Only still to hunger on.
>
> Poor I was, and sought for riches,
> Something that would satisfy,
> But the dust I gathered round me
> Only mocked my soul's sad cry.
> Well of water, ever springing
> Bread of life, so rich and free.
> Untold wealth that never faileth,
> My Redeemer is to me.
>
> Hallelujah! I have found him
> Whom my soul so long has craved!
> Jesus satisfies my longings;
> Thro' his blood I now am saved.
>
> (Clara Tear Williams [1858–1937])

Ironically, as God sometimes has it, the person who loses huge amounts of money, and heaps unfair suffering upon loved ones, wives, husbands, children, may be closer to reaching out for the intervention of God in Jesus Christ than the morally smug, the gambling-clean.

Only by losing does a person discover the riches that will never be lost. In fulfilment of Jesus' saying – winners lose and losers win.

The uncertainty of riches (Jas. 4:13–16) links into the truth of the folly of living solely for gain. Strangely, of all our negative desires, greed is the narrowest, i.e. one dimensional in its hope. The farmer who looked to larger future profits replaced a modest silo with a larger silo. His hope was to make substantially more. What Jesus faulted him for was not for being future-oriented but for not being future-oriented enough, i.e., he missed anticipating the potential loss of living for greed (Lk. 12:18). Therefore, our occupation with making money should be tempered with 'give us this day our daily bread' (Mt. 6:11).

12.

Winning in Christ

How we view Jesus is far more important than whether wagering has any value. In Pascal's perspective, the ultimate wager is betting the Bible is right. Our decision, however, should not be made like a mindless dice throw, spin of a wheel, or the flip of a coin.

In the New Testament various features of Jesus together form a unified conviction that Jesus was God in human form. Willing to bet that Jesus was all that the writers claimed? Those who decide not to go with Jesus in the New Testament documents make a poor choice, a bad decision, and have gambled unwisely. The smart approach is to investigate the evidence first-hand and find out for ourselves.

But for those who get into the historic Christian gospel discover it is less a gamble and more a venture with small risk. Not the risk of losing our souls, but the risk of losing self-pride, the risk of losing a self-centered existence. But in accepting Jesus' Lordship we discover more excitement than the high stakes any earthly gamble could produce.

Preoccupation with and absorption in winning money on earth can be our worst downfall. The great tragedy of modern times is that everyone is over-concerned about making money, winning money, saving money, growing money, spending money, even investing money, and has not turned to the central direction of his or her inner life. These folk long for the gospel of wealth rather than seek the wealth of the Christian Gospel.

Diversions may not only occupy but dominate our spare time. We may plunge into activities and entertainments to forget the big picture, our most crucial choice. But we cannot ultimately avoid dealing with Jesus Christ. Now or later we are answerable to God after we have been confronted with the historic personage of Christ and frequent New Testament claims to His Lordship. It is foolhardy to seek serial earthly fun and not address ultimate issues, such as our relationship with God, such as union with Christ and our connection with him.

One cannot avoid Christ forever. Wisdom says be open to him. If we go through life, banking on Christ's claims about himself, and they prove to be a hoax, then we have lost some time and investments. But if we go through life and ignore Christ and he turns out to be all that he said, then we hit tragic spiritual insolvency, and encounter our greatest loss.

Non-gamblers, who avoid Christ, are the biggest gamblers of all. Obviously, getting the anti-gambler to part with his money, if he or she doesn't have a philanthropist heart, is as difficult as getting ginger ale out of an orange. Such people would not think of playing the ponies or of buying a lotto ticket, but nevertheless they gamble with their very destiny.

Where do we strike it rich?

Where do people seek a glorious present or a fabulous future? The worst bet is to seek fortune in everything but Christ. People bypass Christ as if he were a has-been, a distant figure in a far-away culture, a dry historic personage with no dynamic, devoid of interest.

Sometimes, however, the greatest wealth is found where least expected. Ruth Sheldon Knowles, a US oil consultant, chronicled a series of fascinating stories about oil wildcatters or gamblers.[1] In the wake of Edwin L. Drake, who began the first commercial oil well (near Titusville, Pensylvania) in 1859, for instance, was Captain Anthony F. Lucas, an Austrian immigrant who had a hunch that oil might be locked in the unlikely place of salt domes. He started drilling near Beaumont, Texas, and in 1901, struck Spindletop.

Within weeks, no fewer than six gushers, that could produce more oil than the rest of the world combined, were struck. Spindletop spouted some 50 million barrels, and spawned the then three greatest oil-producing companies: Humble, Texas, and Sun. Oil has been found in a number of unlikely places. Harry Sinclair liked to drill in cemeteries or places where blackjacks grew, hunches that netted him a $700 million oil empire.

Too few consider that seeking the Christ of the New Testament is where we best drill for personal riches. In the Christ, formerly judged dull, we discover a resource for this life and the next that never runs dry. Unlike subterranean oil deposits, Jesus keeps on producing, here and hereafter, without any chance of running dry. A probe of the New Testament record yields a hit upon gold that never tarnishes or loses its value.

In contrast is the sad, blind belief in illusory lucky feelings motivating the occasional as well as the habitual gambler. Whether one bets infrequently or regularly, gambling losses diminish one's sense of worth, acceptance, and sense of divine love. The gambler feels the odds against him are overwhelming and he indulges in self-hate, and that self-hate propels him deeper into gambling debts. Even the so-called safer bets in stock investment can leave a person unfulfilled, for money and material things will not quench the thirst of humans for their Maker.

Mathematical probability is indifferent as to who experiences its patterns. 'The laws of chance are indifferent to the name of the winner.'[2] But in Christianity our welfare is not a matter of indifference to God. God is involved in charting our lives. God planned ahead for our salvation and secured it in the pro-active saving deeds of Jesus Christ.

Just because we don't fraternize with gamblers or visit gaming sites doesn't mean we don't gamble with our destinies. We may be mentally tricked by false ideas far away from gambling dens. Paul referred to this in Ephesians 4:14. Below are two modern translations.

> 14 As a result, we are no longer to be children, tossed here and there by waves, and carried about by every wind of doctrine, by the trickery of men, by craftiness in deceitful scheming (NASB).

> 14 Then we shall no longer be children, or tossed one way and another, and carried hither and thither by every new gust of teaching, at the mercy of all the tricks people play and their unscrupulousness in deliberate deception (NJB).

The words 'trickery' (NASB) and 'tricks people play' (NJB) refer to gambling. We gamble, Paul warned, when 'we are carried about by every changing wind of teaching, by the "dice playing" of men, with cunning skill in the way of seduction' (Eph. 4:14 paraphrased).

The King James Version uses the word 'sleight', a translation of the Greek word *kubeia*, from which we get our English word 'cube', meaning 'wicked dice playing', referring to 'intentional fraud'.[3] Ephesians 4:14 is the only New Testament usage of *kubeia*.[4]

Cubes were used as dice for gambling. And at that time there was no regulation about the manufacture and construction of the dice. Dice were sometimes loaded, weighted, or purposefully made to be unsymmetrical to give an advantage to the gambler. Fraud was a part of gambling then. People won by deceit.

The verses surrounding Ephesians 4:14 refer to mental risk-taking in society's stream of ideas where there is potential seduction. Others may take advantage of our ignorance and draw us in to wager our beings with seemingly credible ideas, which turn out to be a false hope.

What are our chances?

God never wants us to think that our salvation is the result of an indifferent fate, a coin toss, a straw pull, a random draw. Our lives are too precious to be gamed away and committed to chance. God has taken an active role on our behalf. Because of who he is and what he has provided, we have the hope of eternal life.

A major 'snafu' happened at American Family Publishers, an organization that markets all kinds of magazines. Millions of US home owners are on their mailing list and they make a yearly appeal to sell magazines at reduced rates with the hook that they may hold a 'lucky' number that will bring them free millions. There is hardly a household not on their mailing list. Strangely, they even have God on their mailing list. And where did they find God? In Sumter Country, Florida. In the mail they notified God that he may be very, very rich.

A sweepstakes notice arrived at the Bushnell Assembly of God [in February, 1997] announcing God, of Bushnell Fla., was a finalist for the $11 million top prize.

'I always thought he lived here but I didn't actually know,' said Bill Brack, pastor of the church about 60 miles north of Tampa. 'Now I do. He's got a P.O. box here.'

'God, we've been searching for you,' American Family wrote in the letter, as first reported by the local weekly newspaper, the *Sumter County Times*.

The message was centered between two round seals requesting God to 'come forward'.

If God were to win, the letter stated, 'what an incredible fortune there would be for God! Could you imagine the looks you'd get from your neighbors? But don't just sit there, God.'

Pastor Brack said his 140-person congregation is considering whether to mail in the entry. The church could use the money.

If they win, Pastor Brack said, he'd settle with American Family for 10 percent on the dollar and call it even.

And if American Family chooses a different winner?

'God would be disappointed,' Pastor Brack joked.[5]

Pastor Brack knew God would not be disappointed. God would laugh that any promotional company could expand his fortune. After all, his wealth is so vast he needs no supplements, no donations. In addition, he has no need for investment for his riches to grow. He owns all already.

33 Oh, the depth of the riches of the wisdom and knowledge of God!
How unsearchable his judgments,
and his paths beyond tracing out!
34 'Who has known the mind of the Lord?
Or who has been his counsellor?'
35 'Who has ever given to God,
that God should repay him?'
36 For from him and through him and to him are all things.
To him be the glory forever! Amen (Rom. 11:33–36 NIV).

God's interest is not in building his wealth, but in sharing it! He is the donor, and man is in need of his wisdom-wealth.

Three texts in Ephesians speak of God's wealth, and of how we share in it as we participate in Christ.

18 I pray also that the eyes of your heart may be enlightened in order that you may know the hope to which he has called you, *the riches of his glorious inheritance in the saints* (1:18 NIV).

7 in order that in the coming ages he might *show the incomparable riches of his grace, expressed in his kindness to us in Christ Jesus* (2:7 NIV).

8 Although I am less than the least of all God's people, this grace was given me: to preach to the Gentiles *the unsearchable riches of Christ* (3:8 NIV).

Spiritual riches outlast any worldly holdings. Access to God's storehouse, the vault of Christ's wealth, is a goal humans should seek. Our amassed fortunes cannot fulfil our deepest longings and our greatest needs. Gamblers have forgotten to apply to God for the wealth that eludes them in their 'jackpot' quests. He is both giver and guarantor of the inner riches, eternal life.

Christ did not conduct his life by following personal whims, but in a commitment to the will of his Father. He was not gambling with his life, but he had a grip on it. He knew who he was and why he came. (The disciples had a hard time latching on to what he said about what was ahead for him and them.)

Jesus was not God's dice thrown on the world, but the arrival of the all-knowing incarnate Son bent on fulfilling his Father's plan. We are not making a gamble when we put our lives in Christ's hands. He was ahead of the future.

He was in control of all time – past, present, future – as the Apostle Paul consistently and cogently argued in his letters.

Especially in John's Gospel, Christ himself was in possession of himself, aware of the dynamics that plotted his arrest and death, fully assured Satan's schemes would backfire and result in his own undoing. No one took his life, he laid it down. It was not that Christ was tricky in the way he played his hand. He was a planner in partnership with the other members of the Trinity. He was both outrider and general, pivotal participant in envisioning, effecting, and executing the redemption of his church. He was the redemptive Lamb ready to win the release of innumerable lost humans.

Our search for wealth in Christ is not secured or enhanced by thinking of his legacy as having better odds over a rival system. Jesus just doesn't fit into the question of good odds vs. poor odds. Why? – because of the meaning and application of odds. Refer back to the meaning of odds: a quick review of the significance of odds from Chapter 10 reminds us that there are two kinds of probability.

Probability has two senses: The first sense is what concerns gamblers. It is statistical probability. Statistical probability is based on the long-run stability of frequent ratios. In everyday gambling ventures, how many times will the dice come up in favour of the player? The second concept of probability has to do with the degree of likelihood a proposition or position is right, based on given evidence. Probability #2 has to do with intellectual, moral, and spiritual values. Whereas the gambler is concerned with the statistical probability of winning, an empirical concept, a world-view evaluator is concerned with the inductive probability that a moral judgment is more likely right than wrong.[6]

Do odds apply to Jesus?

Jesus is not a better figure to trust because of mathematical odds. He is Lord and Saviour not because of occurrences and statistics, but because of divine revelation. The non-Christian thinker often can't accept that a supernatural God exists, that he is capable of self-revelation. But that divine self-revelation was made through Old Testament spokespersons, and finally in the person of Jesus Christ. Jesus' uniqueness and supremacy expressed in his self-revelation forms the foundation of his durability and dependability. Of course, if uniqueness is associated with and judged by a single instance, then Christ's bodily resurrection catapults Him to the topmost or lead position of greatness, for according to the apostle Paul, Christ was the first in resurrection (Col. 1:18).

Therefore, it is both improper and unnecessary to access Jesus' value, worship stature, and role because he gains more points than others in popularity ratings. Strictly speaking, judging Jesus by odds is a false and inappropriate means of assessment. If that is the basis for our judgment then that would mean we rely on the method of those in Jesus' lifetime who considered him expendable. When Jesus lived, the majority of spiritual leaders felt he was a fraud. Calculation of Jesus' claims, on the basis of his contemporaries, would mean he was not the Messiah, Saviour, and Lord.

But Jesus' titles were rendered authentic, not on the basis of human comparisons and calculations, but because of divine certification/verification. We mis-speak in putting odds on Jesus' life and ministry, as if his rating is the result of a long series of percentage odds. Whether the odds are good or poor depends on percentages, numerical calculations, and volume.

Statistical tabulations don't apply to Jesus, for he was in a distinctive category. His moral glory is not established because he edged out others in a poll. Christ is incomparable. He stands alone. He is not just another man in the series of humanity. His worth is not enhanced or judged by how he stacks up to X number of individuals throughout history.

Even numerous and repeat miracles, *per se*, do not establish his dignity and authority. His supremacy and titles of deity are due to his inherent uniqueness and Person.

On the basis of odds, Jesus had no chance of resurrection, for everyone before him had died. Jesus underwent death, but unlike any other person he was resurrected. No one has been resurrected like Jesus. He truly died on the cross, and he arose from death, alive. That the Christian faith is a credible and superior system stems from Christ's resurrection. Otherwise, as St Paul suggested, if Christ be not risen, our faith is in vain (1 Cor. 15:14).

To have odds, there must be legitimate comparisons. Jesus was not like other men. His inherent dignity was not something he grew into, fabricated or foisted on his followers. Deity was endemic to his nature. Therefore, good odds/poor odds (chance comparison) is foreign to the subject of our estimation of him. Our Lord was unique.

The second sense of probability applies to Jesus

Christian probability has less to do with statistics than with substance, or the truthfulness of the accounts, the truthfulness of the message. How probable is it that the gospel of Jesus' death, burial, and resurrection actually happened and is unrepeatable? We are out of the realm of mathematics and into the realms of factual accuracy and personal evaluation.

Does Christianity discount or deny that probability applies to Christ's Saviour role? How does high probability compare to the certainty reflected in Christian witness from the days of the apostles to the present? What is the Christian position on probability?

Probability is about the content of Jesus' character and the likelihood of his claims as a faith-risk. What counts after our lives are finished, when the final divine audit is in, is not that we accumulated a fortune, nor even that we were good stewards. More importantly, the key determining factors are the probability of Christ being what he claimed and that we belong to him. The cash we earn, save, or win has no relationship to our eternal felicity or loss of it. Those rich on earth can be paupers in eternity. There is no direct correlation between successful investments on earth and successful entrance into heaven at death.

When it comes to our eternal destiny, which for Christians is a new beginning, everyone wants to be a winner. Bet to win is the pattern of every gambler. Each gambler wants to be and won't be satisfied without a win. Winning is not just the best thing, it is everything. Winning in Christ is not due to luck, but to God's pre-emptive redemptive activity and mercy.

Touting fiscal wins and economic gains can leave us unfulfilled. Jesus asked that famous question: 'What shall it profit a man if he gain the whole world, but forfeit his life?' Since in the final analysis, the purpose of life is not financial comfort but conformity to God, contact with and enjoyment of God, we must therefore risk our destiny on Jesus' reliability and resurrection. Are Christ's claims trustworthy? Christianity does not spring from speculation, it stems from reliable and real history. Personal exposure to Scripture is essential to Christian salvation.

Historical certainty substantiates the highest probability of the New Testament having continuing relevance and reliability. Historical evidence indirectly honours Christianity's claims to be true. Before we see ourselves on the winning side, judge the probability of Christ being right, of being what is claimed for him in the New Testament.

Jesus did not quake at the cross or on the cross because it was futureless. He did not gamble with his life, but saw that nothing but good would issue out of the evil ordeal. He saw the prospect, the good goal, of the redeemed hosts. It was part of the joy set before him. Precisely because Jesus knew life was not a gamble with his Father on the throne, is why we can commit ourselves to God without a worry. He takes care of our past, our present, and our future.

13

Can a Christian Ever Gamble?

Some consider the urge to bet to be as old as the human race; that it was in the garden of Eden that our first parents fell for the bad odds of a four-flushing serpent and gamed away Paradise.

We have, of course, no artifacts or textual clues that gambling took place in Eden. But we do know gambling was an ancient pastime. Archaeologists have discovered dice in the excavations of ancient Nineveh.

Ancient artifacts

Board games, though not mentioned specifically in the Bible, have been found in a number of archaeological excavations. . . . Inlaid gaming boards were known from Ur as early as the twenty-sixth century B.C. Likewise, game boards and boxes have been uncovered from Egypt dating to the third and second millennia B.C. One Egyptian set is fully preserved. Of the ten ivory playing pieces five were carved with dogs' heads and five with jackals' heads. These pieces were apparently moved around a playing board with numerous holes for the pieces. Three astragali (animal knuckle bones) served as the dice to determine moves. Game boards have also been found in Palestine. An ivory board from Megiddo is largely circular with fifty-eight holes for pieces to move along. A limestone game board from Tell Beit Mirsim has fifteen ruled squares and ten playing pieces of blue faience, five cone-shaped and five tetrahedrons. It also has a small die in the shape of a truncated pyramid, with numbers on the four sides. Unfortunately, no evidence remains to indicate how these games were played. However, games must have been enjoyed as much in biblical times as checkers, chess, backgammon, and similar games are today.[1]

Dice with numbers on four sides were found thousands of years before Christ's birth. Dice dated to the early second millennium BCE at Gaza and Tell Beit Mirsim were shaped like truncated four-sided pyramids and numbered with from one to four dots only.[2] A gaming board was found on the isle of Crete dated to 1800 to 1650 BCE.

In the ancient city of Rome gaming tables were found in the corridors of the Coliseum. Emperors Augustus, Caligula, Claudius, Nero, and Domitian, all of whom had plenty of extra money, gambled regularly.[3] 'Tacitus, the Roman historian who lived about AD 100, noted that gambling was very common among the tribes of Germany.'[4] In the ruins of Pompeii, in Italy, gambling tables were found beneath the lava.

Jews had form of dice called *urim* and *thummim* (see Chapter 4, footnote 7). The high priest officially decided matters of state significance through these two dice-like objects. This was a far cry from gambling, per se. There was no gambling, as such, sanctioned by the use of the *urim* and *thummim*.

Jewish historians have pointed out that 'while the Hebrews were . . . acquainted with gambling (Judges 14), it was only from mishnaic days onward that the rabbis took a definitive attitude toward gambling'.[5] The Jews of Medieval Europe were known to engage in lotteries, betting by cards, and wagering by dice.[6] 'While public opinion looked down upon it, all the private and communal efforts to stem the tide of gambling did not stop Jews from indulging frequently.'[7]

Morality questions

Gambling is entertaining, if not entertainment, but is it evil? Is gambling an innocent pastime or an immoral activity? When Christians vehemently lambast lotteries are they not falling into the excess of US prohibitionists in the twenties who declared liquor the big evil? Is a neutral dice throw 'an odious vice'?[8] Is gambling naughty or just knotty? Is cessation of all wagering the ideal God desires humans to aim at and achieve? Or is a basic occupation with materialistic lifestyle expressed by some in wishing to get-rich-quick the real problem? Or is the more basic human problem a desire to live independent of everyone including God?

Should gaming for gain be condemned as sin? A realization that gambling was something to repent of was part of the religious conversion of US frontier evangelist Peter Cartwright, a Methodist [1785–1872]. (Cartwright, an evangelist to whom President Abe Lincoln liked to listen, was an itinerant, horse-riding preacher of a bygone age in Ohio and Kentucky when they were wilderness.) Cartwright was known to be fiery. Gambling at cards was one topic which brought him to a quick boiling point.

I was a very successful young gambler; and though I was not initiated into the tricks of regular gamblers, yet I was very successful in winning money [at cards]. This practice was very fascinating, and became a special besetting sin to me, so that, for a boy, I was very much captivated by it . . . O, the sad delusions of gambling! How fascinating, and how hard to reclaim a practiced gambler! Nothing but the power of Divine grace saved me from this wretched sin.[9]

Unlike Peter Cartwright, others see the use of their money in wagering as a diversion rather than a dreadful sin. On the other hand, those who never were drawn into various forms of gambling still regard it as part of a larger evil enterprise. They look at the organizers of gambling and they wonder. Look at the characters who back, run, and promote gambling operations! Gambling critics refuse to give gaming a clean bill of spiritual health because of its connection with the wider picture of sensualism, materialism, and self-indulgence.

From a Christian viewpoint the impropriety of gambling is established, many contend, by organized crime's stake in gambling operations. One criterion used in determining the morality of gambling is the company it keeps. Since criminals crowd to gambling, the argument is, it must be evil. Fred J. Cook was convinced that gambling draws crooks faster than sugar-water draws wasps. In the 1960s he wrote in *A Two Dollar Bet Means Murder*, 'Gambling is the heartbeat of organized crime both on a local and a national scale'.[10] Illegal gambling operations are traditionally off-limits to Christians.

A gambling obsession revolts many Christians' sense of frugality, responsibility, and spiritual commitment. They are sure gambling is a sin. Surprisingly, however, not every Christian is convinced that all forms of gambling are prohibited and pronounced wrong by God. They ask, 'What about the miniscule gambling element in investments?' Lurking behind the huge affair of making money through stocks is whether financial investments avoid gambling. (See Chapter 3 where this was looked at in detail.)

Moral outrage should be muted if playing the stock market is a form of gambling. It seems stock investments carry a strand or show a trace of gambling DNA. *Stocks, while not of the same species as gambling, are of the same genus. As house cats are not lions (species), yet both are cats (i.e. of the same genus).* Risk-taking does not prove gambling, but stock investment can be a gambling event.

What about Jesus' commendation of those who wisely risked investment of their money (Mt. 25:14–30)?[11] Even if the passage makes no veiled reference to wagering, what if a person takes the wealth earned through investments and takes the family for a vacation to Monte Carlo or the French Riveria, or in the other direction, to a gambling city such as Nevada's Las Vegas? Would that be an instance of the use of good money in a questionable area?

According to the US National Gambling Commission, an overwhelming majority of Americans (more than 89% in 1995) regard casino gambling an acceptable activity.[12] In 1995, approximately 50 million people played the slot machines at least once.[13] In 1996, Americans visited casinos 176 million times.[14] Britons, apparently, have an equally broad and accepting view of legal lotteries. Losses through lotto in the UK are considerable, for it has been calculated that Britons in 1988, for instance, averaged out to the equivalent of $200 loss per person, compared to the equivalent of $230 in Japan.[15]

To be entertained a person doesn't need to take a jet to Europe. Anyone can gamble through the internet and at the local store or lottery outlet. In the same report, 82 per cent of US gambling is in lotteries. 'Nationwide [US], total [lottery] sales [in 1996] reached $34.2 billion, a 7 per cent increase over 1995.'[16]

The lottery is both a national and a local game, as is sports wagering. In the US, 26 per cent bet on 1995 sports events. With the proliferation of teams and games, and

with the accessibility of wagering venues the amount
defies accurate calculation.

Pensioners who are solvent and have been successful
sometimes succumb to day-trips to casinos. They have,
they believe, discretionary money for various forms of
entertainment. And within that permissibility they see
nothing wrong with spending money at gambling without expecting to make any money in return.

Tracking down Christian gamblers

How many of the gambling public – in the UK as well as
the US – are Christians? According to some definitions
of Christians, a true Christian never gambles. Even if
we acknowledge that a few Christians occasionally
wager, we can never know exactly how many true
Christians gamble.

On top of that I've wondered how honest some Christians are about gambling. Again, what do you consider
gambling? All queries should begin with defining gambling. Only after we know what gambling is can we determine whether or not we have gambled. We may agree on
what gambling is, but to maintain privacy we'll decline to
admit having gambled.

Do Christians gamble?

In *Reader's Digest* a humorous anecdote, ascribed to a
J.E. Bedenbaugh, told of the comment of his grandmother,
a staunch US Southern Baptist, who had made sure he was
always in church and Sunday School. He said, 'When I
switched to the Episcopal Church after marriage, she challenged me: "What's wrong with the Baptist Church,
son?". '

' "Well," I explained, "Carole and I flipped a coin to see
if we would go to her church or mine, and I lost." '

' "Serves you right," said my grandmother. "Good Baptists don't gamble." '

Good Episcopalians have and do gamble! (And if Baptists made a full disclosure, it would be found that some, if not many, of them do too!)

What may surprise many modern Christians is that some colonial American Christians, Baptist and Episcopalian, saw nothing but good in lotteries. Start with the sterling Father of the US, the first President, George Washington. He may have resisted lying as a youth ('I cannot tell a lie'), but as an adult, he easily and freely gambled at cards and horses.

President Washington passionately warned against the evils of gambling ('Gambling is the child of avarice, the brother of iniquity, and the father of mischief'), but he bought the first lottery ticket to build the new capital.[17] And he gambled at the racetrack and with cards. Gambling, then, was a rich man's diversion and a gentleman's privilege.

Washington fitted into the pattern of Virginia's great planters. He bet on horses. In late seventeenth- and early eighteenth-century Virginia, gentlemen spent a good deal of time gambling:

The great planters' passion for gambling, especially on quarter-horse racing,[18] coincided with a period of far-reaching social change in Virginia. Horse-racing generated far greater interest among the gentry than did the household games. Indeed, for the great planters and the many others who came to watch, these contests were pre-eminently a social drama. The great planters dominated [the quarter-horse races]. In the records of the county courts we find the names of some of the colony's most prominent planter families – Randolph, Eppes, Jefferson, Swan, Kenner, Hardiman, Parker, Cocke, Batte, Harwich (Hardidge), Youle (Yowell), and Washington.[19]

Washington visited the Williamsburg Jockey Club where he bet. Also, he bet on horses at Annapolis (his 1772 diary recorded a loss there). 'Gambling was a recreation, like a good meal among friends or a leisurely hunt in the woods – a pleasant pastime when hard-working planters got together.'[20]

Washington's diaries leave a paper trail, for in them he regularly entered his losses and wins at cards.[21] 'Both men and women gambled at cards. Mrs Thomas Jefferson had a long run of bad luck, but George Washington gallantly lost money – perhaps to put the ladies in good humor.'[22] One historian pointed out that the same table in 1776, where Washington penned an order that his soldiers did not gamble, on other occasions was where he bet at cards.[23] And, the revolutionary soldiers' uniforms and weapons, noted Frank Fahrenkopf, Jr., were secured from gaming revenue.[24] Washington set the tone for the typical hypocritical politician, making a public denunciation but practising the vice in private. That inconsistency continues to emerge in modern government positions.

Diarist Philip Vickers Fithian [born 1747], a plantation tutor of the Old Dominion (Virginia), referred to a Tuesday afternoon of boat racing. One boat had five oarsmen; the other had six, all Negroes, upon whom small bets were made. After the boat of Captain Benson (with five oarsmen) won, a Captain Purchace 'offered to bett ten Dollars that with the same Boat & same Hands, only having Liberty to put a small Weight in the Stern, he would beat Captain Benson'.[25]

'Can Christians gamble and *not* violate God's law?' Colonial American Christians didn't take long to answer that question. And it was often a surprising 'yes'. Some colonial Christians thought lotteries good things because lotteries benefited their churches and their Christian colleges (Harvard, Yale, the College of New Jersey – later called Princeton). Although the Quakers fought lotteries in Pennsylvania, two Philadelphia churches (St Peter's and St Paul's), however, received £3,003 and 15 shillings. Other Anglican parishes benefited, too, in the 1756 lottery in Carlisle, York, Reading, Molatten, Chichester, and Concord.[26]

Of course, because of the good causes, Christians supported lotteries as benevolent acts. But Christians were gamblers for other reasons than that Christian missions were funded. Social good outside the church was also a Christian goal.

Betting on quarter-horse races aside, public lotteries evolved into a more Christian approach to meeting social needs. Admittedly, some of the early lotteries were conducted to promote merchandising schemes, and to profit a few of the persons who had the right ticket. One lottery was held to get a person out of debt. He would sell tickets, a lot of tickets, more than what he would expect for his house, and have enough left over to pay all his bad debts and keep his house. According to historian John Ezell 'most' of the 'early projects . . . were merchandising schemes', such as that of Alexander Kerr, who advertised in the Virginia Gazette, in 1737, a raffle of diamonds in his Williamsburg jewellery store.[27]

In the US, the States were the primary beneficiaries of lotteries. Between 1776 and 1789, there were one hundred lotteries, and by the year 1815 there were 620 new lotteries. Between 1815 and 1840, there were 412 lotteries. All these eased the tax burden of the average citizen.[28] But there was the hidden burden some felt of justifying lotteries before God. What helped pave the way for lottery acceptance was the eventual acceptance that insurance was not a violation of trust in God's rule.

Insurance a form of wagering?

Does insurance go against God?

Openness to accepting mathematical chance within the providence of God came about, albeit slowly, in regard to the debate over the moral propriety of insurance. The attitude of willingness to accept the lottery principle, in a sense, was an extension of the gradual acceptance of insurance by Christians. David L. McKenna noted,

> 'During the mercantile period in the Middle Ages, insurance was invented for merchants who sent their goods to sea against the odds that the ships would be attacked by pirates. Church fathers opposed insurance because God controlled the destiny of ships as well as men. Not only did insurance show a lack of faith – it was gambling on the will of God. But today Christians do not consider insurance an 'actuarial numbers racket'; it is used as an example of commendable stewardship planning.[29]

Today anti-gambling Christians justify buying insurance on the basis that one tries to 'eliminate the problems caused by what is unpredictable'.[30] But that same argument can be used to justify buying a lottery ticket!

Petersen claims that to gamble is to 'exploit chance'. (Most anti-gamblers, however, would view the gambler as being exploited by chance.) Petersen claimed that insurance does not exploit anyone. He should have few buyers of that position. Rather, it seems, the insured exploit the insurance company by getting what they did not fully pay for, if they die young or earlier than expected.

Insurance is a hedge against the unanticipated premature loss of life and limb. Unlike gambling, however, in life insurance (other than term insurance) you can get back what was paid in by cashing in the policy, or you can borrow against it. The law of averages works in favour of the insurance companies being profitable to themselves. Those with no life, health, or other insurance are the real gamblers and those covered by policies are not gamblers.

Apparently, modern Christians have mixed opinions about gambling, yet they are universally keen on insurance. They may recognize lottery playing as gambling, but they don't think insurance is intrinsically evil.

Christian gamblers?

Dr James Dobson, founder of the US Colorado Springs immense Focus on the Family Ministries, mentioned one of his visits to Las Vegas. He and his wife even refused the two free rolls of coins given them when they checked into their hotel.[31] From what else he wrote we may safely assume he didn't spend his own money in the casinos either.[32]

Is that typical of Christians and of modern evangelicals? Or will an evangelical Christian play the slots or buy an occasional lottery ticket? Bill Hybels, pastor of the patently evangelical, now world-famous, Willow Creek Community Church in suburban Illinois, surveyed his Sunday morning congregants and found that nearly 20 per cent of the respondents had participated in some form of gambling.[33] (The survey did not specify how gambling was defined!)

Dennis P. McNeilly, a psychologist at the University of Nebraska's Omaha Medical Center, pointed out that churches sponsor bus trips to casino venues.[34] In Kansas City, some churches have banquets at their floating casino.[35] Richard J. Klemp, director of government affairs for the corporate office of Harrah's Casino in Memphis, said that a lot of church groups gamble, including delegates at the 1998 annual convention of the Black Baptist group, the National Baptists, held in Kansas City.[36] What about Christian elderly in nursing homes which sponsor bingo?

Twenty per cent of the Willow Creek attenders admitted to gambling in the last year that they surveyed the membership. I suspect that was a gross *under*estimation. One has to admire the honesty of the late Wayne E. Oates, Senior Research Professor at Louisville Southern Baptist Seminary, in reference to some Kentucky Christians on Derby Day, one of the more famous horse races in the world. He wrote:

> Many people indulge in gambling only on special occasions, primarily for the fun of sharing in a pastime with friends and associates. For example, Christians and unbelieving secularists gather in backyards on Derby Day in Louisville to watch the Kentucky Derby run on television. A backyard betting pool is formed, and people who never bet at any other time do so for fun. When Derby Day is over, they never think about gambling again until the next Derby Day. If they win, they congratulate themselves on being lucky, for they know little or nothing about horses and the secrets of 'the odds.' Very strict religionists would call this a terrible sin that separates one from God. However, common sense would see it as a fun-filled pastime.[37]

Christians may gamble year-round and not realize they have engaged in a gamble. If insurance is a gamble and speculative stocks are gambling, then 98 per cent of Christians gamble! 'Never that high!' someone says. OK, you've got me. No one, to my knowledge, has surveyed a sizable slice of professing Christians on the rightness or wrongness of gambling in all its forms. I've made a guestimation.

Christians bet in at least four ways

Christians bet? You bet. Astonishing numbers of church-goers are giving in and gambling. Part of the problem is that wagering infiltrates all of life. The lottery issue aside, insurance aside – Christians gamble without knowing it. If gambling goes on in stocks, then my high guestimate of how many Christians gamble is probably on target.

In addition, what about the gamble in pension programmes? Most Christians, I suspect, belong to a pension plan. Every pension is invested in stocks, most into a certain percentage of speculative stocks, too. It is money earned from stocks that future retirers will receive. In the case of pensions, pension members are willing to let professional stock-market experts invest their money. I belong to a pension plan I know invests in the stock market. So in my pension programme I'm a secondary-level gambler. I pay professional stock-market managers to invest my money wisely.

My pension programme is gambling on a secondary level. The problem with this claim, however, is that while the pension personnel make investments, they are not involved in classic wagering, and therefore are not promoting or practicing gambling. Admittedly, investing is not wagering. Not all gambling is wagering.[38] Risking with potential financial gain or loss, however, makes for a partial form of gambling in pension programmes and in other investments, not just straight wagering, *per se*.

When brokers are paid to invest money, isn't that promoting gambling? Brokers are middlemen or 'asset allocators and trading managers [who charge fees of usually] 2 per cent to 4 per cent of assets per year, [and] relieve [me] of making the ultimate decision'.[39]

On a much smaller level, participation in the endless magazine sweepstakes (cf. the lotteries of *Readers' Digest*,[40]

*Consumers' Report, Publishers' Clearing House, American
Family Publishers* [cf. Ed McMahan/Dick Clark – 'You may
be a Millionaire!'] – and *Sweepstakes*), in which the odds of
winning are next to nil, is at the bottom of the gambling
scale. The money participants put out is minimal for post-
age. Again, it is not a wager, but resorting to a form of
lottery.

Lottery is indeed a recognized form of gambling. Instead
of spending money on expensive chocolate, some use that
money on a lotto ticket. Instead of the chocolate passing
from lips to hips, they say better 'kiss off' a dollar or a pound
in the lottery than surrender a pound in chocolate candy.
Critics of lotteries would say: whereas the chocolate pounds
or dollars go 'to the waist', lotto money immediately goes 'to
waste' and with nothing to show for it.

How many Christians see no problem in money spent
on lotteries? I first met a lottery winner in church. When I
was pastoring Miners Mills (Welsh) Congregational (my
first church) of Wilkes-Barre, Pennsylvania, the church
organist, a Welsh lady, a Mrs Evans, I recall, won a spank-
ing-new Plymouth car one year in a sweepstake. I saw the
car. I saw Mrs Evans' grin. Lottery chances are always
slim, but then there are winners.

Several years ago I attended a conference of ministers
in Toledo, Ohio. There were public plenary sessions as
well as seminars. At the opening plenary session – a ques-
tion-and-answer period – there followed the inaugural
presentation by the California pastor/president of Master's College and Seminary, Dr John MacArthur, Jr., a well-
known evangelical spokesman. He was the main attraction. Fortunately, before the dialogue session was ended, I
got in the last question.

On one of the open microphones I asked him his
views on gambling. I was especially interested in what
he said to my follow-up question about stocks and

gambling. He voluntarily disclosed that a generous supporter once gave him stock worth $10,000. He admitted not having any interest in checking the stock market and even in keeping the stock. He decided to turn in the stock for cash. He didn't gamble to get the stock, but he did gamble in getting rid of it, for he discovered after he sold it that the stock increased in value, the next year, to $100,000![41]

Ever gamble? Ever admit to it? Like John MacArthur, Jr. we may have gambled without knowing it. What we make of God, how we view Him, determines how we end viewing Scripture. A popular view of Scripture is to see it as on a par with other human writings. That reduces Scripture to just another opinion and not the revelation of the Lord. According to the view that Scripture is not the final authority, then vice is limited to social dimensions and ramifications.

We gamble that we are right in our neglect patterns. Of course, dropping bad habits takes a back seat to reliance upon the Word and grace of God to cleanse our records, purge our spirits, infuse us with spiritual life, and make daily contact with Christ as natural as breathing.

Gross sins usually stun. Ordinarily, gambling or gambling losses, however, don't leave people guilt-ridden. Small money for a lotto ticket isn't missed. (And maybe there is no reason to feel guilty that we should *spend* money by a small wager. *Spending* is not sinning, necessarily.) Overall, small gambles don't rank high with guilt feelings, compared to adultery and murder. Unlike adultery, gambling is not an attack on the integrity of the marital bond. Unlike murder, the occasional gamble does not threaten your longevity. All these factors are true.

But rather than the problem being gambling, or a gambling obsession there may hide a greater problem, i.e., one's spiritual orientation reflected in the gravitation to gambling or the pride one takes in not having gambled or in not having a gambling problem. At least in the eyes of the authors in Scripture, it would seem that far worse than gambling is our gravitation to living independent of God, an obliviousness toward reliance on God and trust in Christ. The greater sins are often missed.

The fact that people gamble without guilt does not establish that it is not a sin. This view, of course, flies in the face of today's ways of calculating wrongs, which claim that now that the state is a bookmaker, lotteries are endorsed and gambling legitimized, the taint of sin is gradually removed. Government laws don't establish what constitutes sin, but God's laws do, as revealed in the Bible.

On another level, some say gambling, if considered a sin at all, does not bother people if not committed to excess. Because excess is missing does not mean sin is absent. Again, excess is not the sole criterion in determining the rightness or wrongness of an action. From a biblical viewpoint one's total absorption with worldly things, success, wealth, power, and pride about one's actions or abilities is a grave concern. Sure, the outlet of wagering may be a key sin which points to our state or predicament of sinfulness. But one's inner orientation away from God is always the main offence, the chief problem with humans. It is that spiritual state which needs to be challenged and changed. With some people, that orientation works itself out in a compulsion to try to win at wagering, or it works itself out in a compulsion to being self-righteous crusaders against wagering. Gambling or the presence of self-righteousness that they have no such addiction are really only symptomatic of a far deeper void, of a far more lamentable condition.

A lot of people probably breathe a sigh of relief they did not live in other days, when preachers took to the pulpit to berate gambling and gamblers.

Sermonic scorching

Take, for instance, the heated protests against gambling in the pre-Reformation period. Italian Dominican Girolamo Savonarola [1452–1498] scalded his Florence audience with warnings against gambling. Professor Villari, in his classic biography, supplies a Savonarola peroration:

> If you see persons engaged in gambling in these days, believe them to be no Christians, since they are worse than infidels, are ministers of the evil one, and celebrate his rites. They are avaricious men, blasphemers, slanderers, detractors of others' fame, fault-finders, they are hateful to God, are thieves, murderers, and full of all kinds of iniquity. I cannot permit ye to share in these amusements; ye must be steadfast in prayer, continually rendering thanks to the Almighty in the name of our Lord Jesus Christ. He that gambles shall be accursed, and accursed he that suffers others to gamble; shun ye their conversation, for the father that gambles before his son shall be accursed, and accursed the mother that gambles in her daughter's presence. Therefore, whoever thou art, thou shalt be accursed if thou dost gamble or allow others to gamble; thou shalt be accursed, I tell thee, in the city, accursed in the fields; thy corn shall be accursed; and thy substance; cursed the fruit of thy land and thy body, thy herds of oxen and thy flocks of sheep; cursed shalt thou be in all thy comings and goings (extract from Sermon 10).[42]

The problem with denunciations of one type of activity is to leave hearers with the false impression that if they clean up that one fault, break off that one habit, they will achieve reconciliation with God. On that basis then, moral improvement would replace or render unnecessary the divine implantation of new life which Jesus called the experience of eternal life, the qualitative life of God in time in us, which is the chief component for those who enter heaven (Jn. 3:1–10).

Have denunciations of gambling ever matched the steam that Savonarola generated? In the calmer Victorian age, another Catholic, Bernard Vaughan, SJ, politely suggested gambling depleted the prodigal son's inheritance (Lk. 15:11–32). Father Vaughan saw gambling in the phrase that the prodigal 'wasted his money'.

> . . . the evil of gambling . . . is to be found in the liability to abuse; in the almost magnetic hold it gets of a man, robbing him of mind, of heart, and of will-power. . . . Once a man begins to spend more upon this pleasure than he can afford to spend on it, he is indulging in vice.[43]

A formal disavowal, rather than an excoriation, seemed the way in colonial Virginia. The colonial Protestant, Revd William Stith [1707–1755] was probably flattered to be asked to speak before the Williamsburg, Virginia burgesses on the subject of gambling (cf. his sermon entitled 'The Sinfulness and Pernicious Nature of Gaming'), on 1 March 1752. Based on Exodus 20:17, his sermon was on the sin of covetousness. It had four parts: covetousness towards neighbours, country, family, and oneself. John M. Findlay saw in the sermon an eagerness to tone down the wickedness of gaming as 'a loss of self control . . . to preserve the right of self-determination by refraining from extensive gambling'.[44] Was gambling wicked itself or wicked only if taken to extremes?

The sermon, however, gave concessions to the standard Puritan distaste for gambling. The Rector of Henrico Parish concluded: 'In gambling you have run into the worst of sins, and God out of his great love for you, sends his dog the devil to worry and torment you, that you may return.'[45]

Although pleased to have his sermon requested and printed, he must have entertained a sense of ineffectiveness for the wealthy Virginia planters had no intention of abandoning their quarter-horse races. 'Gambling relationships were one of several ways by which the planters . . . preserved class cohesion. By wagering on cards and horses they openly expressed their extreme competitiveness, winning temporary emblematic victories over their rivals without thereby threatening the social tranquillity of Virginia.'[46]

The earliest anti-gambling sermon

But homiletic denunciations against gambling were much older than either the Florentine singeing or the Virginian finger-wag. The earliest post-biblical anti-gambling sermon was a pseudo-Cyprianic tract entitled *De aleatoribus*. A copy is dated between the eighth and the tenth centuries.[47] In it gambling clergy and laity were thumped pretty hard. It is more typical of today's anti-gambling rigorists.

The ancient sermon, at one point, thunders: 'The game of dice is an obvious snare of the devil. He presides over the game in person . . .'[48] In England, sixteenth-century dicing had its critics, too: Sir Thomas Elyot, in *The Book Named the Governor* (1531), warned against dicing: 'I suppose there is not a more plain figure of idleness than playing at dice. For besides that therein is no manner of exercise of the body or mind, they which do play thereat must seem to have no portion of wit or cunning, if they will be called fair players.'[49] John Northbrooke in his *Treatise wherein Dicing, Dancing. . . Are Reproved* (1577), expressed the view that card-playing was not so evil as dicing because there was less trust in chance.[50]

Attitudes in some corners of Christianity, on the use of dice, haven't changed drastically from earlier opposition. Tony Evans, President of the Urban Alternative, in Dallas, Texas, wrote of his own youth: 'The church in which I grew up included people who would not allow any board games if dice were involved because it was viewed as gambling.'[51]

Why the dice themselves, 'usually made of ivory, occasionally of bone', became a target is puzzling since 'the business of making dice, and articles of a similar nature, was one followed by Christians'.[52] The use of the dice, in one sense, is irrelevant. The core issue is the purpose of the toss and how what turns up is regarded.

Every American NFL (National Football League) game begins with the toss of a coin. In England and Europe similar tosses are made quickly to determine who gets the ball first. The option for the team representatives is to choose who goes on offence and who plays the first series of plays whether as offence or as defence, depending on how the coin lands and how the referee presents the options. 'Tossing a coin to determine choice of ends or innings in a game is not gambling.'[53]

Still – one wonders. Indoors, numerous Christians enjoy the innocent parlour-game Monopoly, an all-time popular home entertainment board game. Two other board games advertising themselves as Christian also use dice.[54] Few think it harmful to toss dice in these games. To move a piece on a game board is not teaching our children to gamble.

Christianity, however, of the severest variety has come down hard on hard dice. The eighth- or tenth-century sermon said: 'O dice-player who claims to be a Christian, whoever you are, you are not a Christian, because you participate in the sins of the world.'[55] Again, the game of dice was said to be a 'mortal sin', as well as 'the enemy of your fortune'.[56]

More questions emerge: Are dice the Devil's teaching tools, something to ban or to rail against? What about the three non-pejorative verses in the Book of Proverbs about dice throwing? Also, isn't there a place for allowable fantasy and traditional fiction? If telling the story of Santa Claus is a childhood fantasy, not a lie, is a game of chance played for amusement not gambling or the semblance of gambling?

The US's largest business feeds off the gullible poor and the greedy rich – both of whom entertain a slim hope of becoming instant millionaires. Without a dice thrown, gambling wins hands down.

A recent scientific telephone poll of 1,010 Americans (with an error margin of 3 percentage points), on 22–25 July 1999, found that just fewer than half, or 47%, believed saving and investing of income was the most reliable route to wealth. And one quarter of those polled held that the best chance to build wealth for retirement was by playing the lottery.

In reality, gambling can quickly make more people poorer than richer. The Lutheran Advocacy Ministry in Pennsylvania notes gambling's detrimental impact on the poor:

> The Lutheran Coalition on Public Policy believes that the expansion of legalized gambling is a poor public decision because it will not establish justice, further human rights, or promote the general welfare.[57]

But poor chances of winning are not enough to dissuade the struggling poor from seeking to be delivered from their economic struggles. That is why the lines are long to buy lottery tickets in the run-down sections of our cities. Buying weekly rub-off lottery tickets will take away the possibility of having more wholesome foods on the table, especially when income is marginal. The poor, even the poor Christian, may reply that his or her chances of ever earning mega-millions would never happen in two life-times so why not try? That may be what edges him or her toward risking a spare dollar for a lotto ticket. The poor feel trapped. They feel helpless. For such people, lotto ticket buying is a cry for deliverance.

Senior citizens who have plenty to live on, and figure they will never live long enough to spend it all, also find playing lotto or visiting a casino no hard choice. A 67-year-old woman from Cleveland, Ohio, who took a bus to Rising Sun, Indiana's Grand Victoria riverboat, said, 'When you get to be our age, you don't have a lot of money worries'. Others on the same bus said they were going for the excitement. And part of the excitement was on playing the slots, the cost of which they chalk up to vacation spending.[58]

Inducements aimed at pensioners at Harrah's floating casino in North Kansas City, include 'preferred boarding', and double gold card points on Mondays and Thursdays. In Missouri, the largest category, 36 per cent, are between the ages of 51 and 65.[59]

That's the trend in most gambling states. Senior citizens see gambling as 'action', a boredom chaser. It used to be that they would pack bingo halls to socialize with their friends in the same plight. Now, they board buses, which a Wisconsin gambling director called 'mobile senior citizen centers'.[60] Or they stay at home and buy daily lotto rub-off tickets. Widowed women who drop quarters or nickels into slot machines, get lampooned by casino staff as 'granny grinders'.

Most fixed-income pensioners strictly budget their 'fun money'. According to Indiana's Argosy floating casino marketing and sales director, Gary Johnson, senior citizens spend the least money on gambling of any group of patrons.[61]

Neophyte gamblers look for books which they hope will help them avoid pitfalls or tell them how to beat the house. The new magazine *Chance – The Best of Gaming –* serves the same purpose. Some forms of gambling[62] do not work on chance alone, but require mental skill, mathematical knowledge, and keen memory, not just a thick money roll, full bank account, or a credit card.

Lotto playing requires no brain power. (Other games that depend on pure chance are roulette, raffles, bingo, and the dice game called craps.) The main attraction to gambling is its entertainment for many people. Traditionally, entertainment does not require intellectual concentration. Some don't care to spend the time in learning how to play and how to win by bluffing and bidding. Hence games that require skill, time, and mental agility (such as poker, bridge, and pinochle) have no attraction and are bypassed.

It seems a touch of fatalism draws people to games based on pure chance. Since Christians have historically stressed the value of mental skill over sheer muscle or even the miracle of good odds, one would think those games that require cranial talent would have more appeal to Christians, but such is not the case. Perhaps, they reason that it is better to leave the results entirely in God's hands rather than gain through one's skill. (That is more fatalistic, rather than a predestinarian justification, for traditional predestinarians question whether reliance on God is shown in gaming for gain.)

Dr Timothy Warren, professor of pastoral ministries at Dallas Seminary, Texas, not only warned of the dangers in gambling, but also proposed six conditions and/or cautions for Christians faced with the wagering option:

If you consider gambling a form of entertainment similar to gardening, fishing, watching baseball, or attending a concert, then you might be able to participate. If you can steward a wager expecting to lose, enjoying the game itself, then gambling might be a 'safe' liberty for you. 'So whether you eat or drink or whatever you do, do it all for the glory of God' (1 Cor. 10:31).

If you don't consider gambling a form of giving, then gambling might not become a problem.[63] Some people think of gambling as 'giving' to their favorite charity. . . Still, it may be better to make an outright donation than to confuse gambling with giving. 'Each man should give what he has decided in his heart to give, not reluctantly or under compulsion, for God loves a cheerful giver' (2 Cor. 9:7).

If you don't view gambling as an investment strategy, then you might be able to take part. Some people, however, suppose that buying a lottery ticket is a smart investment program. The chances of that person becoming a millionaire would be much better if he or she invested $10 a week over 40 years. 'Dishonest money dwindles away, but he who gathers money little by little makes it grow' (Prov. 13:11).

If you do not consider gambling a form of earning, then you might be free to indulge. Some people, however, dream of making money gambling. . . 'Then [Jesus] said to them, 'Watch out! Be on your guard against all kinds of greed: a man's life does not consist in the abundance of his possessions' (Lk. 12:15).

If you can gamble without becoming addicted, it might not be a sin for you. Some people can pay out a provident amount, perhaps weekly or yearly, and stop at that. Others can't stop once they start. . . 'Like a city whose walls are broken down is a man who lacks self-control' (Prov. 25:28).

If you can gamble without encouraging a brother or sister in Christ to participate in gambling against their conscience or to become addicted, then you might be free to gamble. The basic issue of

Christian liberty is, 'Can I participate in this activity to the glory of God because I am not harming, but rather, helping myself, my weaker brothers and sisters in Christ, and the cause of Christ in this world?' 'Therefore let us stop passing judgment on one another. Instead, make up your mind not to put a stumbling block or obstacle in your brother's way' (Rom. 14:13).[64]

Whatever kind of gaming suits a person, there are always built-in hazards. From games least dependent on chance to those totally dependent on chance, willy-nilly, a player can be sucked into the economic whirlpool of the illusion of winning or be whipped by the hard reality of poverty brought on by excessive wagers.

As in the prevention of igniting highly flammable fuel, so there must be built-in, mental reminders, scrupulously followed safety guidelines, to prevent one's explosion into aggressive gambling.

How to avoid gambling spending sprees is a worthy goal. Hedges against spendthrift gambling must go along with hedges against spending sprees. Whether shopping or gaming one must never spend one's credit cards to their limits. Responsible Christian stewardship means our wealth is the Lord's and how we use it is our accountability. Financial counsellors advise compulsive buyers to consolidate their debts and duties, and always set limits on spending.

Whenever gambling costs go beyond occasional small change, then one is beginning to let gambling become a master. Scripture calls us always to think of others. Any opportunity for gain should have the welfare of others in mind. The occasional gambler must be thoughtful as to how his actions affect his immediate family.

Occasional Christian lotto players should have self-imposed rules which reflect an honest commitment to

Christian moderation, and a willingness to put extra effort into direct donations to Christian and social causes. Here are some minimal, some simple spend-little cautions and commendations. They should help prevent flings but not fence off the fun.

1 Consider lotteries, bingos, and raffles that support social and spiritual services. Whereas other forms of gambling mostly benefit casino operators and professional gamblers (national and state gambling taxes and voluntary charitable donations cut into some of their profits), church bingo and raffles are used to meet their budgets. But that alone is not a sufficient criterion in judging a good use of money. Does not giving directly to causes without regard for payback make direct stewardship contributions more godly, less selfish? The raffle buyer is dividing his desire – not waiting for a heavenly reward; he or she wants to win that quilt and help the church at the same time!

2 Small amounts only should be bet lest other needs are deprived. Small change is all one should wager. Wagering more does not increase the odds in winning in lotteries; therefore, further money is a waste unless you see it as going toward the public good. Occasional, small-stakes gambles must never escalate to a regular outlay lest it become a habit, an enslavement.[65] Experts warn 'spend enough to amuse yourself and never more than your budget allows'.[66]

3 The best ethical stance, many argue, is that the better bettor refrains from the numbers games (small bets) and lotto tickets. (To such, 'good gambling' is an oxymoron.) 'Dishonest money dwindles away, but he who gathers money little by little makes it grow' (Prov. 13:11, NIV). Aim to accumulate small amounts over time in order to invest in higher-yielding

Conditional Deposits (CDs). Some who can save little may of necessity first start a savings account, then buy CDs, then take matured CDs to buy stock. Others advise the use of the Money Market and skip using CDs. Proven stocks are always the best bet.

4 For every bet, triple or quadruple the amounts and give directly to supporting the agenda of the kingdom of God. Others over self is the Christian way.

5 Any money won should be regarded as the Lord's and generous gifts should be made from the winnings to Christian causes. Certainly, state, federal, or national government will see to it that they get their share. Christians should want to return to the Lord what is already his. Ten per cent was the minimum in the Old Testament. Today, many Christians give more than a tithe, a tenth.

6 If you win money in a lottery, invest your winnings to make more money. (See Chapter 2 on the relevance of Matthew 25:14–30 to the gambling debate.) Reinvestment should be primarily where you can earn more – such as in land purchases, businesses and stock investment.

Opponents of gambling warn that easy winners experience hard times. And they have ready a number of horror stories of surprising bad luck following a gambling 'killing'. On high-dollar lotto winners, Rex Rogers comments that, 'Their new notoriety produces long-lost relatives asking for handouts, lawsuits from complicated marriages and divorces, loss of privacy, harassing or threatening phone calls, and tax problems.'[67]

Newspaper clippings and media coverage tend to pick up on these reversals of fortune. Such coverage focuses on negatives. Do lotteries have a stranglehold on society, rather than offering a helping hand to the populace? How one sees government and state profits goes back to the question of perspective: is the glass half-full or half-empty? Pound/dollar amounts send us back to the basic question, 'What's the glass size?'

Those against gambling see terrible aftermaths. Those neutral or sympathetic to winners tend to see good results and the new and bright beginnings. One reporter was of the opinion that 'amid the fog of dueling statistics, conflicting theories and contradictory conclusions, one point is clear: neither side is above twisting the facts to prove its position'.[68]

Pitting good stories against bad on lotto winnings is not the way to argue against the legitimacy of wagering. Of course, many anti-lottery Christians don't see any benefits from lotteries. There is a reluctance to admit to good done for or through lotteries and lotto winners.

Historically, lottery earnings and winnings have helped the poor, directly and indirectly. Consider the case in the US of a pre-civil-war black, Denmark Vesay, who won a lottery. He was noted for his 'great physical strength and unusual intelligence'.[69] Yet the sea-captain was still a slave. In 1800, he won $1,500 in the East Bay lottery draw. With $600 he purchased his freedom and never bought another lottery ticket. He saw his winning as God's blessing. Vesay acknowledged the lottery win as a gift from God.[70]

A clergyman, already free, though possibly not rich, years earlier bought a lottery ticket. New York City held a lottery in July 1762, offering £20,000 in prizes, from a whopping £5,000 for first prize to smaller amounts. The draw was held inside City Hall. The diary entry of Revd Samuel Seabury, father of the famous Bishop Seabury [1729–1796], the first bishop of the Protestant Episcopal church in America,[71] saw God's goodness in his small winning. Samuel Seabury, the elder, recorded in his journal in 1762:

The ticket No. 5866 in the Light House and Public Lottery of New York, drew in my favor, by the blessing of Almighty God, 500 pounds sterling, of which I received 425 pounds, there being a deduction of fifteen per cent; for which I now record to my posterity my thanks and praise to Almighty God, the giver of all good gifts.[72]

Nine years earlier, in England, the physician-pastor, Revd Dr James Clegg [1679–1755], in contemplation of his death, at the age of seventy-four, wrote in his 1753 diary:

My concern was for ye continuation of ye means of Salvation in these parts after my Decease, but God can provide, and on him I rely. With a view to this I have a Ticket purchased for me in the Irish Lottery. If Providence shall favour me with a Prize, I have determined that one halfe of it shall be applied for that use or to some other that shall appear more pious and charitable.[73]

Do modern lottery winners publicly credit and praise God when they win? Every winner should consider Floyd Pearson of McPherson, Kansas, who saw God's goodness in winning $100,000 in a lottery ticket he almost threw out.

People magazine reported: 'Pearson, who plans to donate some of his windfall to church projects, attributes his win to something more than happenstance. "I believe", he says, "that God has a hand in everything that happens to me." '[74]

Christians, hearing or reading of others winning, are hopefully happy for winners and are not wickedly envious. We especially rejoice when the poor and disadvantaged, and struggling couples have the burden of economic hardship lifted from their shoulders with a substantial prize.

By the same token, we feel pain that the poor foolishly spend the little they have on games that have little guarantees. Ironically, the only persons who have the luxury of gambling live in relative luxury. For ages gambling has been the pastime and recreation of the rich. Those who win lotteries should feel some obligation to distribute their wealth to social and spiritual causes that assist, intervene, and improve life for the needy in whichever nation they belong.

14

The Summing-Up

Lotto: Fun or Folly? has attempted to go beyond gambling's excesses and dangers, and its societal ramifications, to look at how it relates to all of life and all of Scripture.

Anti-gambling rhetoric is no guarantee one will reflect much upon or absorb biblical texts. In our slap-dash times a shrinking number of people seem to give a hoot about hefty doses of historical perspective even from Christian history. My book is not an apology for legalized gambling enterprises. It is, however, an antidote to an unthinking approach.

Good Christians must go beyond a glib repetition of rigorist anti-gambling pronouncements. Everyone is better off when moral standards are both monitored and modulated. And, for those who claim to be Christian, what we have dealt with should challenge thinking to be realistic and more in line with God's self-revelation in Scripture.

I am not a cheerleader for the gaming industry, nor an advocate for government lotteries and casino owners. I don't represent any lobby for or against gambling. Indeed, in *Lotto: Fun or Folly?* no segment of society has been exempt from critical comments and philosophical analysis. Christians and secularists, and those with a mix of those values – whether gambling proponents or gambling opponents – have not been spared.

Four key issues have been raised: Firstly, what is gambling? Secondly, is God excluded from the gambling equation? Thirdly, what forms of gambling cannot Christians escape? And lastly, what gambling directives should Christians develop?

Comparisons

Older casinos and hotels in the US gambling mecca, Las Vegas, are being torn down, making room for new facilities. The rapid removal of the old has been accomplished by co-ordinated, simultaneous implosions, reducing the structures to rubble within a few seconds.

What has been missed in both old and new gambling venues is a cash implosion. The cash implosion that accompanies habitual gambling is never filmed. Lives implode upon themselves without people blinking an eye. The media report divorces, embezzlement, bank robbery, children sent to foster homes, but it is near impossible to catch every dimension of self-implosion.

Like hotels that tumble inward when the charges are fired, careers and family investments have fallen and gone flat. The emotional effects, which are similarly irreversible, cannot be eased by some faded memory of the social interaction, fun, excitement, and rush from gaming. What has been spent is thrown away, lost forever. The gains are gone; savings and reserves sucked up; pocket-money gone 'puff'.

Some see a causal relationship between increasing bankruptcies and gambling. Statistics seem to prove it. Spending more than one earns is the culprit. Hungry shoppers, however, can also waste wads of money through needless purchases as swiftly and unwisely as in gung-ho gaming. But gambling alone is not what produces bankruptcy.

The Christian is not exempt either from bankruptcy or from the temptation to wager. At the same time, anyone who puts cash down for a wager is not affirming that there is no God and that only chance and probability exist. Christian and non-Christian alike are subject to the laws of probability.

As we have noted, gambling has degrading side-effects. It destroys homes and ruins careers by siphoning off essential money. Over-indulgence in wagering in lotteries and casinos doubtless produces some economic disasters. A wise wagerer never empties his or her wallet or bank account, or spends their credit limit in leisure gaming.

Moderation spares us from sad side effects. A disciplined table guest who drinks wine doesn't guzzle down an entire bottle. One glass is enough. A sip may be sufficient.

Solid Christians are justifiably divided on the significance of chance and its relationship to financial risks.

The models for risk and gambling

Lotto: Fun or Folly? should give pause to blanket condemnation of the lottery principle. If chance-taking with the roll of dice is universally wrong, was God's approval of lot-casting misplaced? Proverbs 16:33 would then become an embarrassment instead of a point of admiration. Excess in gambling depends wrongly on God's refusal to use mathematical probability.

How much one knows contributes to determining whether invested money is a gamble or not. Life is full of surprises. Sometimes solid companies have gone under, and the market has both slumped and crashed. What a person brings to a decision determines whether or not it is a gamble. Factor that into the equation as to what is gambling, and how much one is willing to risk. Christians not only keep a tight rein on their tongues, eyes, and ears, but see that God's interest in them includes their money clips and bank accounts.

The inter-relationship of gambling and risk can be illustrated by several models, theological, biological, and social.

Theological model

First, for readers with an acquaintance of Christian theology, take the distinctions, for instance, on the inner nature of the Christian Trinity and Jesus' deity and humanity. Theologians use the categories of essence and substance. Risk and gambling come close to resembling the difference between the valid distinction in Christian theology between the substance of Persons in the Trinity and the essence belonging to the separate Persons, the jointly shared deity between the members of the godhead.

Or take the distinction between Jesus' Person and his nature. In the Chalcedonian formulation the Person of Jesus is not his nature. But, for purposes of discussion, they cohere or coexist in the one Being. The real Jesus is not divided into two Jesuses. So the substance of gambling has the essence of risk. And the substance of risk is a gambling event. These classic theological distinctions are, doubtless, unfamiliar to many who are knowledgeable about many other things.

Biological model

A second model may be easier to relate to. Think of the biological model of symbiosis. In biology, symbiosis is the close union of two dissimilar organisms. One cannot talk of one without including the other. A symbiotic relationship seems to exist between gambling and risk.

As illustrated in the above analogies, the walls separating the legal definition and the loose definition of gambling are not fixed as in the courts, but are fluid as in a playing-field. Those who attempt to keep gambling out of stock investments are proposing a relational rift between two similar entities and dynamic realities, risk and gambling.

The social model

Mathematical odds shake warning fingers in the face of every gamble that doesn't require some skill. For many, the odds against winning, which are overwhelming, never seem to deter the compulsive gambler. The full range of gambling decisions is replete with abundant instances of faulty judgment based on superstition, fatalistic hope, and bi-polar personality traits. Luck is always bogus, but chance is real.

Chance increases or decreases as our knowledge and skills increase or diminish. For instance, if I were to decide to enter the business of international shipping, the more knowledgeable I become about the business, the less I will let business decisions result from chance, and, therefore, the more likelihood I shall succeed.

The more I know about a company the more I reduce risk in buying its stock. What we learn of a company does not reduce its own risk, of course. Only the wise decisions of the company can ensure its continuance and growth. Only a company can reduce its real risk. What we take on in becoming a shareholder is becoming a partner with the company's actual risk. What we know of a company does not reduce the company's risk, but gives us reassurance about the company's future. In buying stock in the company we assume their risk. Thus, we should cease a total condemnation of chance, for chance is a function in physical reality and is included in God's rule (review the arguments in Chapter 9).

A cautious endorsement of minimal financial risk-taking has potential personal and social good. So long as there is a hedge of moderation in place there is little chance for individual, familial, and societal collateral damage.

I have mentioned before the Anglican Kenneth Escott Kirk [1886–1954], one-time fellow of Trinity College, and later Bishop of Oxford, who drew a comparison between the ethical issue of wine drinking and gambling. Like wine aged in the cellar, the comparison is still valid despite the passage of decades. And it is worth repeating:

> In general the attitude of the Church has been to regard betting as a thing indifferent [in theology this is called *adiophora*]. . . With [the proviso of certain instances of excess and abuse], betting is treated in traditional theology as 'allowable'. There is nothing praiseworthy in it, but on the other hand a Christian cannot be blamed for indulging in it in strict moderation. It is in all respects analogous with what we euphemistically call the question of 'drink'. A Christian may 'drink', but he must never drink to excess; so he may bet, but he must not bet to excess.[1]

The more biblical position on gambling is similar to a biblical position on the use of wine. As Scripture urges the moderate use of wine,[2] so it would advocate a moderate reliance on drawings and wagers. Total abstinence from wine drinking is not the Christian approach, rather moderation is. As a glass of wine is no great evil, so a modest wager is no great sin. Total abstinence with alcoholic beverage, some insist, is the biblical way. Others, probably the majority of Christians, however, submit upon sound biblical evidence that a little wine for one's 'oft infirmities' is not killing, but invigorating. Therefore, moderation in chance-taking or gambling is the Christian approach, not total abstinence.

Ironically, the American Methodist minister, the Revd Thomas Grey, a fiery anti-casino crusader, as much as admitted that Bishop Kirk's comparison is on target. Grey said:

> We're going to find out one day – if we don't already know it – that casinos and gambling are a lot like drinking too much liquor. It might taste pretty good at the time but you wake up with a heck of a hangover the next day. I'm afraid that next morning is on the way for America.[3]

A Christian approach to gambling, like a Christian approach to the use of wine, sees excess destructive and moderation constructive.

Christians have been known physically to attack occasional lotto players and berate lotteries. Lotteries, to them, fail to deliver high percentages to social programmes. Admittedly, the percentage of profits that go directly to continue and promote state social programmes are or seem minuscule. Yet that small percentage is billions, itself a hefty total. 'Casinos and racetracks make greater contributions to employment, but in terms of direct contributions to government budgets, lotteries stand alone.'[4]

On the other hand, casino profits pour into the accounts of the owners. But not entirely, for by law casinos are taxed. 'Lottery advocates emphasize their games return an average of 32 per cent of their sales revenue to state governments, while only about 9 per cent of casinos' profits go to the states.'[5]

The lower tax percentage which the state levies on all casino profits, and which goes to support state budgets, many reject as sufficient social justification of casinos. And when one adds that the total contributions of casinos to social projects, such as regional schools, universities, and hospitals, tend to be proportionately lower than revenues from the lotteries, some ask how much stock should be attributed to their generosity. Gambling critics see societal donations as largely token promotional strategies to enhance the casinos' public image.

But neither casinos nor lotteries can match the benefits of stocks to improve the lot of individual citizens. Indeed, Episcopal Herbert Waddams argued that 'it is morally unhealthy that such huge sums of money should be used for gambling, when so much misery and undernourishment remains unrelieved in the world'.[6]

Where should we put our excess money, i.e., money after supporting the church and paying the bills? Instead of casting our blue chips and silver coins before the altars of instant riches in our favourite gambling centres, we should invest our money in profitable stocks. It's better stewardship (cf. Chapters 2 and 3).

Because of the foresight of countless Christian benefactors Christian institutions and missions have received in donations, trusts and bequests many millions of dollars to strengthen Christian missions and to spread the Good News. The importance of investments and profits, in part, should be to fortify and further Christ's evangelistic and educational mission in the world.

We may not like the comparison, but the reality is what counts. Stock investment is still the best bet. Anyone who wants to maximize his profits turns to stock investments.

The average person has more invested in the market than in the house that shelters him. Stock account for more than 40 % of the average household's financial assets, more than in any period in history. The percentage of adult Americans who own stock has risen from 10.4 % in 1965 to 43 % today.[7]

Some wise investors

The wisdom of investment over simple wagering was reinforced in the US when the estate of a deceased Brooklyn engineering professor was estimated at $800 million. How did Professor Donald Othmer and his wife, Mildred, who lived modestly, acquire such wealth? 'In the 1960s, the Othmers each invested $25,000 with Mr [Warren] Buffett. In the early 1970s they received shares worth $42 each in Berkshire Hathaway, [Buffett's] investment and insurance holding company. The stock now is worth $77,200 a share.'[8]

The recommendation of stocks as the best bet across the board, however, is done with the realization that stock can't escape 'how the dice roll'. Although God is in charge of our lives, He does not refuse to use probability and variations. Investors hope the economy stays well and investments and fortunes are not squandered or siphoned away.

Gambling, like a colour spectrum, stretches to the left and right of centre. At either extreme there is much or little risking. Every risk is a percentage gamble. Solid, blue-chip stocks seem safest. As with each throw of the dice, so with each corporate decision, the company's worth and value goes up or down.

Enormously wealthy, Warren Buffett, whose net worth was last reported to be 14 billion, made his fortune in stocks and in buying companies. He said: 'The market, like the Lord, helps those who help themselves. But, unlike the Lord, the market does not forgive those who know not what they do.'[9]

One cornerstone principle of Buffett's investments is 'know the company in which you invest'. Peter S. Lunch's summary sounds like a Buffett creation: 'Many people invest in a way similar to playing poker all night without ever looking at their cards.'[10]

Big gamblers are, however, in the end big losers. Huge outlays at bet windows or card tables are a waste of wealth, time, and energy. But the occasional gambler who may not care about his small wagers, can be overly occupied with self and substance. He, too, can have a fixation on riches.

Christians operate on two levels: the physical level of participation in risks, but also in the mental/spiritual level of understanding that gaming is only a game. Also, Christians hold that there are higher stakes than those played in gaming, that one's indifference or involvement in Christ has a bearing upon one's ultimate welfare.

The model of spiritual risk-taking

Occupation or obsession with winning may signal a serious spiritual deficiency. The typical casino 'junkie' does not go to church, does not read the Bible, or pray (except perhaps for the elusive jackpot!). Usually daily buyers of lotto tickets pray only to win.

Scripture's warnings about a life immersed in materialistic gain are not taken seriously. Whereas monetary gambling can leave you penniless when engaged in to excess, gambling that God's Word is wrong can leave you eternally hopeless. *Lotto: Fun or Folly?* addresses the need of the financially well-off to be rich toward God. As a Christian thinker I am as much concerned about spiritual gamblers as about financial gamblers.

Many who have gone to casinos say they've enjoyed the times of relaxation and social interaction. Fun is one of the themes pushed by the gaming industry. Without giving unqualified endorsement of gaming, the Episcopal theologian, Herbert Waddams, admitted: 'The best case that can be put in favour of gambling is that it is a form of innocent pleasure.'[11]

Lottery buyers and casino patrons say they feel a rush in gambling that they don't even get in sexual encounters. Gambling centres and lotto outlets, however, cannot begin to put into your heart, soul and mind the gratification from the knowledge of God in Scripture. While we are most concerned what God gets out of our worship, the worship of God is enormously enriching to us.

Most US casino/hotel rooms have Gideon Bibles, either KJV or NKJV. They are left unused, and the resort visitor is deprived of an inner wealth that outlasts the hilarity and frivolity of bright lights and happy music. If you want to add to your life without deducting from your assets, spend time reading the Scriptures. There you will read about divine providence. There you discover that so-called Lady Luck does not exist and cannot do for you what God can. A personal God, not an abstract principle, is behind who you are, what surrounds us in the splendour of the universe, and what happens to us as we live. God is not a statistical force, but our loving Father. We belong to God. We owe him our full attention and our complete trust.

The spin-off from Bible reading is much better than anything from a roulette wheel. From Scripture we experience a wholeness and newness that no gambling can comprehend, duplicate, or exceed. Unlike gambling, we win in Christ, because he has laid down his life. Christ supplies us unlimited salvation and he does not withhold from his own, i.e., those who seek him earnestly and energetically. Christ's giving is not based on *quid pro quo* (this for that). He gives of his grace and redemption freely: what he has for us is far better than anything promised by earthlings and lasts forever.

Spellbound by the dazzle of showplace entertainments and the glitter of success, many feel certain they can get along without God. Therefore, a conventional reaction is: why get excited about news of a grace-granted salvation?

Society is being short-changed on the merits of the inner spiritual life. Instead, people are being relentlessly bombarded with new material diversions. St Paul's warning in 1 Timothy 6:9,10 has special application in our times:

> People who want to get rich fall into temptation and a trap and into many foolish and harmful desires that plunge men into ruin and destruction. For the love of money is a root of all kinds of evil. Some people, eager for money, have wandered from the faith and pierced themselves with many griefs (NIV).

The prophet Isaiah asks of everyone whom the Lord has blessed with discretionary wealth:

> Why spend money on what is not bread,
> and your labour on what does not satisfy?
> Listen, listen to me, and eat what is good,
> and your soul will delight in the richest of fare.
> (Isa. 55:2 NIV)

Appendix

Changes in US Roman Catholicism regarding charity gambling

Bingo has always been popular in many American Catholic churches. It began in the midst of the famous economic depression in the United States in 1934. It became a key money-making method for Catholic churches in the Depression. 'By 1939 fewer than a dozen out of 200 Catholic and Episcopal bishops prevented the use of bingo as a fund raiser.'[1] Of the 26 million Americans estimated to be bingo players by 1950, many of them met in church basements or church educational buildings to support the churches' budgets.[2]

In the state of Ohio, not-for-profit organizations such as churches are allowed to sponsor bingo and some other games of chance as long as profits go entirely to the organization. In the Ohio region in which I live, just across the border from Kentucky, the following report is worth notice. 'In Kentucky, the Division of Charitable Gaming says 52 Catholic churches, schools and service organizations in northern Kentucky sponsor bingo games as fundraising events.' In 1996, 50 of the 105 licensed charitable gaming organizations in Boone, Campbell and Kenton counties were affiliated with the Catholic church. 'Those same Catholic groups accounted for 42 per cent of the $36 million in gross receipts collected by charitable gaming organizations in Northern Kentucky, records show.[3]

The presumption is that all Roman Catholics approve of wagering to raise money. But that is not established by the facts. While there has been a general acceptance of charity-gaming, even with hierarchical permission, there is not a unanimous consensus among the Roman Catholic clergy.

In the 1950s Archbishop Stritch of Milwaukee was an ardent critic of bingo as a means of raising church revenue.[4] In 1959 Richard Cardinal Cushing, one-time Archbishop of Boston, said: '[Gambling] does not create new sources of revenue, but rather draws from those which already exist in ways which tend to disturb the normal and healthy process by which economic prosperity is promoted . . . it creates serious temptations to theft in those who handle money which does not belong to them, and because it stands in the way of prompt and systematic payment of debts and other obligations of justice . . .'[5] In the 1970s, a priest with a parish of 350 members in Los Angeles, California, had doubts about using games to raise money. He said, 'If money can only be raised to support our work through gambling, I seriously question how important, relevant, and effective we are.'[6]

In Canada, 1993, a courageous Catholic bishop turned down money from a bingo/lottery. Bishop Denis Croteau of the diocese of Mackenzie-Fort Smith in northern Canada refused a $19,000 donation from an affiliate of the Knights of St Columba for improvements to a spiritual life centre in the Yellowknife area in the north-west. Why? Because the money came from bingo and the sale of 'Nevada tickets' – a form of lottery in which winning tickets have matching symbols similar to those on slot machines. Bishop Croteau said: 'I hate the thought of taking money from poor people to run the church.'[7]

Signs indicate that Catholic stewardship reform is spreading.

Recently, in Kentucky's Roman Catholic Covington Diocese new rules about the use of games of chance in stewardship have been introduced. Depending on the country, region and diocese, Roman Catholics show varying degrees of acceptance of some forms of gambling to meet their budgets. Covington Diocese guidelines 'prohibit the use of such games as blackjack, roulette, craps, keno, baccarat, and poker at church fund-raisers.'[8] Although the official Catholic moral stance of permissibility is intact, casino types of gambling are deemed inappropriate and imprudent for their church.

Traditionally, the Roman Catholic's position is that a wager is not inherently evil and that 'though a luxury, [gambling] is not considered sinful except when the indulgence in it is inconsistent with duty.'[9] Addictive or compulsive gambling is a sickness that needs to be treated. Bingo playing could be a compulsion, not just a way to spend time and socialize.

Roman Catholic festival practices in Northern Kentucky used to allow casino-type gaming, such as slot machines, roulette, blackjack, craps, keno and baccarat. Bishop Robert Muench of the Diocese of Covington has acted on the recommendation of a 15-member council that all types of casino-style gambling be barred in the fifty-two diocesan churches. The new policy severely curtails the use of casino gambling at church and school fund-raising.[10] ' "Ultimately, the popular pull-tab games would be eliminated, too, under the proposed policy change", Father Sacksteder said.'[11] The move to return to the voluntary support of Catholic members is welcomed by all those interested in spiritual renewal in the parishes. The article continues:

'While the proposed change is driven partly by the church's opposition to legalized gambling in Kentucky, it also reflects the church's renewed emphasis on stewardship, or church members giving of their financial resources, time and talents', Father Sacksteder said.[12]

The Diocese of Covington, KY, 'plans to eliminate bingo as a primary fund-raiser for Catholic churches and schools'.[13] The Revd Thomas Sacksteder, spokesman for the diocese, said, 'The bottom line is: Yes, bingo's going to go someday. It's just a matter of when.'[14] Perhaps the same reform directive will appear in other dioceses of the Catholic Church across the nation.

Increasingly, Christians of all denominations recognize that it is better to give money directly to Christian missions than to hope for a windfall from bingo or other games of chance or figure that though they don't win, a net profit goes towards the church. 'Benevolence, not bingo, is the church's duty to the needy.'[15]

Both Catholics and Protestants recognize that bingo diminishes if not ruins motivation for work. A youth counsellor was asked, 'What will it do to a 12-year-old boy to win $100 at bingo?' The counsellor paused, and said, 'That boy will never again be happy delivering papers for $2 a week.'

The hope of many within Catholicism is that annual 'festivals' might become less game-oriented entertainments, and money-making gimmicks, indeed that 'festivals' would be linked regularly with faith and furthering spiritual devotions.

Questions for Discussion

Chapter 1

1. Are definitions important? And who determines whether a definition is allowable?
2. What is the range of definitions on gambling? In deciding ethical questions should questions of usage be important?
3. Rex Rogers gives as reason # 6 for not gambling: 'Gambling is a form of theft.' How is gambling theft when the placing of a wager (money) is voluntary? How is it theft when there are no grounds for arresting the person placing the bet?
4. Is the legal definition of gambling enough?
5. Review the varieties of gambling. Where is gambling going?
6. Do people gravitate to gambling or are they lured, attracted through pre-conditioning?
7. Fun is explained by many as the main reason for gambling. But is gambler-satisfaction a useful product? Is it more truly fun or folly?
8. How do these outlets for gambling impact upon individual Christians, upon churches, and upon communities?
9. Have churches masked their own gambling practices under the guise of stewardship games?

10. Is compulsive gambling more likely to grow when Christians condone gambling?
11. The chief argument for allowing gambling is that it is a game, a form of recreation. Is that the lure in gambling? In the appeal for free food, fun, and fortune, how does fun rank as a leading motive to gamble? Should a Christian rank fun as a justification for gaming?
12. Deeper questions than its legality are involved in gambling: what about its morality? If gambling is part and parcel of every risk-decision, even where money is not involved, does that make every decision necessarily evil?

Chapter 2

1. Does the Bible berate gamblers or condemn gambling? How can you explain the absence of condemnation in biblical times when wagering was all around them?
2. Should churches resort to the lottery principle such as in raffles to raise money?
3. What other Bible passages speak to a more intentional approach to success in making money?
4. Are Bible passages on greed specifically focusing on gambling?
5. Are misers as bad as gamblers?
6. Why is Matthew 25:14–30 relevant to the gambling debate? Is non-work wicked?
7. Can wagering be justified from that passage? Does it allude to stock investment or would stock investment fit into a legitimate way of multiplying the money?

8. Discuss the interpretation of Ivan Zabilka of Isaiah 65:11 and 12 who wrote:

   'Gambling is specifically in view in Isaiah 65:11–12, where it says that those who "spread a table for fortune" are destined for the sword'

   (*The Lottery Lie: Gamblers, Money and Hungry Kids*, 1998, p. 121).

   Compare this to Dr Gilmore's explanation of the same passage in the text of Chapter 2.

Chapter 3

1. Talmage once said, '. . . the man who deals in "fancy" stocks, or conducts a business which hazards capital. . . is a gambler . . .' Is that true?
2. Rex M. Rogers contended that 'compulsive gamblers only rarely play the stock market'. Is he wrong? Why?
3. Are stock purchases partly gambling, even if not identical with typical wagers?
4. What four major arguments emerge against counting stock shares as a gamble?
5. Justin Mamus asks, 'Is Wall Street so pure at heart that investing has no element of gamble to it?' What do you think?

Chapter 4

1. Casting lots in Bible times was done to settle disputes, to come to closure on ownership. But was it a form of gambling? Do you have to have money to gamble? If casting lots was not an evil, why is gambling wrong?

2. Discuss Ezekiel 21:21.
3. Discuss Nehemiah 7:1–5a.
4. By lot, Jonathan was found to be the (unwitting) violator of his father's oath (1 Sam. 14:42). Was he?
5. The Urim and Thummim (or ephod) were also oracular media, but answers were restricted to 'yes' or 'no' (1 Sam. 23:9–12; 30:7–8; Num. 27:21). The same results could be gained by casting lots (Lev. 16:8; Num. 26:55–56). Was wagering right under the nose of the High Priest and without a word of condemnation? What was the significance of the Urim and Thummim? Is there any similarity between the ancient High Priest deciding issues and ministers counselling?
6. Look up the following verses: [a] Numbers 26:52–56; 27:12; [b] Deuteronomy 33:8–11; [c] Joshua 7:13–15; 14:1–5. What similarities are there? What kind of relationship, if any, do you detect?
7. The casting of lots (cf. Josh. 14:2) would not decide the size of the respective territories then, but only where the tribes would settle in Canaan. If a tribe were large it would have a large area but only the lot would decide whether it would be in the north, centre, or south. These lots were most likely the Urim and Thummim of the High Priest (cf. Ex. 28:30). Was the implication of Urim and Thummim that God is directly involved in chance?
8. What possible advantages did the Hebrews see in casting lots? Why would they resort to a method that permeated pagan cultures? And what advantages did the early Church see in casting lots (Acts 2:26)? What was it about 'casting lots' that would cause Old Testament patriarchs and New Testament saints to both allow and practise it? What value was associated with it? Didn't it short-cut rational process? Wasn't it an unthinking way to resolve issues? Was there anything

attractive about casting lots that appealed to persons of faith in God? Does casting lots give justification to modern gambling?

Chapter 5

1. Lloyd Douglas [1877–1951] took Jesus' seamless robe as the central theme for his novel *The Robe* (1942). The soldiers gambled for it. Was it gambling or were they just passing the time? Was it gambling when no money was exchanged? Can one gamble without money being put up front?

2. Some use the argument that gambling is wrong because, though it is a 'something', it is too small a something to be an equitable basis for getting a huge something in return. Is this a valid objection? This amounts to the view that a disproportionate exchange is immoral. Is that right?

3. Some see it as a chance to have made some money through resale. So some have speculated that greed drove them to gamble. Working from the model of the seamless robe it assumes the seamless garment was valuable. Is that so? Or was it too common to be thought of any value?

4. Except for the pagan and superstitious use of lots, casting lots for mundane gain is never condemned in Scripture. In cases of deadlocks and ties, lots were cast (Prov. 18:18). If you grant that the soldiers did not fight over the clothes, that they did not try to swindle the others out of the prize, did their use of a dice throw elevate their actions?

Chapter 6

1. To choose a surgeon whose record for patient survival is poor is not only a risk, it is a gamble, a gamble in which the odds are against you. Do you agree? How does one weed out what is a gamble and what is a wise choice?

2. Is marriage ever a gamble?

3. Farmer Merrill Thornton of Osceola, Iowa, saw himself as a crazy gambler. He said: 'I'd never put $1,000 down on the table over a hand of poker, but here I am gambling thousands or more every year on something that isn't even as sure as that.' Should farmers think of themselves as gamblers?

4. Perhaps the most famous Old Testament risk-taker was Abraham, who 'went out, not knowing where he went' (Hebrews 11:8). But the 'gamble' in Abraham did not leave him even after he arrived in Canaan, for as Genesis 23:1–20 relates, he was 'the first person in the Bible to recognize land as individual property that can be improved, purchased, and sold'. Is a real-estate purchase ever a gamble?

5. Jesus himself likened his crucifixion as both the epitome and end of his risk-taking on earth. The verb, ordinarily translated 'to lay down' in John 10:11,15,17, could mean 'to risk' as well as 'to give'. Would it be a slur to consider Jesus' choice of going to the cross a gamble? Why?

6. How does the involvement of Jesus in his own destiny come through in the Gospel of John? Why was he not described as a hapless victim of circumstances and more the orchestrator of events? Was the cross an elevation or a denunciation of Jesus?

Chapter 7

1. Significant space has not been given to Puritans in recent Christian books on gambling. Is that a loss? How relevant is the Puritan controversy to today?

2. Puritan diaries fill out how gambling was viewed in a way Puritan lectures on moral issues don't. In reviewing the cited diaries, what observations can you make?

3. *The Larger Catechism* asked, 'What are the sins forbidden in the eighth commandment?' (The commandment against stealing.) Answer: The sins forbidden in the eighth commandment, besides the neglect of the duties required, are '. . . *wasteful gaming* [emphasis added]; and all other ways whereby we do unduly prejudice our own outward estate, (Prov. 21:17, Prov. 23:20–21, Prov. 28:19) and defrauding ourselves of the due use and comfort of that estate which God hath given us (Eccl. 4:8, Eccl. 6:2, 1 Tim. 5:8)'. Which way did the Assembly lean on the matter of lotteries? Or can a judgment not be rendered on *The Larger Catechism*?

4. Thomas Gataker [1574–1654] is a little-known Westminster Assembly participant, yet in his own age he was highly esteemed. He seemed to take a position opposite that of *The Larger Catechism*. From his writing on the subject, what would you say?

5. In his sermon on Proverbs 16:33 the Calvinist Royalist Robert South [1634–1716] distinguished between two views of chance: one non-Christian, the other Christian. Was this valid?

6. Cotton Mather [1663–1728] represented those then and now who say gambling is taboo for a Christian. Are lotteries a misuse of God's sanction and commandments?

7. Should good from lotteries be overlooked, denied, or minimized? Or should it be acknowledged and appreciated? If all lotteries are evil, what do you say about house lotteries?

Chapter 8

1. Probably the most thorough treatise ever written on the nature and use of Bible lots was by the English Puritan, Thomas Gataker [1574–1654]. Reread and ponder his arguments. Find any problems with his positions? Which are proven? Which doubtful?
2. Where is 'chance' referred to in the Bible? How does that fit in with the stress in Scripture on divine ordination?
3. 'Angels in heaven have their charges by Lot assigned them, who shall rule this or that Province, who tend this or that person, who govern this or that church' (cf. Dan. 10:13,21; Mt. 18:10; Acts 12:15; Rev. 1:20). Are lotteries in heaven's rule?
4. 'The use of Lots in games is not in itself or of itself a sin either against Piety or against Charity.' So said Gataker. Can you agree? Why do you disagree?
5. Gataker took exception to William Perkins' and others' view on Lots. How effective were Gataker's arguments in your opinion?
6. 'The use of Lots was not spoiled by human wickedness, nor spoiled absolutely or universally, for the acts of the Creator and the acts of a creature must be kept separate' (226). Therefore, in casting lots there is 'no tang or taint at all of impiety, or blasphemy' (226). What do you think of this position taken by Gataker?

7. 'In these words the Holy Ghost manifestly not only allowed and approves the use of Lots in such cases, but commends it unto us as a wise and discrete [discreet] course of the taking away of controversies and questions in this kind, and the preventing of lawsuits or other quarrels that thence otherwise might arise.' (Gataker, 'On Proverbs 16:33'). Are lawsuits preventable by the casting of lots?

8. Why would a lawsuit work better than the casting of lots?

9. How well did Gataker argue his case? How convincing is his position?

Chapter 9

1. Is gambling a permissible amusement or a social evil?

2. Does chance automatically rule out God's sovereign control?

3. What is the position of R.C. Sproul?

4. How does it compare with Thomas Gataker? With Robert South?

5. Discuss Isaiah 65:11's reference to dependence on 'the hollow gods of supposed good fortune'.

6. The two usages of chance are reflected and advanced in Scripture. Watch for it. Perhaps the text that bears most immediately on the two aspects of chance is Proverbs 16:33: 'Lots are cast into the lap; The decision depends on the LORD.'

7. The role of chance keeping randomness alive and probabilities intact does not precede or supersede God. *Chance is God's instrument, not to destroy determinism, but to destroy man's ability to predict with certainty.* True?

8. William S. Pollard, as a Christian physicist, grappled with the problem of the place of chance in God's world. Does his view deny predestination? providence?
9. Should one knock the book of Ruth 2:3 (KJV) where it says, 'As it happened, she came to the part of the field belonging to Boaz'?

Chapter 10

1. Probability has two senses: describe and explain them.
2. What are the odds in casino games . . . in the 1970s . . . in the 1990s?
3. Is it true that in gambling probability doesn't play favourites?
4. In colonial times lotteries supplied the struggling colonies with an educational edge. What institutions directly benefited from lotteries?
5. Would one-cause lotteries be more moral? Do church raffles escape the moral connotations of secular lotteries?
6. What about house lotteries? Should they be condemned?

Chapter 11

1. Why do people gamble?
2. Rex Rogers says: 'Gambling maximizes covetousness.' Does that apply to the casual, occasional lotto player?
3. Proverbs 10:22; 11:4; Matthew 6: 24; Luke 12:15; Colossians 3:5; 1 Timothy 6:10, 17: read and relate to the topics of greed and gaming.

4. Is the lure of the lottery merely extravagance or the drive to be delivered from the pain of poverty?
5. Church raffles are often used to raise money for churches. Should they?
6. What inner or eternal good does heaping up money bring?

Chapter 12

1. The modern world is money-mad. Which is better: the gospel of wealth, or the wealth of the Christian Gospel?
2. Where do we strike it rich? Where do people seek a glorious present or a fabulous future?
3. Read Ephesians 4:14. Was Paul risking criticism by using an object from the gambling world?
4. Name the three texts in Ephesians that speak of God's wealth, and of how we share in it as we participate in Christ.
5. Does Christianity discount or deny that probability applies to Christ' Saviour role?
6. Anglican Kenneth Escott Kirk [1886–1954], one-time Fellow of Trinity College, later Bishop of Oxford, drew a comparison between the ethical issue of wine-drinking and gambling. Agree or disagree? Why?
7. Warren Buffett, whose net worth was last reported to be $14 billion, said: 'The market, like the Lord, helps those who help themselves. But, unlike the Lord, the market does not forgive those who know not what they do.' Is this biblical?

Chapter 13

1. Some say gambling is easily recognized to be evil by the company it keeps. True?
2. Is it a sin to gamble?
3. 'Can Christians gamble and *not* violate God's law?' Colonial American Christians didn't take long to answer that question. And it was usually 'yes'. Do you think they took the right position? How would you say they were inconsistent, if at all?
4. Is insurance an insult to God's providential care?
5. In what ways do Christians gamble and not know it?
6. Apparently an early Christian saw nothing wrong in the manufacture of dice. What should a modern card factory worker do: quit or stay producing cards?
7. Take Professor Warren's six criteria on whether or not to gamble. Is that kind of approach biblical? Which arguments would you throw out? Why? Which ones, if any, would you say are 'on target'?

Notes

1. Weighing up the Gambling Pound

[1] 'Funny money' is counterfeit money. 'Play money' is fake money, money used in pretend games. 'Fun money' is real money used to finance recreation, played away without anticipating financial gain. Most of those who used their discretionary funds for gambling justify it as 'fun money'.

[2] 'Bowing Down to Chance', *Sword And Trowel* (published by Metropolitan Tabernacle, London), No. 1, 1994; reprinted: *Sword And Trowel*, No. 3, 1999., pp. 14, 15. The article lists 15 rapid-fire objections to gambling.

[3] Isaac Watts, *Logic* (Morgan, PA: Soli Deo Gloria Publications 1724, 1996), p. 83.

[4] Gilbert Keith Chesterton, *All I Survey: A Book of Essays* (New York: Dodd, Mead & Company, 1933), p. 233. Chesterton's distinction should not be dismissed as frivolous, for Pascal once wagered that by being in the world one must bet one's life on whether there is or is not a god. As Jeff Jordan summarized: 'If one bets against God and wins, one gains very little. But if one loses the bet, then the consequences may be horrendous' (Jeff Jordan, (ed.), *Gambling on God* [Lanham, MD: Rowman & Littlefield Publishing, Ltd., 1994], p. 1).

[5] John Scarne, *Scarne's New Complete Guide To Gambling* (NY: A Fireside Book (Simon & Schuster), 1974), pp. 9f. distinguishes between seven types of gamblers: [1] the occasional gambler; [2] the degenerate or habitual gambler; [3] the skilled gambler or gambler hustler; [4] the professional gambler or gamble operator; [5] the gambler cheat or crook; [6] the gambler chiseler; [7] the system gambler who 'lives in a dream world all his own, believing that it is only a question of time until he finds an infallible betting system which he can use to amass a fortune' (p. 10).

[6] Fredreka Schouten, 'Internet gambling under fire', *The Cincinnati Enquirer*, Feb.11, 1999, A-9.

[7] *International Gaming & Wagering Business* journal (*IGWB*), August, 1997, pp. 63–66.

[8] Ibid., p. 64.

[9] Tomas M. Martinez, *The Gambling Scene: Why People Gamble* (Springfield IL: Charles C. Thomas Publisher, 1983), p. 107.

[10] Larry Burkett, *Christian Financial Concepts: Money Matters*, May 1997, Issue 233, p. 1. Burkett may be referring to William M. Bulkeley's statement in the *Wall Street Journal*, 14 July 1992, 'Video Betting, called "Crack of Gambling", is spreading.' cf. Viveca Novak, 'They Call It Video Crack', *Time*, 1 June 1998, p. 58.

[11] Rex M. Rogers, *Seducing America*, p. 35.

[12] Barry M. Horstman, 'Personal casinos: Net bets', *The Cincinnati Post*, 20 September 1997, 4-A.

[13] Brett Pulley, 'With Technology, Island Bookies Skirt US Law', *The New York Times*, 31 January 1998, A-1.

[14] Ibid.

[15] *Time*, 2 June 1997, p. 61.

[16] B. M. Horstman, 'Casinos here to stay, but fight won't go away', *The Cincinnati Post*, 20 September 1997, 4-A.

[17] Ibid.

[18] *IGWB*, August, 1977, p. 48.

[19] Ibid., pp. 48, 49.

[20] Ibid., pp. 49–51. *IGWB* covers the current pressures being used to change the 1994 Congressional ban.

[21] Donald Janson, *The New York Times*, 2 September 1979, 'Casino gambling has done wonders in the service of Mammon in the center of Atlantic City, but it has brought a sharp decline in membership and attendance at churches of all denominations here.' Recent studies of the effect of commercial gambling in Atlantic City show that the 'mild recovery Atlantic City enjoyed in 1994–1995 ran into the sand in 1996'. Like the tide in plain view 'Atlantic City's future has receded' – leaving it the meagre gains from day trips instead of the prosperity of a destination resort (*IGWB*, August 1997, pp. 25, 26). See George Sternlieb with Jane W. Hughes, *The Atlantic City Gamble* (Cambridge, MA: Harvard University Press, 1983), 215 pages. Casino business has not raised the economic strength of Atlantic City. It is 'still a festering slum, with 15% unemployment and no movie theater' (*Business Week*, 9 November 1998, 38E4). The unemployment rate compares to three times the national average unemployment rate of 12.7 per cent ('1997 Annual Average Labor Estimates by Municipality', New Jersey Department of Labour, Office of Labour Planning and Analysis, cited by James Dobson, 'Family News', *Focus on the Family*, January 1999, p. 3).

[22] Rachel Melcher, 'Churches say casinos exact stiff price', *The Cincinnati Enquirer*, 12 June 1999, B-1.

[23] Ibid., B-7.

[24] *IGWB*, August, 1977, p. 28.

[25] Ibid., p. 29.

[26] The Macmillan Company, *Encyclopaedia Judaica* (Jerusalem, Israel: Keter Publishing House, Ltd., 1971), Vol. 1:301.

[27] Rex M. Rogers went further. He had four more reasons why gambling should be rejected by every Christian.

[28] Tony Evans, *Tony Evans Speaks*, p. 41.

[29] T. De Witt Talmage, *500 Selected Sermons* (Grand Rapids: Baker Book House, 1900, 1957), Vol. 6:188.

[30] T. M. Martinez, *The Gambling Scene*, op. cit., p. 54. See also Jim Orford, *Excessive Appetites* (A Psychological View of Addiction) (Chichester, NY: Wiley, 1985), 367 pages.

[31] T. M. Martinez, *Gambling Scene*, op. cit., p. 39.

[32] Rachel Melcher, 'Riverboat casinos awash with retirees', *The Cincinnati Enquirer*, 12 July 1998, E-1.

[33] Edmund Bergler, *The Psychology of Gambling* (London: Bernard Hanison Ltd., 1958), p. 7.

[34] It is huge elsewhere, too. For instance, the Dutch State Lottery and the Dutch Giro Lottery 'attract 2 million and 1.2 million players monthly'. (See Willem Albert Wagenear, *Paradoxes of Gambling Behaviour* (London, UK: Lawrence Erlbaum Associates Publishers, 1988), Chapter 5.

[35] For reasons of space there are minimal references to race-track and sport gambling in *Lotto: Fun or Folly?* On these forms of gaming, see *IGWB*'s August, 1997, journal supplement, pp. 34–37, 64–68.

[36] 'When you combine revenue from all spectator sports, such as baseball and football and hockey with revenue from other leisure activities for which Americans spend money, such as movie box office totals, theme parks, cruise ships and recorded music, that combined total is still less than the revenue from gambling'. (*ICWB*, Background Paragraph of Resolution: 'Raising Moral Objections to State Sponsored Gambling', 18 May 1996).

[37] Rachel Melcher, 'Problem gamblers hard to identify and hard to count', *The Cincinnati Enquirer*, 19 June 1999, A-4.

[38] Rachel Melcher, 'Riverboat casinos awash with retirees', *The Cincinnati Enquirer*, 12 July 1998, E-1.

[39] Ann Fabian, *Card Sharps*, p. 11.

[40] R. Melcher, ibid. John Sheldon III, director of marketing and entertainment at Grand Victoria Casino and Resort in Rising Sun, Indiana, said, 'Average folks (come) here for entertainment'.

[41] T. M. Martinez, *The Gambling Scene*, op. cit., p. 103. Martinez coined the expression 'TV game-bling.' 'The offspring of the marriage between gambling and the media is the TV game show' (ibid., p. 105).

[42] James H. Gilmore; B. Joseph Pine II, 'Beyond Goods and Services: Staging experiences and guiding transformations', *Strategy & Leadership: A Publication of Strategic Leadership Forum* (Cleveland, OH: Strategic Horizons LLP, 1997), May/June 1997, Vol. 25: No. 3, entire, and Pine/Gilmore, 'Manager's Journal', *The Wall Street Journal*, 4 August 1997, A-18. See B. Joseph Pine II, James H. Gilmore, *The Experience Economy: Works is Theatre & Every Business a Stage* (Boston, MA: Harvard Business School Press, 1999).

[43] Jim Howell, 'West Ohio Follows Grey into gambling Fray', *United Methodist Review*, West Ohio Edition, Vol. 13, No. 15, 12 July 1996, pp. 1f.

[44] Barry M. Horstman, ' "Player tracking" finds those who bet (lose) big', *The Cincinnati Post*, 15 September 1997, 4-A.

[45] For those who cannot consult a US print copy or a library Reference copy, use the Internet: www.ngisc.gov.

2. The Bible on Gambling

[1]   Robert Horton made an unfounded comparison
      between selling stock and robbery. He took the refer-
      ences in Proverbs against stealing as a reference to stock
      traders. He claimed stock traders fed off others' misfor-
      tunes, thereby 'robbing them'. ('Proverbs', *The Exposi-
      tor's Bible* [London: Hodder & Stoughton, 1895] p. 23).

[2]   NIV. Chapter 8 focuses on the significance of these
      texts.

[3]   Norman Geisler, in his book *Gambling*, p. 114, cited
      Proverbs 13:11: 'Wealth from gambling quickly disap-
      pears; wealth from hard work grows' (*Living Bible*). But
      the Hebrew text does not have the word 'gambling'.
      The Hebrews did not have a word for gambling. Prov-
      erbs 13:11 refers to sudden fortune, which could be an
      inheritance or gift from a living person; it need not be
      wealth from winning a bet.

[4]   Ivan Zablika, *The Lottery Lie: Gamblers, Money and Hungry
      Kids* (Anderson, IN: Bristol House, Ltd., 1998), p. 121.

[5]   Joseph Addison Alexander [1809–1860], *Commentary
      on Isaiah* (Grand Rapids: Zondervan Publishing House,
      1953), Vol. 2:446.

[6]   Franz Delitzsch [1813–1890], *Biblical Commentary on the
      Prophecies of Isaiah* (Grand Rapids: Wm. B. Eerdmans
      Publishing Co., 1954), Vol. 2:482.

[7]   Herbert Carl Leupold [1892–1922], *Exposition of Isaiah*
      (Grand Rapids: Baker Book House, 1972), Vol. 2:364. E.
      J. Young: 'Perhaps there is an intended contrast
      between spreading out the tables for meals and bowing
      down to be slaughtered'. (*The Book of Isaiah* [Grand
      Rapids: Wm. B. Eerdmans Publishing Co., 1972], Vol.
      3:510.)

[8]   David L. McKenna, 'Gambling', *Christianity Today*, 8
      June 1973.

9   Henry Chafetz, *Play the Devil: A History of Gambling in the United States from 1492 to 1955* (New York: Bonanza Books, 1950), p. 254.

10 *The Cincinnati Post*, 7 June 1997, 4-C.

11 *The Philadelphia Evening Bulletin*, 3 October 1966, p. 2.

12 Alan Haynes, 'The First English National Lottery', *History Today*, 29:613, September 1979.

13 'Lotteries Relegalized', *The Economist*, 263:25, 30 April 1977.

14 Wm. Petersen, *What . . . about Gambling?*, p. 5.

15 Herbert Waddams, *An Introduction to Moral Theology* (New York: Seabury Press, 1964), p. 219.

16 H. P. Howington, cited in R. Coggins (ed.), *The Gambling Menace* (Nashville, TN: Broadman Press, 1966), p. 23.

17 Personal correspondence.

18 Donald Carson, 'The Gospel of Matthew' in *The Expositor's Bible Commentary* (Grand Rapids: Regency [Zondervan], 1984), Vol. 8:516.

19 Ibid.

20 Frederick Dale Bruner, *Matthew: The Churchbook* (Dallas: Word Publishing, 1990), Vol. 2:902.

21 D. Carson, *Matthew*, op. cit., p. 516. Also suggested in the Revised English Bible.

22 Leon Morris, *The Gospel According To Matthew* (Grand Rapids: Wm. B. Eerdmans Publishing Co., 1992), p. 631.

23 D. Carson, *Matthew*, op. cit., p. 516, however, believes there is no reference to investment of money in a lending agency. Carson, however, provides no textual prohibition against earning through loaning out. Leon Morris argued, however, that *toxos* refers to 'loaned money at interest'. (Morris, *Matthew*, op. cit., p. 631, note 43.

24 Ibid.

25 Lycurgus M. Starkey, Jr., 'Christians and the Gambling Mania', *The Christian Century*, 27 February 1963, p. 269.

[26] Carl F. H. Henry, *The Christian Mindset In A Secular Society: Promoting Evangelical Renewal & National Righteousness* (Portland, OR: Multnomah Press, 1984), p. 138.

[27] Wayne E. Oates, *Luck: A Secular Faith* (Louisville, KY: Westminster Press, 1995), pp. 6, 68, 74, 77, 79, 87, 95, 100, 102, 103.

[28] Rex M. Rogers, *Seducing*, p. 63.

[29] Ibid., p. 93.

[30] Ibid., p. 68.

[31] Tony Evans, *What A Way To Live: Running All of Life by the Kingdom Agenda* (Nashville, TN: Word Publishing, 1997), p. 415.

[32] I. L. Zabilka, *The Lottery Lie*, p. 125.

[33] R. M. Rogers, *Seducing*, p. 94.

[34] David L. McKenna, 'Gambling: Parasite on Public Morals, *Christianity Today*, 8 June 1973, p. 4.

[35] A. Fabian, *Card Sharps*, p. 10.

[36] T. Evans, *What A Way To Live*, p. 415.

[37] D. Bruner, *Matthew: Churchbook*, p. 905.

[38] Bob Russell, 'Take The Risk', *Preaching Today*, Christianity Today/Leadership, 1995.

3. Is Stock Investment Gambling?

[1] Henry Ward Beecher, *Lectures to Young Men*, (Philadelphia: Henry Altemus, 1895), p. 136.

[2] 'Repentance always implies abhorrence of sin. It of course involves the love of God and the forsaking of sin. The sinner who truly repents does not feel as impenitent sinners think they should feel at giving up their sins, if they should become religious. Impenitent sinners look upon religion in this way: that if they become pious, they should be obliged to stay away from balls and parties, and obliged to give up theatres,

or gambling, or other things that they now take delight in.' Charles Finney, *Lectures on Revivals*, Lecture 18: 'Directions to Sinners', [1835], p. 364.

[3] Charles Finney, *Lectures to Professing Christians* (1878), Chapter 3, 'Doubtful Actions are Sinful', pp. 40, 41.

[4] T. De Witt Talmage, *500 Selected Sermons* (Grand Rapids: Baker Book House, 1900, 1957), Vol. 6:181. On Talmage's life see his posthumously published autobiography, *T. De Witt Talmage – As I Knew Him* [the concluding chapters by his wife] (New York: E. P. Dutton and Company, 1911). One of my former seminary professors, Dr George Handy Wailes, had – as a young man – heard Talmage. Wailes had high praise for Talmage, one of the most popular preachers of his era. He was, in Wailes' view, an amazingly able orator.

[5] Ibid., Vol. 10:181.

[6] Ibid., Vol. 10:182.

[7] William Adamson, *The Life of Joseph Parker, D.D.* (New York: Fleming H. Revell Co., 1902), p. 314.

[8] T. De Witt Talmage, *500 Selected Sermons* (Grand Rapids: Baker Book House, 1900, 1957), Vol. 17:234.

[9] Rex M. Rogers, *Seducing America*, p. 94.

[10] Henlee H. Barnette, 'Gambling', *Baker's Dictionary of Christian Ethics*, editor Carl F. H. Henry (Grand Rapids: Canon Press/Baker Book House, 1973), pp. 257, 258.

[11] Vicki Abt, James F. Smith, Eugene Martin Christiansen, *The Business of Risk* (Lawrence, KS: University Press of Kansas, 1985), p. 259.

[12] Justin Mamis, *The Nature of Risk: Stock Market Survival and the Meaning of Life* (Reading, MA: Addison-Wesley Publishing Company, 1991), p. 113.

[13] Vicki Abt, James F. Smith, Eugene Martin Christiansen, *The Business of Risk*, op. cit., p. 259.

[14] Justin Mamis, *The Nature of Risk: Stock Market Survival and the Meaning of Life*, p. 90.

[15] William J. Petersen, *What You Should Know About Gambling: A Christian Approach to Problems of Today* (New Canaan, CT: Keats Publishing, Inc., 1974), p. 80.

[16] 'The stock market can be a gamble, especially if you do not know what you are doing. There are people who gamble on stocks and lose their socks.' Geisler, *Gambling*, p. 79.

[17] Wayne E. Oates, *Luck: A Secular Faith* (Louisville, KY: Westminster Press, 1995), p. 7.

[18] Rex. M. Rogers, *Seducing America*, p. 94.

[19] Ibid.

[20] Ibid.

[21] Larry Burkett, *Christian Financial Concepts*, (May, 1997), p. 1.

[22] See Chapter 2 for an examination of the Matthean passage on investments.

[23] George Gilder, *Wealth & Poverty* (San Francisco: Institute for Contemporary Studies, 1983, 1993), p. 68.

[24] John Train, *The Midas Touch* (New York: Harper & Row Publishers, 1987), p. 46: 'The gambler, to a greater extent than the aggressive speculator, will take a leap into the unknown, trust that his experience and intuition will give him a big winner. [That there is a close relationship between investment risk and investment reward] would be true if the efficient market theory were correct. It is not true in skillful, value-oriented investment.'

[25] Kenneth M. Morris, Alan M. Siegel, *The Wall Street Journal Guide to Understanding Money & Investing* (New York: Lightbulb Press, 1993), p. 133.

[26] Ann [Vincent] Fabian, *Card Sharps, Dream Books, & Bucket Shops: Gambling in 19th-century America* (Ithaca: Cornell University Press, 1990), p. 6.

[27] Wayne E. Oates, *Luck: A Secular Faith* (Louisville, KY: Westminster Press 1995), p. 77.

28 Justin Mamis, *The Nature of Risk*, p. 104.

4. Casting Lots Through the Ages

1 N. Geisler, *Gambling*, p. 119.
2 Rex M. Rogers, *Seducing America*, p. 59. Yet there is minimal material on casting lots in Rogers' work. He essentially raised the matter only to drop it.
3 *NIV Study Bible* (Grand Rapids: Zondervan Publishing Co., 1985) pp., 710, 1367 notes.
4 P. J. Achtemier, *Harper's Bible Dictionary*, (San Francisco: Harper & Row, Publishers, Inc. 1985).
5 Ibid.
6 Ibid.
7 Ibid. Of significance is a thorough 1986 doctoral dissertation by Cornelius Van Dam, *The* Urim *and* Thummim: *A Means of Revelation in Ancient Israel* (Winona Lake: Eisenbrauns, 1997), Van Dam argued convincingly throughout his monograph that the *Urim/Thummim* was not the same as casting lots (Ibid., 35–37, 199, 216, 261, 262). The distribution of the tribal land was through lot, not the *Urim/Thummim*. Lot-casting had divine guidance but was not used for divine revelation.
8 Ibid. Walter C. Kaiser, Jr., Peter H. Davids, F. F. Bruce, Manfred T. Brauch, *Hard Sayings Of The Bible* (Downers Grove, IL: Inter-Varsity Press, 1996), p. 331.
9 Tomas M. Martinez, *The Gambling Scene: Why People Gamble*, op. cit., p. 5
10 Walvoord, John F., and Zuck, Roy B., *The Bible Knowledge Commentary*, (Wheaton, Illinois: Scripture Press Publications, Inc., 1983).
11 Walter C. Kaiser, Jr., Peter H. Davids, F. F. Bruce, Manfred T. Brauch, *Hard Sayings Of The Bible*, (Downers Grove, IL: Inter-Varsity Press, 1996), p. 331.

[12]   James Luther Mays, Ph.D. (ed.) *Harper's Bible Commentary*, (New York: Harper & Row, Publishers, Inc.) 1988.

[13]   See Chapter 8, p.120.

[14]   Marvin R. Vincent [1834–1922], *Word Studies in the New Testament* (New York: Charles Scribner's Sons, 1914), Vol. 2:81, 82.

[15]   M. Henry, *Matthew Henry's Commentary on the Bible*, (Peabody, MA: Hendrickson Publishers, 1991).

[16]   Summarized from ibid.

[17]   Marvin Vincent, *Word Pictures in the New Testament*, Vol. 1: 287 on Luke 1:9.

[18]   Herman Hanse, 'lagchano', G. Kittel, (ed.) *The Theological Dictionary of the New Testament* (Grand Rapids: Wm. B. Eerdmans Publishing Co., 1967), Vol. 4:1.2

[19]   Ibid.

[20]   Michael Fleeman, 'Terror in the Heartland: The McVeigh Trial', *The Cincinnati Enquirer*, 23 April 1997, A-10.

[21]   See Chapter 8 of *Lotto: Fun or Folly?* where I summarize Gataker's Chap. 10. There I note: 'One of the most intriguing sections was his treatment of "Bible" lottery (340–346). (This was pre-Wesley practice!)'

[22]   Christopher P. Gavaler, 'The Empty Lot', *American Indian Quarterly*, Spring, 1994; 18: 2, pp. 215, 217, 221, 222, 226. Works cited: John Heckewelder, *Thirty Thousand Miles with John Heckewelder*, edited by Paul A. W. Wallace (Pittsburgh: Pittsburgh University Press, 1958); Earl P. Olmstead, *Blackcoats Among the Delawares*(Kent, OH: Kent State University Press, 1991); Paul W. Wallace, 'Introduction', *Thirty Thousand Miles with John Heckewelder*, op. cit.

[23]   Joseph Edmund Hutton, *A History of the Moravian Church* (London: Moravian Publication Office, 1909). John Taylor Hamilton, *History of the Moravian Church: the Renewed Unitas Fratum, 1722–1957* (Bethlehem, PA:

Interprovincial Board of Christian Education, Moravian Church in America, 1967). And don't miss the last two: Charlotte B. Mortimer, *Marrying by Lot: A tale of the Primitive Moravians* (New York: G. P. Putnam, 1868), Clarence E. Beckel, *Early Marriage Customs of the Moravian Congregation in Bethlehem, Pennsylvania* (Allentown, PA: Pennsylvania German Folklore Society 1938).

24 John Wesley, *Works of John Wesley: Journals* Vol. 1, 14 October 1735–29 November 1745, p. 169.

25 John Wesley, *Works of John Wesley: Addresses, Essays, Dialogues*, op. cit., Vol. 8:522, 525, (Address: 'Principles of a Methodist').

26 For this and following references, see William D. Buursma, 'Casting Lots For Church Leaders', *Leadership*, 6, 3, Summer, 1985, pp. 99, 100.

5. 'Gambling' at Golgotha

1 Ralph Gowers, *The New Manners and Customs of Bible Times*, (Chicago: The Moody Bible Institute of Chicago, 1987).

2 Josef Blinzler, *The Trial of Christ* (Westminster, MD: The Newman Press, 1959), p. 243.

3 Matthew 27:35; Mark 15:24; Luke 23:34; John 19:23, 24.

4 Rex M. Rogers, *Seducing America*, op. cit., p. 60.

5 Kenneth Escott Kirk, *Conscience and Its Problems: An Introduction to Casuistry* (New York: Longman's Green and Company Ltd., 1927), p. 313.

6 Raymond E. Brown, S.S., *The Death of the Messiah* (New York: Doubleday, 1994), Vol. 2:956.

7 Mentioned by B. F. Westcott in his classic commentary on the English text of John (p. 275).

8. Klass Schilder, *Christ Crucified* (Grand Rapids: Wm. B. Eerdmans Publishing Co., 1940), p. 177.

9. Flavius Josephus, *Antiquities of the Jews*, III. 6.4.

10. Frederick W. Krummacher, *The Suffering Savior* (New York: Robert Carter and Brothers, 1855), p. 369.

11. William Barclay, *Daily Study Bible, The Gospel of John* (Phila.: The Westminster Press, 1955), Vol. 2:297.

12. Raymond E. Brown, S.S., *The Death of the Messiah* (New York: Doubleday, 1994), Vol. 2:957.

13. Ibid., Vol. 2:957, 958.

14. C. H. Spurgeon, *Metropolitan Tabernacle Pulpit*, Vol. 45:319. There is no evidence anywhere for the contention that the dice had any of Jesus' blood on them.

15. Charles H. Spurgeon, *Morning and Evening*, (Oak Harbor, WA: Logos Research Systems, Inc., 1995).

16. Charles Haddon Spurgeon, *The Gospel According to Promise* [on Matthew 27:35].

17. Henry Ward Beecher, 'Gambling and Gamblers', *Lectures to Young Men* (Philadelphia: Henry Altemus, 1895) p. 135.

18. Richard Allen Bodey, 'A Bag With Holes', *Christianity Today*, Vol. 2, No. 6, 23 December 1957, p. 17.

19. For a modern instance, see D. James Kennedy's sermon, 'What's Wrong with Gambling?' (Fort Lauderdale, FL: Coral Ridge Ministries, n.d.), p. 3.

20. Frederick W. Farrar, *The Life of Christ* (New York: A. L. Burt Company, 1874), p. 501.

21. See Marvin Vincent, *Word Studies in the New Testament*, Vol. 2:285. Alfred Edersheim suggested the four parts to be: headgear, sandals/shoes, long girdle, and a coarse *talith* or outer mantle. A. R. S. Kennedy, argues that Jesus was led barefoot to Golgotha. See Raymond E. Brown, S.S., *The Death of Jesus* (New York: Doubleday, 1994, Vol. 2:954–956).

22. Thomas Gataker, *On the Nature and Use of Lots: A*

Treatise, Historical and Theological (London: John Haviland, 1627), p. 218. See also p. 100.

[23] Henry Alford, *Greek New Testament* (Chicago: Moody Press, 1856, 1958), Vol. 1:899.

[24] Scholars debate whether Psalm 22 created the gambling detail or whether Psalm 22 illustrated and reinforced the detail. I am of the persuasion that Jesus fulfilled what was foretold. It was neither contrived nor coincidental. Other parts of Psalm 22 found fulfilment in Christ which could not be contrived or created, such as the conversion of Gentile nations on account of him (22:26–32).

6. Is Risk-taking Gambling?

[1] T. M. Martinez, *The Gambling Scene*, op. cit., p. 55.

[2] *The Billings Gazette*, 23 March 1978, A-1.

[3] *The New York Times*, 9 October 1979, A-6.

[4] *People*, 3 March 1979. Women block out the risks of plastic surgery, but there are plenty: facial paralysis, infection, skin perforation, hair loss, blindness, even death by pulmonary embolism.

[5] Bruce Schneier, *Applied Cryptography* (New York: John Wiley & Sons, Inc., 1994), p. 16.

[6] *Statistical Abstracts of the United States, 1996* (Washington, D.C.: US Department of Commerce, 1996), p. 101.

[7] *Time*, 6 December 1976, p. 65.

[8] Tony Evans, *Tony Evans Speaks out on Gambling & the Lotto* (Chicago: Moody Press, 1995), pp. 8, 10.

[9] See Chapter 3 on the controversy of whether or not stock investment is a gamble.

[10] Tony Evans, op. cit., p. 23.

[11] David L. McKenna, 'Gambling: Parasite on Public Morals', *Christianity Today*, 8 June 1973, p. 4.

[12] Elizabeth Achtemeir, *The Committed Marriage* (Philadelphia: Westminster Press, 1976), p. 51.

[13] Moyers has since changed his ecclesiastical credentials. He is currently a member of the United Church of Christ.

[14] *The Billings Gazette*, 3 August 1975, B-4.

[15] John Scarne, *Scarne's New Complete Guide to Gambling* (New York: Simon and Schuster, 1974), p. 6.

[16] Scarne, *Guide To Gambling*, op. cit., p. 1.

[17] Charlotte Olmsted, *Heads I Win, Tails You Lose* (New York: The Macmillan Co., 1962), p. 60. 'Women gamblers now make up one out of every four persons being treated by Gamblers Anonymous. An astonishing one out of every three gamblers is a woman.... Unlike men, most women who wager tend to be closet gamblers, and more than three-fourths list escape as a dominant reason for gambling.' Geisler, *Gambling*, op. cit., p. 88. Sandra LeSourd, *The Compulsive Woman* (Old Tappan, NJ: Chosen Books, 1987), p. 233, puts the percentage of compulsive women gamblers higher, at one-third of all compulsive gamblers. Barbara Deane says women are gambling more and many are unable to quit. See 'Risking It All: Women and Gambling', *Woman's Day*, Vol. 59. No. 4, Feb. 1, 1996, p. 43.

[18] Rachel Melcher, 'Riverboat casinos awash with retirees', *The Cincinnati Enquirer*, 12 July 1998, E-2.

[19] Rogers, *Seducing America*, op. cit., p. 44.

[20] Ibid., p. 121.

[21] *The Philadelphia Enquirer*, 12 June 1972, B-8

[22] Rogers, *Seducing America*, op. cit., p. 32.

[23] Barry M. Horstman, 'Chasing Instant Riches', *The Cincinnati Post*, 15 September 1997, 4-A.

[24] Stephen and Amanda Sorenson, *Living Smart, Spending Less: Creative Ways to Stretch Your Income . . . and Have Fun Doing it* (Chicago: Moody Press, 1993), p. 23.

[25] See pages 121, 122 of Chapter 9 ahead for Gataker's use of the expression.

[26] Ben E. Johnson, *Getting Lucky: Answers to Nearly Every Lottery Question You may Ask* (Chicago: Bonus Books, 1994), p. 47.

[27] John Ezell, 'The Lottery in Colonial America', *The William and Mary Quarterly*, Vol. 5; No. 2, April, 1948, p. 194.

[28] Ibid., p. 197.

[29] Carl Sifakis, *The Encyclopedia of Gambling* (New York: Facts on File, 1990), p. 187.

[30] Michael J. Walsh, 'Responsible Gaming', Louisville's *The Courier-Journal*, 12 August 1998.

[31] Paul Zane Pilzer, *God Wants You To Be Rich: How and Why Everyone Can Enjoy Material and Spiritual Wealth in Our Abundant World* (New York: Simon & Schuster, 1995), p. 27.

[32] Hebrews 11:24, 25, *NIV*.

[33] George Lawson, *An Exposition of Ruth* (Evansville, IN: Sovereign Grace Publishers, 1805, 1960), p. 43.

[34] Charles Haddon Spurgeon, *New Park Street Pulpit*, Vol. 4 (1858): 479.

[35] James Swanson, (ed.) *New Nave's Topical Bible*, (Oak Harbor, Washington: Logos Research Systems, Inc., 1994).

[36] Joachim Jeremias, *Jerusalem in the Time of Jesus* (Philadelphia: Fortress Press, 1979), p. 267.

[37] Gerhard Kittel, ed., *The Theological Dictionary of the New Testament* (Grand Rapids: Wm. B. Eerdmans Publishing Co., 1974), Vol. 9:638. cf. also TDNT, Vol. 6:491; Vol. 8:155.

[38] Karl Barth, *Church Dogmatics* (Edinburgh: T & T Clark, 1939), I/2, p. 622.

[39] Edward Schillebeeckx, *Jesus* (New York: Vintage Books, 1981), p. 643.

[40] Martin Bucer, *Instruction in Christian Love*, (Richmond,

VA: John Knox Press, 1952) Paul T. Fuhrmann (transla-
tor) p. 52.

7. Puritan Ponderings

[1] William Ames, translated out of the Latin, *Conscience
with the Power and Cases* [divided into five books] (London: Printed by Edward Deering for I. Rothwell, T.
Slater, L. Blacklock, 1643), pp. 60, 61. The whole work,
of over 292 pages, 6½ by 5 inches in size, is a series of
questions and answers in the typical Puritan format.
Baxter's work had a similar title: *Cases of Conscience*.

[2] Rex M. Rogers' one paragraph of only 11 lines omits the
diversity of opinion within top-level Puritan thinking.
His cryptic summary, unfortunately, is misleading. It
follows, fairly closely, the views of Cotton Mather (see
below) on gambling, without mentioning the admission of the role of chance in Puritan theologians
(*Seducing America*, op. cit., p. 30). Scattered select
Matherian arguments are found in Ivan Zabilka, *The
Lottery Lie: Gamblers, Money, and Hungry Kids*, (Anderson, IN: Bristol House, Ltd., 1998) pp. 110, 175, 179.

[3] Laura A. Smoller, 'Playing Cards and Popular Culture
in Sixteenth-Century Nuremberg', *The Sixteenth Century Journal*, Vol. 17; No. 2, Summer, 1986, p. 189.

[4] Ibid., pp. 188, 189.

[5] Ibid., p. 189.

[6] Martin Luther, *Luther's Works: Table Talk*, edited and
translated by Theodore G. Tappert (Phila.: Fortress
Press, 1967), Vol. 54: 206.

[7] J. K. S. Reid, trans., *Calvin: The Theological Treatises*
(Phila.: Westminster Press, Library of Christian Classics, 1954), p. 82.

[8] L. A. Smoller, 'Playing Cards', op. cit., p. 190.

9   See Alan MacFarlane's introductory essay 'Diary-keeping in seventeenth-century England', to *The Family Life Of Ralph Josselin (1671–1683): A Seventeenth-Century Clergyman* (London: W. W. Norton & Company, 1970) pp. 3–14.

10 On the friendship between Pepys and Evelyn, see John Drinkwater, *Pepys: His Life and Character* (Garden City: Doubleday, 1930). For Pepys on gambling: *The Complete Diaries*: on visits to the gaming house – Vol. 2 (1661):211–212; refuses to gamble – Vol. 4 (1663):87; lotteries at court – Vol. 5 (1664):214–215; other lotteries – Vol. 5 (1664):269, 276, 279, 299–300, 323; wins books – Vol. 7 (1666):8; gambling at court and inns – Vol. 9 (1668–69):2–4, 9, 71. For a brief but good biography of Evelyn see Florence Highham's *John Evelyn Esquire: An Anglican layman of the seventeenth century* (Naperville, IL: SCM Book Club, 1968).

11 See the now rare, John Evelyn, *The History Of Religion* (London: Henry Colburn, Publisher, 1850) 2 volumes.

12 The 17th-century spelling peculiarities are retained in the citations from Evelyn diaries. John Evelyn, *The Diary of John Evelyn*, selected, edited by John Bowle (New York: Oxford University Press, 1985), p. 193. Wm. Bray edition of the Evelyn diaries, *Diary and Correspondence of John Evelyn*, R.R.S. (London: George Routledge & Sons, Ltd., n.d.), p. 250.

13 Ibid., pp. 238, 239, 323.

14 J. Bowle (ed.) *Diaries*, op. cit., pp. 320, 321.

15 Westminster Assembly, *The Westminster Larger Catechism*, (Oak Harbor, WA: Logos Research Systems, Inc., 1995).

16 'The clerical dynasty of the Gatakers, father and son, lectured for 66 years; Thomas, Sr. lectured at Christ Church Newgate from 1579 to 1593, and Thomas, Jr. [the one we are treating] lectured first at Lincoln's Inn

from 1602 to 1611 and then across the river at Rotherhithe from 1611 until his death in 1654', (p. 199, Paul S. Seaver, *The Puritan Lectureships* (Stanford, CA: Stanford University Press, 1970)). See Benjamin Brook, *The Lives of the Puritans* (Soli Deo Gloria Publications, 1813, 1994), Vol. 3:200–222.

[17] James Reid, *Memoirs Of The Westminster Divine* (Edinburgh: The Banner of Truth Trust, 1811, 1982), Vol. 1: 305. Daniel Neal, *The History of the Puritans* (Minneapolis, MN: Klock & Klock Christian Publishers, 1837, 1979) Vol. 2:643.

[18] Irvonwy Morgan, *Prince Charles's Puritan Chaplains* (London: George Allen & Unwin Ltd., 1957), p. 109.

[19] Several university libraries have Gataker's work on lots. One is at the University of Las Vegas; the one I used was at Lehigh University at Allentown, PA.

[20] Ames had more to say on lotteries in his work, *Conscience with Power and Cases* (1643) cited at the start of this session.

[21] Robinson never made the trip but said farewell to the Plymouth colony when they left Holland. Robinson's article on casting lots is found in his works: Robert Ashton (ed.) *The Works of John Robinson* (London: John Snow, 1851), Vol. 1:201–204 where he explores, however briefly, the similarity between oath and lot.

[22] William Ames, *The Marrow Of Theology*, translated from the 3rd Latin edition and edited by John D. Eusden (Philadelphia: Pilgrim Press, 1629, 1968), p. 18. Gataker, however, does give a defence of his position against this charge.

[23] Ibid., p. 273. The wager was a legitimate way of settling a conflict of interests. As Ames saw it, lotteries became evil when it was used as an easy and repeated way to make gain.

[24] Ames, *Conscience*, op. cit., pp. 60, 61.

[25] Reid, *Memoirs*, op. cit., Vol. 1:294.

[26] John T. McNeill, *A History of The Cure of Souls* (New York: Harper & Brothers Publishers, 1951), p. 265.

[27] N. H. Keeble and Geoffrey F. Nuttall, *Calendar and Correspondence of Richard Baxter* (Oxford: Clarendon Press, 1991) Vol. 1 (1638–1660): the pertinent correspondence is nos. 124, 144, 189.

[28] Richard Baxter, *The Works of Richard Baxter*: The Christian Directory (Pittsburgh: Soli Deo Gloria Publications, 1673, 1990), Vol. 1:840 (The quotes are from Chapter 19, Part 4, Title 5: 'Cases of Conscience about Lusory Contracts').

[29] Cotton Mather, *Winter Meditations: Directions How to Employ the Leisure of the Winter for the Glory of God* (Boston: Benjamin Harris, 1693), p. 11.

[30] Richard Baxter, *The Certainty of the Worlds of Spirits* (London: T. Parkhust, 1691), pp. 223, 224. Interestingly, in the same work Baxter refers to Cotton Mather's *Life of Mr. Eliot*, the New-England Evangelist (ibid., p. 244).

[31] John M. Findlay, *People of Chance: Gambling in American Society from Jamestown to Las Vegas* (New York: Oxford University Press, 1986), p. 18. In my research I found that Findlay wrote the fullest and best chapter on the history of gambling in colonial times.

[32] Cited by Lilly C. Stone, 'English Sports and Recreations', Louis B. Wright, Virginia A. LaMar, (eds) *Life and Letters in Tudor and Stuart England* (Ithaca, NY: Cornell University Press, 1962), p. 433.

[33] Findlay, *People of Chance*, op. cit.

[34] Horton Davies, *Worship and Theology in England*: II. From Andrewes to Baxter and Fox [1603–1690] (Grand Rapids: Eerdmans Publishing House, 1975, 1996), Vol. 2:173–175, ibid., Vol. 3 *From Watts and Wesley to Maurice, 1690–1850* (1961, 1996), p. 66. Peter Toon, *God's Statesman: The Life and Work of John Owen* (Exeter, UK: The

Paternoster Press, 1971) described South as 'a noted opponent of Protestant nonconformists' (p. 62). '[South's] learning was ample; his mind clear, strong and intense. . . . His invective is sharp, cutting, and by no means just . . . the freshness, vigour, and splendid movement of his style gave him an assured place among the great masters of English prose.' (Edwin Charles Dargan, *A History of Preaching*, Vol. 2:166, 167).

[35] Robert South, *Sermons* (Philadelphia: J. L. Gihon, 1853), Vol. 1:139, 163, 248, 350.

[36] South, *Sermons*, Vol. 1:121. See Chapter 8 where discussion focuses on South's contribution to the chance/providence debate.

[37] Gataker, pp. 130, 131.

[38] Ames, *Marrow*, op. cit., p. 18, note 38.

[39] Asbury, *Sucker's Progress*, op. cit., p. 73.

[40] Mather, *Winter Meditation*, op. cit., p. 10.

[41] Ames, *Marrow*, op. cit., pp. 4, 5, 296.

[42] Findlay, *People of Chance*, op. cit., p. 21 (citing Mather via Perry Miller).

[43] Mather, *Winter Meditations, Directions How to Employ the Leisure of the Winter for the Glory of God* (Boston: Benjamin Harris, 1693), pp. 10, 11.

[44] Jacob Rader Marcus, *The Jew in the Medieval World: A Source Book* (Cincinnati, OH: Hebrew Union College Press, 1938, 1990), p. 418.

[45] Gataker, *Lots*, op. cit., p. 237.

[46] Bruce C. Daniels, *Puritans At Play: Leisure and Recreation in Colonial New England* (New York: St. Martin's Press, 1995), p. 178.

[47] Ibid., p. 176.

[48] Ibid., p. 181.

[49] Information on early American lotteries can be found in the present work 88, 89, 113, 114, 209, 279 (#31).

[50] Daniels, op. cit, p. 182.

[51] Clyde Brian Davis, *Something For Nothing* (Philadelphia: J. B. Lippincott Company, 1956), p. 38.

[52] Asbury, *Sucker's Progress*, op. cit., p. 72.

[53] Davis, *Something For Nothing*, op. cit., p. 39.

[54] Asbury, *Sucker's Progress*, op. cit., p. 73.

[55] Daniels, *Puritans At Play*, op. cit., p. 182.

[56] Asbury, *Sucker's Progress*, op. cit., p. 76.

[57] Ibid., p. 74.

[58] Daniels, *Puritans At Play*, op. cit., pp., 182, 183.

[59] Asbury, *Sucker's Progress*, op. cit., p. 78.

[60] Julie Ralston, '15 chosen to buy houses for $1', *The Cincinnati Enquirer*, 25 June 1997, B-5.

[61] Rogers cites the Maryland local volunteer fire department lottery in 1992, which raised $4.1 million and spent $3.3 million to run the event, and Tennessee ran a charity bingo in 1988, which generated $50 million, but only $1 million reached charities (Rogers, *Seducing*, op. cit., p. 79).

[62] Findlay, *People of Chance*, op. cit., p. 30.

8. Thomas Gataker's, *On the Nature & Use of Lots*

[1] 'Lusorious' is no longer used today (obsolete). *The Oxford English Dictionary*, Vol. 1 (Compact Edition) (New York: Oxford University Press, 1971) pointed out that it was derived from the Latin, *lusor*, player, and related to the play aspect of wagering. One writer noted 4 kinds of lots: political, military, lusorious, and divinatory. Gataker used the word originally in 1619 in the first edition of his book on lots. T. Godwin used it first in 1613. Lusorious meant recreational; we would say, 'fun money'.

[2] In his massive (1,100 pgs) *magnum opus*, Jeremy Taylor (1613–1667) *Ductor Dubitantium, or the Rule of*

Consceince in All Her General Measures; serving as a great instrument for the determination of Cases of Conscience (1660), Book Four, Jeremy Taylor in dealing with the same question, takes the same position as Gataker. One wonders about how much Gataker's work influenced him.

9. Luck: Chance or Providence

[1] Kenneth S. Kantzer, 'Gambling: Everyone's a Loser', *Christianity Today*, 25 November 1983, p. 13.

[2] Frank Scoblete, *Break The One-Armed Bandits: How to Come Out Ahead when you play the Slots* (Chicago: Bonus Books, Inc., 1994), pp. 143, 145, 147.

[3] John Scarne, *Scarne's New Complete Guide to Gambling* (New York: Simon & Schuster, 1974), p. 25.

[4] G. A. Buttrick, (ed.), *The Interpreter's Bible* (New York: Abingdon Press, 1956), Vol. 5: 751 (James Muilenburg exegesis).

[5] Herbert Carl Leupold, *Exposition of Isaiah* (Grand Rapids: Baker Book House, 1971), Vol. 2:364.

[6] Edward J. Young, *The Book of Isaiah* (Grand Rapids: Wm. B. Eerdmans Publishing Co., 1972), Vol. 3:509.

[7] G. A. Buttrick, (ed.) *The Interpreter's Bible*, op. cit., p. 752.

[8] Franz Delitzsch, *Commentary on the Prophecies of Isaiah* (Grand Rapids: Wm. B. Eerdmans Publishing Co., 1877, 1954), Vol. 2:485.

[9] N. P. Howington, 'Biblical Insights', in Coggins, (ed.) *The Gambling Menace*, op. cit., p. 21. Very good background material on the significance of Gad and Meni can be found in Vol. 2:446 of Joseph Addison Alexander's [1809–1860] commentary on the *Prophecies of Isaiah* (Zondervan reprint, 1953).

[10] Wayne E. Oates, *Luck*, op. cit., p. 15.

11 Steven J. Brams, *Biblical Games: A Strategic Analysis of Stories in the Old Testament* (Cambridge, MA: The MIT Press, 1980), p. 5.

12 R. C. Sproul, *Not A Chance: The Myth of Chance in Modern Science & Cosmology* (Grand Rapids: Baker Books, 1994), pp. 1–39.

13 Ibid., p. 5.

14 Thomas Gataker, *On the Nature and Use of Lots*, op. cit., pp. 10, 11.

15 R. C. Sproul, *Not A Chance*, op. cit., pp. 6, 7.

16 Ibid., p. 23.

17 Ibid., pp. xii, 23, 24, 38, 39.

18 Thomas Gataker, *Nature and Use of Lots*, op. cit. pp. 38, 39.

19 Ibid., pp. 10, 11.

20 John Calvin, *Concerning the Predestination of God* (London: James Clarke & Co. Ltd., 1552, 1961), p. 169.

21 Ibid., pp. 163, 164.

22 Matthew Henry, *Matthew Henry's Commentary on the Bible*, (Peabody, MA: Hendrickson Publishers), 1991.

23 Ralph Wardlaw, *Lectures on The Book of Proverbs* (Minneapolis MN: Klock & Klock Christian Publishers, Inc., 1861, 1981), Vol. 3:117.

24 Robert South, *Sermons of Revd Robert South* (Phila. PA: J. L. Gihon, 1853), Vol. 1:121. Gataker, like South, also saw no conflict between chance as a secondary agent and God as the source of all that is. See Chapter 8, pp. 120, 127.

25 Charles H. Spurgeon, *New Park Street Pulpit* (Pasadena, TX: Pilgrim Publications, 1855, 1975), Vol. 1:257 (Spoke Sunday morning, 8 July 1855).

26 William G. Pollard, *Chance and Providence: God's Action in a World Governed by Scientific Law* (New York: Charles Scribner's Sons, 1958), p. 60.

27 R. K. McGregor Wright, *No Place for Sovereignty: What's*

Wrong with Freewill Theism (Downers Grove, IL: Intervarsity Press, 1996), p. 191.

[28] Heinz-Otto Peitgen, Hartmut Jurgens, Dietmar Saupe, *Chaos and Fractals: New Frontiers of Science* (New York: Springer-Verlag, 1992), p. 11.

[29] William G. Pollard, *Chance and Providence*, op. cit., p. 60.

[30] Ibid., p. 55.

[31] Ibid., p. 73.

[32] Ibid., p. 71.

[33] Chapter 8, p. 128.

[34] Chapter 8, pp.119–120. Wayne Oates made the same observation in his *Luck*, op. cit., p. 35.

[35] 'Fortunately' brings up the role of pagan Fortune; 'accident' brings up the historic contrast/conflict with divine providence, and 'charming' refers back to the pagan belief that spiritual powers other than God can change situations.

10. Probability: The Only Sure Thing in Lotto

[1] George Gilder, *Wealth & Poverty* (Santa Ana, CA: Institute for Contemporary Studies, 1983, 1993), p. 267.

[2] M. G. Bulmer, *Principles of Statistics* (New York: Dover Publications, Inc. 1967, 1969), pp. 1–6.

[3] Ann Fabian, *Card Sharps*, op. cit., p. 162.

[4] Ibid., p. 167.

[5] Ibid., p. 161.

[6] Tom Ainslie, *How To Gamble in a Casino: The Most Fun at the Least Risk* (New York: Simon & Schuster, 1979), pp. 20f.

[7] Horace C. Levinson, *The Science of Chance: From Probability to Statistics* (New York: Rinehart & Company, 1939, 1956), p. 24.

[8] Andrew Keith, Barbara Maddux, 'The Lucky Thirteen', *Time*, 10 August 1998, p. 63.

9   William F. Buckley, Jr., *National Review*, 1 September 1998, p. 55.

10   *Time*, 6 December 1976, pp. 54, 65.

11   Barry M. Horstman, ' "Player tracking" finds those who bet (lose) big', *The Cincinnati Post*, 15 September 1997, 4-A.

12   Just below whales are several thousand 'premium players' who typically wager from $100,000 to $250,000 a visit. Brett Pulley, 'Casinos Paying Top Dollar To Coddle Élite Gamblers', *The New York Times*, 12 January 1998, A-1, A-12.

13   Paisley Dodds, 'Gambling ban gets no respect', *The Cincinnati Enquirer*, 12 May 1997, A-6.

14   Kristen Delguzzi, *The Cincinnati Enquirer*, 4 June 1997, B-3.

15   Kristen Delguzzi, 'Editor Awaits Court Date to Plead Guilty to Theft of Christmas Fund', *The Cincinnati Enquirer*, 13 May 1997, B-2.

16   John Scarne, *Scarne's New Complete Guide To Gambling* (New York: Simon & Schuster, 1974), p. 17. For a full examination of probability see M. G. Bulmer, *Principles of Statistics* (New York: Dover Publications, Inc. 1967, 1969), and for the more advanced, consult Arnold O. Allen's *Probability, Statistics, and Queueing Theory* (with Computer Science Applications), 2nd edition (New York: Academic Press, Inc. 1977, 1990).

17   Ross Phares, *Bible in Pocket, Gun in Hand: The Story of Frontier Religion* (Lincoln: University of Nebraska Press, 1964, 1971), p. 69.

18   Stanley Vestal, *Queen of Cowtowns, Dodge City* (New York: Harper & Brothers, 1952), p. 60.

19   H. C. Levinson, *Science of Chance*, op. cit., p. 15.

20   CBS *60 Minutes*, 12 February 1978.

21   H. C. Levinson, ibid., p. 171.

22   Michael Sankey and Timothy O. Russell, *Where to Play*

in the USA: The Gaming Guide (AZ: Facts on Demand Press, 1997).

23 *Time*, 6 December 1976, p. 54.

24 Norman L. Geisler, Thomas A. Howe, *Gambling a Bad Bet: You Can't Win for Losing* (Grand Rapids: Flaming H. Revell, 1990), p. 12.

25 Barry M. Horstman, 'Once It was a Vice; Now it's Entertainment', *The Cincinnati Post*, 13 September 1997, 1-A.

26 *IGWB*, August 1997, pp. 44ff.

27 Associated Press, 'Gaming Rights Asserted', *The Billings Gazette*, 21 July 1992, B-28.

28 Barry M. Horstman, 'Some Communities win with casinos, some lose', *The Cincinnati Post*, 18 September 1997, 6-A. Barry M. Horstman, 'America's biggest casino', *The Cincinnati Post*, 1 August 1998, A-1. The Foxwood casino, which has never closed since its February 1992 opening, houses 5,567 slot machines that take in $7 billion annually. Only 2½ hours from nearly 10 per cent of the nation's population, it draws an average of 50,000 visitors daily; weekend crowds sometimes reach 75,000.

29 Ibid.

30 Ibid. *IGWB*, August 1977, p. 44: 'Tribes are putting gambling revenues into education, health services, better housing and similar social infrastructure.'

31 Barry M. Horstman, 'American's biggest casino', *The Cincinnati Post*, 1 August 1998, 6-A.

32 1530 WSAI, Box 1530, Cincinnati, OH 45201.

33 *People*, 31 March 1997, p. 58. See another reference to Pearson in Chapter 2.

34 Source: John Barwick now of Hazen, ND, USA.

35 Scarne, *Scarne's New Complete Guide To Gambling*, op. cit., pp. 6, 7.

36 Arizona, California, Colorado, Florida, Georgia, Idaho, Kansas, Kentucky, Louisiana, Michigan, Minnesota,

Missouri, New Jersey, New Mexico, New York, Rhode Island, South Dakota, Texas, West Virginia, Wisconsin.

[37] Andrew Keith, Barbara Maddux, 'The Lucky Thirteen', *Time*, 10 August 1998, p. 62.

[38] Ibid.

[39] Ibid., p. 64.

[40] Joe Atkins, 'The States' Bad Bet', *Christianity Today*, Vol. 35, No. 14., 25 November 1991, p. 17. In 1987, 800 people became millionaires through lotteries (Geisler, *Gambling*, op. cit., p. 14).

[41] Suplee's comment first occurred in his guest editorial 'Talk of the Town', *The New Yorker*, 19 December 1988, p. 27.

[42] Barry M. Horstman, 'Lottery sales', *The Cincinnati Post*, 20 March 1999, 6-A

[43] Consult your local library for a Reference copy or see the final report on the Internet: www.ngisc.gov.

[44] Ibid.

[45] The Associated Press, 'Millions in U.S. reportedly pathological gamblers', *The Cincinnati Enquirer*, 19 March 1999, A-5.

[46] Clyde Brian Davis, *Something For Nothing* (Philadelphia: J.B. Lippincott Company, 1956), pp. 38f.

[47] H. C. Levinson, *The Science of Chance*, op. cit., p. 172.

[48] Melanie Colletti, 'Grant Money Disbursed', *Cripple Creek/Victor Eagle*, Vol. 2, No. 12, 18 July 1997, p. 1.

[49] H. C. Levinson, *The Science of Chance*, op. cit., p. 170.

[50] R. Rogers, *Seducing America*, p. 43.

[51] Barry M. Horstman, 'Lotteries are hot, but odds make them a sucker bet', *The Cincinnati Post*, 17 September 1997, A-4.

[52] The sense of G. L. L. Buffon, *Essaie du'arithmetique morale* (Paris: Presses Universitaires de France, 1777, 1954), cited by Thomas M. Kavanagh, *Enlightenment and the Shadows of Chance: The Novel and the Culture of*

Gambling in Eighteenth-Century France (Baltimore, MD: The Johns Hopkins University Press, 1993), p. 26.

53   N. Geisler, *Gambling*, op. cit., p. 19.

54   Julie Ralston, '15 chosen to buy houses for $1.00', *The Cincinnati Enquirer*, 25 June 1997, B-1, B-5.

55   Barry M. Horstman, 'Lotteries are hot', *The Cincinnati Post*, 17 September 1997, p. 4-A.

56   Barry M. Horstman, 'Lottery sales', *The Cincinnati Post*, 20 March 1999, 6-A.

57   Barry M. Horstman, 'Lotteries are hot', *The Cincinnati Post*, 17 September 1997, 4-A.

58   Wm. F. Buckley, Jr., 'Powerball Shmowerball [sic]! New York, July 28', *National Review*, 1 September 1998, p. 55.

11. False Hopes in an Uncertain World

1   Barry M. Horstman, 'Easy betting at casinos threatens horse racing', *The Cincinnati Post*, 19 September 1997, 6-A.

2   John Scarne, *Scarne's New Complete Guide To Gambling*, op. cit., p. 7.

3   D. James Kennedy, 'Is Gambling a Sin?' (sermon), (Fort Lauderdale: Coral Ridge Ministries,), p. 2. See the D. James Kennedy edited essays, *Gambling: America's Hidden Addiction* (Fort Lauderdale: Coral Ridge Ministries Media, 1995).

4   R. Rogers, *Seducing America*, op. cit., p. 68.

5   John Harris, *Mammon: Covetousness, the Sin of the Christian Church* (Swengel, PA: Bible Truth Depot, 1836, 1959).

6   C. S. Lewis, *God in the Dock: Essays in Theology and Ethics* (Grand Rapids: Wm. B. Eerdmans Publishing Co., 1970), p. 52.

7   Karl Barth, *Church Dogmatics* II/1 (Edinburgh: T & T Clark, 1957), II/1, p. 130.

8 All references are from the NIV.

9 Sir Walter Scott, *The Journal of Sir Walter Scott*, edited and introduced by W.E.K. Anderson (Edinburgh, UK: Canongate Classics, #87, 1972, 1998), pp. 76 (select journal entries for 21–22 January 1826).

10 Emile Caillet, *The Dawn of Personality* (Indianapolis, IN: Bobbs-Merrill, 1955), pp. 140f. Selected by *The New York Times Book Review* as one of the 100 best books in 1955 out of 10,000 titles.

11 William M. Sheraton, *It's Faster to Heaven in a 747* (New York: Sheed and Ward, 1973), p. 125.

12 Charles H. Spurgeon, *Metropolitan Tabernacle Pulpit* (Pasadena, TX: Pilgrim Publications, 1976), Vol. 43:596.

13 Post staff report, 'Con man stole $405,000, spent it on lottery tickets', *The Cincinnati Post*, 12 June 1997, 17-A.

14 Barry M. Horstman, 'Gamblers set new record on riverboats', *The Cincinnati Post*, 26 June 1997, 8-A.

15 Tanya Albert, 'River of Cash Floats Casinos', *The Cincinnati Enquirer*, 23 September 1997, A-1.

16 Barry M. Horstman, 'Gamblers set new record on riverboats', *The Cincinnati Post*, 26 June 1997, 8-A

17 *Colorado Springs, The Gazette*, 19 July 1997, Bus.–1. See Patricia A. Stokowski, *Riches and Regrets* (Niwot, CO: University Press of Colorado, 1996), 338 pages (a major study of Blackhawk and Central City, Colorado).

18 'Bingo was legalized in 1937 in Rhode Island, 1949 in New Hampshire, and 1954 in New Jersey. Forty-six states, the District of Columbia, and all the Canadian provinces have now legalized bingo . . . [45% of charity gambling comes from bingo]'. (Rogers, *Seducing America*, op. cit., pp. 42, 101).

19 'Lottery funds gay education', *The Evangelical Times*, June 2000, p.13

20 Richard John Neuhaus, 'Gambling with Gaming', *First Things*, August/September 1999, No. 95, p. 88.

[21] *Time*, 6 December 1976, p. 56.

[22] William Saroyan, *Here Comes/There Goes/You Know Who* (New York: A Trident Press Book, Simon and Schuster, 1961), pp. 145f.

[23] Clyde Brian Davis, *Something For Nothing*, op. cit., pp. 25, 27, 259.

12. Winning in Christ

[1] Ruth Sheldon Knowles, *The Greatest Gamblers* (New York: McGraw-Hill Publishing Co., 1959).

[2] H.C. Levinson, *Science of Chance*, op. cit., p. 32.

[3] Marcus Barth, 'Ephesians' *Anchor Bible Commentary* (Garden City, NY: Doubleday & Company, 1974) Vol. 1:443.

[4] Walter Bauer, Wm. F. Arndt, Felix W. Gingrich, *A Greek-English Lexicon of the New Testament* (Chicago, IL: The University of Chicago Press, 1979), p. 456.

[5] Tom Bayles, The Associated Press, 'Sweepstakes win would be simply divine', *The Cincinnati Enquirer*, 28 February 1997, A-14. In a telephone conversation with Pastor Brack I learned the church never sent in the form, obviously, knowing that God didn't need the American Publishers' money.

[6] M.G. Bulmer (op. cit.), pp. 1–6.

13. Can a Christian Ever Gamble?

[1] 'Games', *Harper's Bible Dictionary*, editor Achtemier, Paul J., (San Francisco: Harper & Row, Publishers, Inc.) 1985. Thomas Gataker, the Puritan, refers to dicing in detail (See Chapter 8).

[2] W.W. Hallo, 'Games in the Biblical World', in *Eretz-Israel*, Vol. 24: 1993, pp. 83–88.

3 William S. Garmon, 'Early Beginnings', in R. Coggins (ed.) op. cit., *The Gambling Menace*, p. 12.

4 Henlee H. Barnette, 'Gambling', in Carl F.H. Henry (ed.) *Baker's Dictionary of Christian Ethics* (Grand Rapids: Conon Press, 1973), p. 2258.

5 Cf. *Encyclopaedia Judaica* (Jerusalem, Israel: Keter Publishing House Ltd., 1971), Vol. 7:299. Similarly, the older *The Jewish Encyclopaedia*, edited by Isidore Singer (New York: Funk and Wagnals Company, 1903), Vol. 5:563 (Article 'Gambling' by Julius H. Greenstone).

6 Ibid.

7 *Encyclopaedia Judaica*, op. cit., Vol. 1:301.

8 Samuel Hopkins [1807–1887], *The Evils of Gambling* (Sermon preached in Montpelier, Vermont, April 19, 1835) (Montpelier: E.P. Walton and Son, printers, 1835), pp. 6, 10.

9 Charles L. Wallis, editor, *Autobiography of Peter Cartwright [1785–1872]* (Nashville, TN: Abingdon Press, 1856, 1984), pp. 311, 332.

10 Fred J. Cook, *A Two Dollar Bet Means Murder* (New York: Dial Press. 1961), p. 61.

11 See Chapter 2.

12 Rogers, *Seducing America*, op. cit., p. 22.

13 Ibid., p. 32.

14 Paul F. Knue, Editorial, *The Cincinatti Post*, 19 September 1997, 18-A.

15 Ivan Zabilka, *The Lottery Lie: Gamblers, Money and Hungry Kids* (Anderson, IN: Bristol House, Ltd., 1998), p. 27.

16 Barry M. Horstman, 'Lotteries are hot, but odds make them a sucker bet', *The Cincinatti Post*, 17 September 1997, 4-A.

17 Some may dispute Washington was a Christian. Although he was a member of the Episcopal church, according to his famed biographer, James Thomas

Flexner, 'Washington's religious belief was that of the enlightenment: deism. He practically never used the word "God", preferring the more impersonal word "Providence".' Volume 4:490 of Flexner's *George Washington: Anguish and Farewell (1793–1799)* (Boston: Little, Brown and Company, 1963, 1972).

[18] Quarter horses are horses that are capable of high speeds up to a quarter of a mile.

[19] T.H. Breen, *Puritan and Adventurers: Change and Persistence in Early America* (New York: Oxford University Press, 1980), pp. 149, 155, 156 in his chapter: 'Horses and Gentleman: The Cultural Significance of Gambling Among the Gentry of Virginia'.

[20] Ibid., p. 151.

[21] Kennet S. Kantzer, 'Gambling: Everyone's a Loser', *Christianity Today*, Vol. 27, No. 8, 25 November 1983, p. 12. Geisler, *Gambling*, op. cit., pp. 13, 55.

[22] John C. Miller, *The First Frontier: Life in Colonial America* (New York: Dell, 1966), p. 104

[23] Walter Wagner, cited in William J. Petersen, *What You Should Know About Gambling: A Christian Approach to Problems of Today* (New Canaan, CT: Keats Publishing, Inc., 1974), p. 27.

[24] Barry M. Horstman, 'Sure bet or fool's gold', *The Cincinatti Post*, 13 September 1997, 4-A.

[25] Phillip Vickers Fithian, *Journal & Letters: 1773–1774*, edited by H.D. Farish (Williamsburg, VA: Colonial Williamsburg, Incorporated, 1957), p. 154.

[26] John Ezell, 'The Lottery in Colonial America', *The William and Mary Quarterly*, April 1948; Vol. 5; No. 2:198.

[27] Ibid., p. 191.

[28] Ibid., p. 199, F/n 39. Wm. Petersen, *What … about Gambling?*, p. 28.

[29] David L. McKenna, 'Gambling: Parasite On Public Morals', *Christianity Today*, 8 June 1973, p. 4.

[30] Wm. Petersen, *What . . . about Gambling?*, op. cit., p. 29.

[31] James Dobson, *Solid Answers* (Wheaton, IL: Tyndale House Publishers, Inc., 1997), p. 366.

[32] Ibid., p. 532.

[33] Joe Atkins, 'The States' Bad Bet', *Christianity Today*, Vol. 35, No. 14, 25 November 1991, p. 17.

[34] John W. Kennedy, 'Gambling Away the Golden Years', *Christianity Today*, 24 May 1999, p. 42.

[35] Ibid., p. 46.

[36] Ibid.

[37] Wayne E. Oates, *Luck: A Secular Faith* (Louisville, KY: Westminster Press, 1995), pp. 69, 70.

[38] See Chapter 3.

[39] Victor Niederhoffer, *The Education of a Speculator* (New York: John Wiley & Sons, Inc., 1977), p. 135.

[40] William Petersen thought it was exploitative for *Readers' Digest* to use sweepstakes to increase their sales (*What . . . about Gambling?* op. cit., p. 6).

[41] May 23 1997, Reformed Theological Conference, Emmanuel Baptist Church, Toledo, OH.

[42] Pasquale Villari, *Life and Times of Savonarola* (New York: Charles Scribner's Sons, 1888), p. 138.

[43] Father Bernard Vaughan, *The Sins of Society* (London: Kegan Paul, Trench, Turbner & Co. Ltd., 1906), pp., 40, 41.

[44] J. Findlay, *People of Chance*, op. cit., p. 28.

[45] Revd William Stith, *The Sinfulness and Pernicious Nature of Gaming: a sermon preached before the General Assembly of Virginia at Williamsburg*, 1 March 1752, and published at the request of the house of Burgesses (Williamsburg: Wm. Hunter, 1752). Stith's sermon *followed* Virginia's legislation against gambling. In 1727, the Virginia House of Burgesses adopted the Statute of Anne, a law passed by the British House of Commons in 1760. 'In 1744 the House of Burgesses adopted a law that

prohibited gaming and betting in public, but once again endorsement seems to have been sporadic at best'. (Ann Fabian, *Card Sharps, Dream Books, & Bucket Shops: Gambling in 19th-century America* (Ithaca: Cornell University, 1990), p. 23).

[46] T. J. Breen, *Puritans and Adventurers*, op. cit., pp. 162 f.

[47] Scott T. Carroll, 'An Early Church Sermon Against Gambling (CPL 60)', *The Second Century*, Vol. 8, No. 2, Summer, 1991, pp. 83–95. Carroll's estimation was that it was written before the mid-third century. German church historian Adolph Harnack regarded Victor (Bishop of Rome, 189–98) to be the author.

[48] Ibid., p. 90.

[49] Cited by Lilly C. Stone, 'English Sports and Recreations', in Louis B. Wright, Virginia A. LaMar, (eds.), *Life and Letters in Tudor and Stuart England*, op. cit., p. 451.

[50] Ibid.

[51] Tony Evans, *Tony Evans Speaks out on Gambling & the Lotto* (Chicago: Moody Press, 1995), p. 8.

[52] William Smith and Samuel Cheetham, *A Dictionary of Christian Antiquities* (London: John Murray, 1875), Vol. 1:709. 'Boldetti, for instance, gives (p. 416) a Christian sepulchral inscription over an ARTIFEX ARTIS TESSALARIE, who is generally considered to have been a maker of dice. (Martigny, *Dict. des Antiq. Chret.*, s.v. "Jesu, Tales de.")'. Ibid.

[53] The Revd Edward Rogers, 'Important Moral Issues in Gambling', *The Expository Times*, January 1964, Vol. 75:4, p. 123.

[54] One was 'Bibleopoly', where 'instead of buying hotels, you build churches, draw "Faith/Contingency" and "Abyss" cards, and even lose a turn by landing on "Go Meditate"!' Also advertised was the game 'Redemption: The City of Bondage', a board game with six set of

dice clearly visible in Christian Book Distributors' *Catalogue # 90073*, May/June, Peabody, MA, 1997, p. 41. Interestingly, many games use a spin-wheel instead of dice. It serves the same purpose without the onus of dice.

[55] Carroll, *Sermon against Gambling*, op. cit., p. 93.

[56] Alice Ann Love, 'Some See Lottery, not Saving, as Best Chance for Big Money', *The Cincinatti Enquirer*, 29 October 1999, A-14, reporting on a poll conducted by the Consumer Federation of America and Primerica, a financial services firm.

[57] 'Gambling', *Lutheran Advocacy Ministry in Pennsylvania*, Harrisburg, PA, adopted 5 March 1984 and affirmed, January, 1993.

[58] Rachel Melcher, 'Riverboat casinos awash with retirees', *The Cincinnati Enquirer*, 12 July 1998, E-2.

[59] John W. Kennedy, 'Gambling Away the Golden Years', *Christianity Today*, 24 May 1999, p. 43.

[60] Ibid., p. 42.

[61] Rachel Melcher, 'Riverbed casinos awash with retirees', *The Cincinnati Inquirer*, 12 July 1998, E-2.

[62] For instance, bridge, poker, and pinochle.

[63] Dr Warren's statement as printed is what he wrote, for he intended to separate gambling from giving. I don't think his condition for gaming here is either a meaningful deterrent or an encouragement to gamble. To me it would make more sense if condition 2 read: 'If you consider gambling a form of giving, then gambling might not become a problem.' How so? Because gambling has a fringe social feedback.

[64] Timothy Warren, 'What Does the Bible say about Gambling?' *Kindred Spirit*, Summer, 1997, Dallas Theological Seminary, Dallas, Texas, Vol. 21, No. 2, p. 5.

[65] See the example of Mr Wilson of Lockland, Ohio, who

became addicted to gambling and embezzled charity funds from his newspaper (Chapter 10).

[66] Andrew Keith, Barbara Maddux, 'The Lucky Thirteen', *Time*, August 10, 1998, p. 64.

[67] R. Rogers, *Seducing*, op. cit., p. 89.

[68] Barry M. Horstman, 'Some communities win with casinos, some lose', *The Cincinnati Post*, 18 September 1997, 6-A.

[69] Herbert Asbury, *Sucker's Progress: An Informal History of Gambling in America from the Colonies to Canfield* (New York: Dodd, Mead, and Company, 1938), p. 83.

[70] Ibid.

[71] Consecrated bishop on 14 Novmber 1784 (p. 29, Allen C. Guelzo, *For The Union Of Evangelical Christendom: The Irony of the Reformed Episcopalians* (University Park, PA: The Pennsylvania State University Press, 1994)). Guelzo has argued, however, that Seabury's consecration was 'at best irregular and at worst fraudulent'. (Ibid., p. 31).

[72] Asbury, *Sucker's Progress*, op. cit., pp. 72, 73. John Ezell gives a descriptive page on the July, 1762, Light House and Public Lottery, the background on how the drawing was done, as well as the diary citation of Revd Seabury in *The William and Mary Quarterly*, April, 1948; Vol. 5; No. 2, pp. 185, 186.

[73] Michael Brander, *The Country Divine* (Edinburgh: The Saint Andrew Press, 1981), p. 60.

[74] *People*, 31 March 1997, p. 58.

14. The Summing-Up

[1] Kenneth Escott Kirk, *Conscience and Its Problems: An Introduction to Casuistry* (New York: Longman's Green and Co., Ltd., 1927), p. 306.

2 G. I. Williamson, *Wine in the Bible and the Church* (Phillipsburg, NJ: Pilgrim Publishing Co., 1976); Andre S. Bustanoby, *The Wrath of Grapes: Drinking and the Church Divided* (Grand Rapids, MI: Baker Book House, 1987); Kenneth Gentry, *The Christian and Alcoholic Beverages* (Grand Rapids: Baker Book House, 1986).

3 Barry M. Horstman, 'Sure bet or fool's gold?' *The Cincinnati Post*, 13 September 1997, 4-A.

4 *IGWB*, op. cit., August, 1997, p. 60.

5 Barry M. Horstman, 'Lotteries are hot, but odds make them a sucker bet', *The Cincinnati Post*, 17 September 1997, 4-A.

6 Herbert Waddams, *A New Introduction to Moral Theology* (New York: Seabury Press, 1964), p. 218.

7 Daniel Kadlec, 'Married to the Market', *Time*, 20 October 1997, p. 72.

8 Frank Eltman, 'Teacher leaves $800 M', *The Cincinnati Enquirer*, 14 July 1998, A-2.

9 Andrew Tobias, 'Letters from Chairman Buffett', *Fortune*, 22 April 1983, p. 140.

10 Robert G. Hagstrom, Jr., *The Warren Buffett Way: Investment Strategies of the World's Greatest Investor* (New York: John Wiley & Sons, Inc., 1955, 1994), [mass market ed.], p. vi.

11 Herbert Waddams, *A New Introduction to Moral Theology* (New York: Seabury Press, 1964), p. 219.

Appendix

1 Ivan Zabilka, *The Lottery Lie: Gamblers, Money and Hungry Kids* (Anderson, IN: Bristol House, Ltd., 1998), p. 175.

2 Ibid., pp. 175, 176.

[3] Stephen Huba and Frank Main, 'Churches to phase out bingo', *The Cincinnati Post*, 24 June 1997, A-4.

[4] I. Zabilka, *Lottery Lie*, p. 176.

[5] Ibid.

[6] Walter Wagner, *To Gamble Or Not To Gamble* (New York: World Publishing Co., 1972), p. 332.

[7] *The Christian Century*, Vol. 110, No. 16, 12 May 1993, p. 514.

[8] *The Cincinnati Post*, 24 June 1997, A-4.

[9] F. O'Hare, 'Gambling,' *New Catholic Encyclopedia* (New York: McGraw-Hill, Company, 1967), Vol. 6:276. T. Slater wrote in the article on 'Gambling', *The Catholic Encyclopedia* , edited by Charles G. Herbermann, Ph.D., (New York: The Gilmary Society, 1909), Vol. 6:375: 'It is not gambling, in the strict sense, if a bet is laid on the issue of a game of skill like billiards or football . . . [It] is not sinful to stake money on the issue of a game of chance any more than it is sinful to insure one's property against risk, or deal in futures on the produce market.'

[10] Stephen Huba, 'Festivals Open Without Gambling', *The Cincinnati Post*, 24 May 1997, A-10.

[11] Cindy Schroeder, 'Diocese May End Gaming', *The Cincinnati Enquirer*, 15 May 1997, B-1. See also Andrea Tortora, 'N. Kentucky Priests Say No Dice to Gambling', *The Cincinnati Enquirer*, 20 May 1997, B-5.

[12] Ibid., 15 May 1997, B-11.

[13] *The Cincinnati Post*, 24 June 1997, Ibid., A-1.

[14] Ibid.

[15] Geisler, *Gambling* op. cit., p. 116.

Annotated Select Bibliography

Ames, William, translated out of the Latin, *Conscience with the Power and Cases* (London: Printed by Edward Deering for I. Rothwell, T. Slater, L. Blacklock, 1643). Rare Puritan book. Five volumes.

——, *The Marrow Of Theology*, translated from the 3rd Latin edition and edited by John D Eusden (Philadelphia: Pilgrim Press, 1629, 1968). Currently in print from Baker Books.

Asbury, Herbert, *Sucker's Progress: An Informal History of Gambling in America from the Colonies to Canfield* (New York: Dodd, Mead & Company, 1938). Somewhat outdated, once-popular historical survey of all forms of gambling in the periods specified.

Baxter, Richard, 'The Works of Richard Baxter' in *The Christian Directory* (Pittsburgh: Soli Deo Gloria Publications, 1673, 1990), Vol. 1:840 (Chapter 19, Part 4, Title 5: 'Cases of Conscience about Lusory Contracts'). Back in print from Soli Deo Gloria Publications. One of the more popular Puritans.

Breen, T.H., *Puritans and Adventurers: Change and Persistence in Early America* (New York: Oxford University Press, 1980). Chapter: 'Horses and Gentlemen: The Cultural Significance of Gambling Among the Gentry of Virginia.' An eye-opening historical study in the colonial American time.

Daniels, Bruce C., *Puritans At Play: Leisure and Recreation in Colonial New England* (New York: St. Martin's Press, 1995). Reflects wide-ranging research; valuable doctoral dissertation.

Davis, Clyde Brian, *Something For Nothing* (Philadelphia: J.B. Lippincott Company, 1956). A secular work of some merit.

Evans, Tony, *Tony Evans Speaks out on Gambling & the Lotto* (Chicago: Moody Press, 1995). Small pamphlet; more a personal statement than an argued position.

——, *What a Way to Live: Running All of Life by the Kingdom Agenda* (Nashville, TN: Word Publishing, 1997). Returns to the theme of lotteries among other reflections, but still brief on the controversy.

Fabian, Ann, *Card Sharps, Dream Books, & Bucket Shops: Gambling in 19th-Century America* (Ithaca: Cornell University Press, 1990). An impressively written work on the nineteenth-century controversies.

Gataker, Thomas, *On the Nature and Use of Lots: A Treatise, Historical and Theological* (London: John Haviland, 1627). Very rare Puritan work. Only in a few libraries in the world.

Geisler, Norman, *Gambling: A Bad Bet* (Grand Rapids: Baker Books, 1990). A small paperback; now out of print and somewhat hard to find. Rex Roger's work is a kind of supplement or replacement of this older work.

Kirk, Kenneth Escott, *Conscience and Its Problems: An Introduction to Casuistry* (New York: Longman's Green and Company., Ltd., 1927). One of the better known Anglican works on *adiaphora* matters.

Mamis, Justin, *The Nature of Risk: Stock Market Survival and the Meaning of Life* (Reading, MA: Addison-Wesley Publishing Company, 1991). A work from the business world.

Martinez, Tomas M., *The Gambling Scene: Why People Gamble* (Springfield IL: Charles C. Thomas Publisher, 1983). One of the more insightful books on gambling. The Foreword is written by Igor Kusyszyn, of the University of York, UK.

Oates, Wayne E., *Luck: A Secular Faith* (Louisville, KY: Westminster Press, 1995). Written from a Southern Baptist viewpoint. Oates doesn't get far into the subject of predestination. It has, nevertheless, some useful personal observations especially on modern secularism.

Petersen, William J., *What You Should Know About Gambling: A Christian Approach to Problems of Today* (New Canaan, CT:

Keats Publishing, Inc., 1974). Long out of print. Sketchy, but stimulating.

Pollard, William G., *Chance and Providence: God's Action in a World Governed by Scientific Law* (New York: Charles Scribner's Sons, 1958). Few seem to have noticed this interesting work by an atomic scientist.

Rogers, Rex. M., *Seducing America: Is Gambling a Good Bet?* (Grand Rapids: Baker Books, 1997). Like Geisler's work Rogers's is pretty heavy on the sociological damage caused by gambling. But it is surprisingly skimpy and sometimes shallow, however, in dealing with the theological controversies involved in gambling. One glaring omission was that after he raised the issue of the casting of lots in Scripture, he dropped it!

Sproul, R.C., *Not A Chance: The Myth of Chance in Modern Science & Cosmology* (Grand Rapids: Baker Books, 1994). A compilation of lectures by a gifted and prolific American Calvinist. Only some chapters relate to gambling issues.

Van Dam, Cornelius, *The Urim and Thummim: A Means of Revelation in Ancient Israel* (Winona Lake: Eisenbrauns, 1997). A monument of research worth consulting.

Zabilka, Ivan, *The Lottery Lie: Gamblers, Money and Hungry Kids* (Anderson, IN: Bristol House, Ltd., 1998). This little-known work was a delightful find. Zablika reflects extensive reading and is useful as a resource. His theological comments, however, are few and fail to reflect an openness to differing interpretations.

Subject Index

Author Index

Scripture Index

Men Behaving Badly

in 1 and 2 Samuel

John Goldingay

ISBN 1-84227-012-5

In his distinctive and stimulating style, John Goldingay brings fresh perspective and new insights to the characters, lives and situations of the 'men behaving badly' in the books of 1 and 2 Samuel. With lively writing and gentle humour, *Men Behaving Badly* illuminates the timeless foibles and phobias of the human condition.

This 'un–commentary' focuses on the characters themselves (rather than on the plot or the theme). By connecting thus with the Biblical story and 'getting inside' the motives and emotions of these men (and women), the author draws the reader to connect with (or disconnect from!) the characters in a new way.

Yahweh is also a strong character participating in the lives of these men as the events of 1 & 2 Samuel slot into the larger picture of the Biblical narrative. 'Irreverently faithful', Goldingay pushes the parameters of traditional biblical exposition to breathe new life into the text and bring ancient truths to people in the 21st century.

Illustrations from films, current events and politics etc. serve to further draw the reader into the character studies…and to consider his or her response to its challenges.

John Goldingay is **David Allan Hubbard** Professor of Old Testament at Fuller Theological Seminary, Pasadena, California. His previous works include *After Eating the Apricot, Models for Scripture, Models for Interpretation of Scripture* and *To the Usual Suspects*.

paternoster press